D0251474

Panasonic

Panasonic

THE LARGEST CORPORATE
RESTRUCTURING IN HISTORY

Francis McInerney

T·T

TRUMAN TALLEY BOOKS

ST. MARTIN'S PRESS ✺ NEW YORK

www.stmartins.com

Design by Phil Mazzone

Library of Congress Cataloging-in-Publication Data

McInerney, Francis.
    Panasonic : the largest corporate restructuring in history / Francis McInerney.
      p. cm.
    ISBN-13: 978-0-312-37137-1
    ISBN-10: 0-312-37137-3
    1. Panasonic Industrial Corp.—Reorganization. 2. Matsushita Denki Sangyo—Reorganization. 3. Electronic industry—Japan. 4. Corporate reorganizations—Japan. I. Title.

HD9696.A3J365533 2007
338.7'621380952—dc22

                            2006053032

First Edition: May 2007

10 9 8 7 6 5 4 3 2 1

For Alexa and Chris

CONTENTS

INTRODUCTION

S<small>OMETIME IN</small> 1992, <small>MY LONGTIME BUSINESS PARTNER</small> S<small>EAN</small> W<small>HITE</small> and I were walking down Park Avenue toward the Helmsley Building when we passed the Panasonic showroom that used to be across from the Waldorf. We were writing a book on why the Japanese economy had stalled a few years before, a stasis from which it is now emerging after more than a decade and a half. We had an hour to kill so we decided to check out the showroom to see how Panasonic was doing.

Our theory on Japan was that while cheap information was allowing smart companies to use information technology to get closer to their customers and become more responsive to them, Japan's main players, no matter how information intense, were for some unclear reason actually moving further away from their customers. This was causing Japanese companies, with the notable exception of the automobile sector, chronic losses of market share around the world and a collapse of sales and profits. Japan was in the dumps.

We thought that if we could figure out the mechanisms of Japan's failings, and compare them to successful business models elsewhere, we could prescribe for managers worldwide a new form of winning organization designed to profit from falling information costs. We did this over a series of three books guided by our longtime editor, Mac Talley, now at St. Martin's.

We were focused on Japan because, a decade earlier, we had directed the staff at our market research company, Northern Business Information (now part of Gartner Group), to prepare and publish an analysis of how Japan would come to dominate the world information industry. We were obviously wrong and wanted to know why.

The Panasonic showroom, ironically full of information technology, fit our theory of Japanese unresponsiveness to customers to a T. The place was a disaster. Products didn't work. The ones that did weren't connected to anything, making them useless. The youngish staff knew nothing, and appeared, as we later wrote, hungover "or worse."[1]

With nothing there worth seeing, we didn't hang around. As we left, Sean said, "I'll bet that the last person to go in there was some Panasonic executive who didn't even know how to use a computer. It's a showroom; they can't sell you anything, and they don't know who can. Besides, who would want to buy Panasonic after that?"

A year later our first book, *Beating Japan*, was published. Not long after, Sean was at home in Connecticut, when a neighbor came by to tell him a horror story about how her sister had just been fired from the Panasonic showroom in New York when a team of executives walked in and shuttered the place.

Sean wisely said nothing.

But it was clear that a fresh, new wind was blowing through the company that owns the Panasonic brand, Matsushita Electric Industrial of Osaka, Japan. This book is about the wind that cleaned out the Panasonic showroom and that is still roaring through one of Japan's largest companies, altering everything in its path. It is also about how I came to play a role in advising Matsushita during the years since.

Panasonic is not about any ordinary restructuring. It is about a company of ¥7.7 trillion ($72 billion) in sales at the time, employing 293,000 people around the world, the tenth-largest industrial company not in oil or autos.[2] It is about a company whose many tens of thousands of products are so universally used that it may have more customers than any firm in history. *Panasonic* is about a company that was 11 percent larger than IBM was when Lou Gerstner began his reworking of that firm. The best way to think of this is what Gerstner would have been up against if he had added a company the size, and complexity, of Apple into the mix. Even this, however, doesn't capture the challenge. Matsushita is so big that it is one of the few companies, possibly the only company, which has a product in just about every home and business in the developed world. The company has operations in almost every country on the planet. The scope of its markets worldwide is a phenomenon: Matsushita makes everything from pencil sharpeners to telecommunications and TV production systems, from batteries to manufacturing production systems, and from flat-panel TVs to car audio and satellite navigation systems, even entire building systems and home interiors. When Gerstner took over IBM, it made computers, admittedly a lot of them. But Matsushita's breadth and size combined made reorganizing the company incomparably more difficult than the task that faced IBM's incoming CEO in 1992.

Not only is *Panasonic* about the largest and deepest restructuring ever done, it is about how this was accomplished without importing an outside CEO like Gerstner or Carlos Ghosn. It is also about turning around a complex and tradition-bound organization in a country that is often thought, mistakenly, to deeply resist radical change. It is about the continuing process of Japanese companies adapting to the competitive forces roiling the markets around them. In this sense, *Panasonic* provides insight into the essential flexibility of Japan and the ability of management there to solve immensely complex global problems. This flexibility could once again reshape world markets just as Japan did in the decades following the Second World War.

Panasonic is also about the largest implementation of my Soccer Ball System for creating and managing information-efficient companies capable of profiting from the highly compressive force of falling information costs. *Panasonic* is the poster child for what can be done for large legacy companies burdened with traditions and obsolete procedures. *Panasonic* is, in addition, about how an operation with many tens of billions in sales can learn how to scale profitably, expanding, like Wal-Mart, into the several-hundred-billion-dollar range. As such, this book leads major industrial corporations into uncharted waters. It is a must read for managers in any large operation seeking increased scale.

In a larger sense, *Panasonic* is about reenergizing a country that entered a prolonged period of economic stagnation when the Nikkei 225 peaked in the final days of 1989, a slump that, because Japan is the world's second-largest economy and strategically placed in Asia, threatens the long-term stability of the advanced world. Matsushita's resurgence, by leading Japan, reduces geopolitical risks and brings growth to the Japanese economy, a win-win for us all.

A quick glance at a map of the world and the headlines in the daily paper tells all: The North Asian rim of the Pacific is a cauldron of instability. Major conflict has torn it apart for over a century. First came European and Japanese colonialism, then the Second World and Korean wars. Mao Tse-tung soon wiped out seventy million of his own people, more than Hitler and Stalin combined, making him the greatest monster in history, and that was during peacetime. Mao's heirs in China and North Korea are struggling with his legacy in complex and unpredictable ways. In short: the area has been ugly since before most of our great-grandparents were born, it looks ugly now, and its future looks uglier still. Insert into this mix an ever-weakening Japan, once the bulwark of regional stability, unable to grab its own reins and get itself back on the road to prosperity, and we have the perfect formula for disorder on a scale that we have never known. And this only half a century after we thought we had entered a period of postwar "normalcy."

That one of Japan's major industrial enterprises should emerge from Japan's malaise and show the country a way forward is a big deal in a picture as unstable as the Pacific today. It is a very big deal. It shows the people of Japan that they do not have to enter a slow, steady decline into eventual irrelevance, something we may think absurd, but that has been a real concern in Japan for some time. For the rest of us, Matsushita's reforms regenerate a pillar of global stability and make the management of peace and economic growth doable, something that has looked less and less likely with each passing year for the last decade and a half.

There are other ramifications as well. It is commonly thought, even by Japanese themselves, that Japan rarely changes without a great deal of outside pressure, usually military. The Japanese even have a word for it, *gaiatsu*: *gai* for outside, *atsu* for pressure. In my three decades of advising Japanese companies, I was often told that companies need *gaiatsu* to reorganize radically enough to secure profitable growth. That this is not true will be amply demonstrated in this book.

However, it is rare enough for a Japanese company to shred every aspect of its corporate operations that what you will read in this book indicates a shift deep in the nation's psychology. And when the world's second-largest economy changes, only fools do not pay attention.

Moreover, for us in the United States, where we are used to major corporate restructurings and the consequences—for good and for ill—to see that the largest such reshaping ever is not here but in Japan where these things are much less common (Nissan's reorganization was led by a foreigner, when Nissan was smaller, and began after Matsushita's) is a big surprise. For those in Europe who look down on the "Anglo-American Model," the discovery that it has spread to a country as powerful as Japan, and perhaps soon elsewhere in Asia, will come as unpleasant news.

We often look to General Electric as the example of examples in continuous corporate realignment. But Jack Welch started off with a much smaller company than Matsushita, and he took two decades to reshape the organization. Lou Gerstner took ten years to rebuild IBM. Matsushita accomplished much the same thing in only six.

The Matsushita that emerged looks nothing like the company of ten years ago. It has none of the same divisions and is run on different lines. It has accumulated significant merger and acquisition expertise, a whole raft of new products with dominant market shares (something it hasn't had in decades), new management, new cost accounting, and new capital allocation systems. The company is growing again and has passed profit milestones it last passed over three decades ago.

How I came to write this book is a story all by itself. Kirk Nakamura, the CEO who led the restructuring, read *Beating Japan* while he was running Matsushita's U.S. operation in the mid-1990s, hit the roof when he read our review of his Park Avenue showroom, and then did something un-American: instead of shooting the messengers, he closed the showroom and sought our advice on how to improve MEI's U.S. operations. Sean (now with Centennial Ventures in Denver) and I then authored a reform template for him called *The Digital Revolution*, the template that gives *Panasonic* its unique insight into why Matsushita made the decisions that it did.

Even this does not really explain how Kirk and I synched up over the following decade and still less why he entrusted his company to my ideas. Having advised CEOs for over thirty years, I'm used to executives who take multiple sources of advice and derisk these in a policy blend that may, or may not, work. Kirk not only took my ideas and made them operationally viable on an enormous scale, but he took them *undiluted.*

It helps that we have similar backgrounds and think similarly. We are both hard money men—a company is about operating sources of cash and little else—and highly structured thinkers. That is to say, we don't look at organizations as sets of two-dimensional performance data. We see them as multidimensional organisms moving through time with complex touch points of cash that must be identified and managed. We ask ourselves not what rate of return is optimal, though, of course, we want to know this, but what shape of organization will produce the best rate of return. This is a subtle but profound distinction because cost cutters, no matter how radical, never come to grips with creating a structure that actually benefits from their cost cutting. For them a sustainable business model is always just out of reach. Kirk and I agree with John de Butts, the late CEO of AT&T, that "the system is the solution."

Our view is that the structure itself is like an airframe that must be constantly redesigned to tolerate the increasing speeds of modern markets. As Kirk likes to say, "there are no taboos."[3] Management must not simply be prepared for change; it must be in change mode every minute of every day.

Early in his career, Kirk made loud noises about restructuring his area of the company, the Nagoya sales operation, for more revenue and profit and got the attention of Matsushita's board. No politically savvy young manager would take such risks. But taking these risks didn't seem to bother him—that's not quite true; it bothered him a lot, but he pushed ahead anyway—and he took to carrying an undated letter of resignation in his pocket for quick use. In a sign of things to come, the Nagoya office was restructured.

I started out, creating a citywide high school student union in Toronto. I began my own high school in the city, which still exists after four decades, went on to university—like Kirk, I studied economics—after which I joined the Royal Bank of Canada. My grandfather joined the Royal just before the First World War, and my father joined in London after the Second World War. With my father, I moved to Paris in the early sixties and joined the bank myself in London in the early seventies, and soon began making unpopular Kirk-like noises.

Here is where we differed. While I saw the bank as a family affair, and Kirk, like all Japanese salarymen, felt the same way about his company, he stuck it out. I left. Kirk fought the ebb tide for decades until it turned. I went out on my own, built a business with Sean White, and moved to the United States.

As a young man in the mid-sixties, Kirk was deeply influenced by the writings of his company's founder, Konosuke Matsushita, about whom you will hear in the first part of this book. At nearly the same time, in 1967, I came under the influence of Marshall McLuhan, whose ideas Sean and I later married up with Konosuke Matsushita's to create the template for Kirk Nakamura's reforms. *Panasonic* will describe this process in detail.

Kirk and I both wound up as foreigners in the United States only a few years apart. No question the United States was a strange world to Kirk. He didn't speak English all that well and had little experience dealing with non-Japanese, let alone in a place as turbulent as the United States. But it was no less strange to me. It may sound odd coming from an Anglo-Canadian, but the United States was the most foreign country I had ever visited, let alone lived in. Where to Kirk the language barrier marked obvious differences, to me the lack of it created a vertiginous, disorienting experience that took a good decade to get used to.

Kirk's home while in the United Kingdom was Sunningdale, southwest of London. I was born in Sunningdale. Kirk is an avid golfer. So am I, and one of my earliest memories is being walked around Sunningdale Golf Course by my father and grandfather as they played.

Kirk and I tend to read the same type of books—on culture,

history, and business—and we both look for new ways of solving problems that no one else has thought of and which many find dangerous even though they are usually a lot less risky than business as usual. The result is that we often have similar notions at the same time. It is not unusual for me to get an e-mail asking for something I am thinking of, or to fly fourteen hours to Japan and walk into a meeting with Kirk, only to have him ask me a question to which I had, for no particular reason, thought of the answer a week or so earlier.

Moreover, we are both focused on the same thing: the relationship between a company's speed and its operating sources of cash. We both understand that an organization's speed is its destiny, irrespective of anything else. A slow organization with a good rate of return is what Michael Dell calls a "pool of cash" just waiting for its profits to be siphoned off by someone faster, leaner, and meaner.

Perhaps because of these similarities, we understand each other. More to the point, we trust each other. When I sat down to interview him for this book, the first thing he said to me was, "You know, if I hadn't met you, none of this would have been possible." While this speaks to a deep relationship, the fact is that, from his earliest days, Kirk was a man with a mission. He was looking for a catalyst. In me, he found one. This book is my memoir of our ten years of work together.

In late 1996, not long after I began advising Kirk while he was running Panasonic North America, in a fit of presumption I concluded that he would soon be CEO of Matsushita. I decided that while I was supposed to be advising him on Matsushita's U.S. operations, everything I suggested, no matter how local in its immediate application, should be useful to him globally as CEO. My job, as I saw it, was to help him get to the top office in his company, and to have a set of strategies that he could implement the day he got there. *The Digital Revolution* was that strategy. *Panasonic* is about how Kirk turned this 128-page strategic outline into an industrial event of unprecedented magnitude spanning the globe across an organization today of 355,000 people.

My work with Kirk fell into four phases. The first, the 1993 book Sean White and I wrote, *Beating Japan*, was the basis for much of what Kirk did in the two years before we started working actively with him. The second, our 1996 template for reform, *The Digital Revolution*, prescribed much of what Matsushita did when Kirk became CEO in 2000. This template itself became our 2000 book, *FutureWealth*. The third, Sean's and my 1995 book, *The Total Quality Corporation*, showed how companies can make money by being green. This became a centerpiece of Matsushita thinking about its products and production methods. Finally, after Sean moved to Centennial Ventures to manage the strategic partners funds we raised for them, I developed the Soccer Ball System of management—just in time, as you will see, for Matsushita to react to the tech crash of 2001.

In the 2001 crash, Kirk faced the prospect of the company being taken over or broken up. As Wellington said of Waterloo, "It was a near run thing." Instead, Matsushita has just recorded its largest operating profit in fifteen years.

Steve Halstedt, chairman of Centennial Ventures, where I am part of the General Partner in two funds, asked me after I started this book, "So, what did Matsushita do to turn itself around?" Searching for a quick answer, I said something vacuous like, "Everything." *Panasonic* is the "everything."

It will become clear as you read *Panasonic* that I have had extraordinary access to Matsushita, perhaps more than any Japanese company has ever granted an outsider. Over the last ten years, Matsushita refused nothing for which I asked. To write this book, I had a large and helpful support team, and excellent translation wherever I needed it.

There are one or two things that might throw readers. The Japanese fiscal year is named for the year it begins, always on April 1, not the year it ends. Matsushita's annual reports, however, use the Western, year-end notation. I used FY to denote the Japanese fiscal year because that is the frame of reference of all those quoted in the book, and it was easier for me to make my text consistent with their comments than to explain the difference repeatedly. Also, Matsushita uses certain phrases, like its desire to be an "excellent" company. To Matsushita, the word means a defined set of operating measures, like profitability, that it takes to mark a company as top-ranked. Other expressions, like "universal design," do not mean what we take them to mean in English, and I have explained these in the text. Others, like "vertical launch," "Victory Products," and "V-shaped recovery," are self-explanatory, as you will see. There is also the Japanese penchant for slogans, like Matsushita's Value Creation 21. I have kept these to a minimum—almost every year has its own slogan and these are posted throughout the company—using only those that are vehicles for clear-cut policies.

I use one or two Japanese terms, like *honsha* for head office and *shacho* for CEO. And you will read in detail that Kirk Nakamura speaks English yet you will note the presence of a translator during my interviews with him for this book. This, he said, is because he wants to be quoted as accurately as possible and that this is best done in his own language. Being bilingual myself, I don't blame him.

While I have advised Matsushita throughout the process of restructuring, my views are my own, are consistent with what I advised management, and, as you will see, are not sugarcoated.

CHAPTER ONE

THE CHALLENGE

THE BEGINNING

On June 6, 1995, two managers from Matsushita Electric Industrial, one of Japan's largest companies, visited Sean White and me in our offices in New York. Masayuki Kusumoto and David Chapin asked if we would speak at a July management conference at their U.S. headquarters in Secaucus, New Jersey, just across the Hudson River. Matsushita's CEO, Yoichi Morishita, was coming from Japan for the occasion, and their U.S. boss, Kunio "Kirk" Nakamura, wanted us to speak. The subject was to be our 1993 book, *Beating Japan*.

We were worried about meeting Kusumoto and Chapin because our comments in *Beating Japan* about the staff at Matsushita's Park Avenue showroom being hungover or worse were pretty hard hitting. We had not met anyone from Matsushita before and we expected a sharp response. The discussion went well for an hour or so and our seminar was arranged. Just before leaving, Kusumoto said that there was one more thing he would like to bring up: our comments in *Beating Japan* about the showroom. Out of his briefcase, he pulled a copy of a talk Kirk had recently given his management and pointed to what he said about our book. The page was too hot to handle. But, to our astonishment, instead of dumping all over us or slamming the company's image doctors, he told his managers in no uncertain terms that there was something wrong with the system and that it must be fixed. Now.

Must be a different kind of executive, we figured.

Beating Japan had been ferociously critical of Japanese management styles, saying, in short, that most Japanese companies were designed to put too much distance between themselves and their overseas customers to engender any hope of long-term growth and profitability. Japanese companies were, for the most part, designed to maximize domestic customer input and to minimize, even extinguish, input from foreign customers. After a good run in automobiles and consumer electronics, the business model of an entire nation was bankrupt.

We reached this conclusion after nearly two decades in the telecommunications business. We built our first company, Northern Business Information Inc., into the world's largest telecom market research house, which we sold to McGraw-Hill in 1988. (McGraw-Hill sold NBI on to Gartner Group some years later.) For several years, our biggest customer had been Japanese telecommunications giant Nippon Telephone and Telegraph.

While running NBI, we noticed something unusual about Japanese companies. The commonplace in telecom was that Japan was soon to emerge as the information industry's dominant force. In the early 1980s we even published a research report saying this was so. Except that Japan didn't become a dominant force. It didn't become much of anything. The more we looked around, the more we noticed that apart from a few laptop computers and some very large machines, Japan didn't exist in computing, or in microprocessors, and certainly not in software.

So we asked the question the other way round. Where *was* Japan succeeding in global markets? In cars, certainly, and in consumer electronics, but in little else. Why? Were its companies doing something right in a couple of industries, like cars and cameras, and something wrong in all the others? If so, what was it, and what could be learned from this? Were other companies around the world making similar mistakes or different ones? If we could map these distinctions, we believed, we could create a grid, or a lens, that would enable us to see the problem in its full set of dimensions and prescribe practical solutions to modern market challenges useful to CEOs the world over.

To add to our certainty that there was something to the Japan question, a cursory overview of Japan's postwar history threw our inquiries into high contrast. Almost from the moment the Americans arrived in 1945, the Japanese authorities realized something that the North Koreans, Iranians, and other nuclear pretenders today do not: *Japan was not defeated by the atom bomb but by the overwhelming force of cheap information technology that made the bomb possible.* Japan moved immediately to secure its postwar position in the information world, pouring tens of billions of dollars in the following decades into computers, semiconductors, and telecommunications. Japan directed the capital budgets of the then government-owned Nippon Telephone and Telegraph, for many years the largest company in the world by market capitalization, into these core sectors.

At the same time government officials, whose "guidance" matters a lot in Japan, were said to have told Eiji Toyoda, the leading light of automaker Toyota, never to export cars. And told Soichiro Honda not to make cars at all. So why did they do well when so many infotech companies did poorly? For most Americans, Japan's postwar misadventures in information technology are simply an example of government trying to meddle in the private sector, messing things up, and wasting taxpayer money. There is some truth to this, and many Japanese will agree. But it is far from the whole story, as we soon discovered.

The year after McGraw-Hill bought our company, we were approached by Nippon Electric Corporation (NEC), a client since 1976, and asked to go to Japan to figure out why the company, which had been a telecommunications pioneer practically since Bell invented the phone, was seeing its once-promising U.S. telecom business stall, then shrink, while competitors were growing fast in the decade of opportunity after the 1983 breakup of AT&T. It made no sense to NEC, and not much to us either, why an early leader in the United States should stumble so badly.

A bit of corporate archeology reveals that NEC was once part of the old Bell System that included the American company Western Electric (now Alcatel-Lucent Technologies) and the Canadian firm Northern Electric (now Nortel Networks). NEC was the first company to introduce computerized telecommunications products into the United States. But Nortel entered the American market after NEC and quickly pushed it aside. So, whatever the issue in the U.S. market was, it wasn't being foreign. There had to be something else.

From our work with NEC, we learned a lot about the operations of Japanese companies. At NBI, we put all the companies we studied on a grid, comparing financials to financials, R&D organization to R&D organization, and sales structure to sales structure, and so on. When we plotted NEC on our grid, anomalies leapt out at us. Places where we expected a large organization, like sales, were tiny. Where we expected to see many fewer people, like R&D, there were lots. And there were equally curious overlaps—places where reporting structures were duplicated, even triplicated, when only one, and sometimes none, were needed.

From this work, we looked at other Japanese companies and quickly realized that NEC's market share problems were common to many and that all the American hysteria in the eighties and early nineties about how Japan was about to roll over the rest of the industrial world, which we had helped foster, was grossly misplaced. Japan was in deep trouble.

Moreover, while the American press was working itself into a xenophobic lather about Japan, the view from Japan itself was quite depressing. Japan's Dow, the Nikkei 225, peaked on December 29, 1989, at 38,916. That day the Dow was at 2,753. By the time *Beating Japan* was published in May 1993, the Nikkei was down to 19,590, having lost 50 percent of its value. By March 2003, when the Nikkei bottomed out, it had lost 80 percent of its value, which would be like the Dow falling to 550 rather than the 8,000 it was at.

Nikkei 1989-2006

NORTH RIVER VENTURES LLC

In the Great Depression, the Dow fell roughly as far as the Nikkei in percentage terms, and bottomed out in about three and a half years. It took the Dow a quarter century to surpass its 1929 highs, and the Nikkei looks set to take as long.

In 1989, Japan entered a prolonged period of economic stagnation from which it is now recovering, and businesspeople there were not shy about expressing their worries. As we were researching *Beating Japan*, they could see clearly that markets had turned against them some time previously and they saw few practical solutions to their problems. Even now, the Nikkei trades at only 40 percent of its 1989 peak and is just reaching its October 1986 level—twenty years ago. You don't have to watch grainy newsreels of soup kitchens and President Roosevelt's speeches to imagine the convulsions in the United States if the Dow today was running at its October 1986 level of 1,800 instead of the record highs it is testing. Japan has been through a rough time and has lost large amounts of its wealth. The fact that it has steered through is testimony to the resilience of the Japanese people. How Japan did so is the story of this book.

The short of our diagnosis of Japan's troubles was simple: when information costs fall, more information is substituted for other factor inputs like land, labor, and capital. Price-performance shifts fast and customers gain large consumer surpluses that move market power from producers to their customers. Cheap information also gives customers more and more control over information generation and dissemination, adding to customer market power. Low-cost information, therefore, allows customers to move quickly to those producers offering superior customer service and greater levels of value added. The faster the cost of information falls, the more dramatic this power shift is, destabilizing markets everywhere. I like to say that Karl Marx was right (sort of): when information costs fall far enough, all power goes from producers to customers.

If you lack a strong customer connection in the first place, you won't see this power shift until long after your market share has shrunk to the vanishing point. Even then, you will see it only retrospectively, like driving by your rearview mirror, as Marshall McLuhan used to say of his fellow Canadians, when there will be little you can do about it. Without a strong customer connection, Japan was seeing its infotech markets disappear in its rearview mirror.

As I will show you in *Panasonic*, designing your organization to profit from fast-falling information costs, rather than being victimized by them, is the key to success. I call this design the Soccer Ball System: an information-efficient company has all its assets and operations are on its surface, as it were, where they touch customers.

Many personal computer makers, for example, have been savaged by Dell's integrated distribution that puts the whole company on the "surface." Of the original PC makers of a quarter century ago, only Apple survives. After decades of lassitude Apple is only now figuring out how to ride the customer power curve with its iPod/iLife combo. All the now gone PC makers were supposed to be sophisticated information companies.

Get the information cost-driven power shift to your customers wrong and, to put it mildly, you have an issue, no matter how hot your technology.

Japan had an issue. *The whole country.* Japan's tech sector was addicted to pumping out ever-cheaper products and the large part of its industry had no overseas customer service relationship to speak of. What had been its differential advantage for decades— efficient manufacturing—was going to lower-cost countries like South Korea and China. Winning companies the world over had superior control over the sales process and deeper customer service relationships than did Japan's information technology sector. Without these customer-facing operations, customer information was not cycling back fast enough, or coherently enough, to be turned into ever more valuable products and services. The size of this gap between Japan and the expectations of its markets was impressive to us. Actually it was shocking; it implied the potential collapse of the world's second-largest economy, the centerpiece of geopolitical stability in the increasingly sensitive Pacific Rim.

Very few others outside Japan saw it this way. One who did was Bill Emmott, the recently retired editor of *The Economist*, who wrote *The Sun Also Sets* in 1989[1] just as the Nikkei was about to go off a cliff. Emmott focused on macroeconomic and policy challenges while Sean White and I looked at business models and how they work. Emmott returned to the subject sixteen years later with a special section in *The Economist*, "The Sun Also Rises," in October 2005.[2] Like *Panasonic*, Emmott points to a resurgent Japan.

When I first met Kirk Nakamura in 1995, a half-decade before he became CEO, Matsushita showed all the outward signs of malaise. Sales were ¥6.8 trillion but operating profits had slid 54 percent to ¥266 billion, from their ¥578 billion peak in 1984 when sales had been 31 percent lower at ¥4.7 trillion. Operating margins that were north of 12 percent in 1984 were south of 4 percent by 1995. They would continue to drift south for five more years, falling another 29 percent.

Late in July 1995, Sean and I were ushered into a large meeting room at Matsushita's U.S. headquarters in Secaucus to give our *Beating Japan* prescription for Japanese companies. The meeting was more formal than anything we were used to: a stage with large flower arrangements, highly orchestrated introductions of President Morishita, Kirk, and ourselves, with entries and exits timed to the second. Our relaxed presentation style—we don't stand at podia reading timed scripts, and we flip back and forth between each other depending on the issue—was maladapted to the occasion. I was sure that we went over badly.

But we must have made at least a passing grade because in June 1996, Kirk asked us to return to Secaucus to advise him on a series of reforms he planned to make.

Matsushita was not the only company in trouble in its sector. Many are still sorting themselves out ten years after Kirk Nakamura began planning Matsushita's long road back. *Panasonic* shows what these firms are up against. The picture isn't pretty and their late start leaves them vulnerable. *Panasonic* shows what it will take to put them on a firm footing.

The *New York Times* reported, for example, that in 1988, Japanese IC makers accounted for 51 percent of the world's supply, and NEC, Toshiba, and Hitachi ran one, two, and three in the market.

Today, Japan gets just over 23 percent share. NEC, which was the largest chipmaker in the world when *Beating Japan* was published, is now the tenth-largest chipmaker.[3] This is a major shift in competitive position that really hurts in a country that spent so much of its national treasure to establish dominance in IC markets.

Caught in Japan's downdraft, Matsushita entered this massive shift in competitive forces as the world's largest producer of consumer electronics. Its products are, as I said earlier, in literally every home and office in the developed world. But Panasonic was a failing global brand, and MEI had stagnating sales, anemic and falling profits, and wobbly operating fundamentals. In one of the most significant course corrections in industrial history, Matsushita broke ranks, drove changes that others would not, and did not look back.

When Kirk invited Sean and me to help him in his U.S. operation, this companywide turnarounds was still a few years off and we were confronted with a long list of numbingly complex issues:

- Morale was poor.
- The simplest procedures were antiquated.
- Half a dozen or more firms had rights to the Panasonic name and all had different strategies.
- Products from these companies overlapped; some were duplicated, even triplicated, and competed for the same customers.
- The company was designed to force-feed sales at the expense of operating free cash flow.
- There was no system for collecting customer information.
- Because there was no customer information, products were designed in a vacuum, and often launched into markets for which there was no certain demand.
- When demand for products failed to materialize, sales operations that had no influence on products were blamed.

- Overseas sales operations learned over the decades to keep their heads down, shuffle paper, and do what they could. Star performers left for better-run companies.
- There were no clear lines of authority connecting customers to decision makers; in fact, we could see no lines at all.
- The North American sales operation, run from Secaucus, had a shadow staff organization in Japan that had no identifiable value.
- Large numbers of products were assigned to Matsushita's sales companies around the world regardless of demand.
- Matsushita had clear leadership in few major product categories; in most it was somewhere between average and an also-ran.
- There was no brand we could point to—was it National, Panasonic, Quasar, NAIS, Technics, Ramsa, or what?—and no strategy for getting one.
- Matsushita lacked any sense of how to manage its customers' experience of its products.
- There was no system of demand creation.
- Advertising had all but ceased and what there was of it was uncoordinated and had no clear theme or company image.
- Major retailers like Wal-Mart were revolutionizing their operations to cut inventory while minimizing stockouts, but Matsushita had no way of supporting this.
- Consolidation in the retail sector meant that the company had many fewer but larger customers, yet had not adapted its sales or production systems to this.
- Nothing the firm did was designed to maximize profitability. In fact, it did the opposite: it force-fed the market large numbers of marginal products instead of concentrating on big-selling profit spinners.
- If MIS had a purpose, we could not figure out what it was. No one seemed able to tell us.

- Management education was almost nonexistent, and the firm was not hiring professionals from the best business schools.
- The firm made only limited attempts to bring in expertise from top-performing companies; and management had become inbred to a dangerous degree.
- Women? What women? Try designing products and selling them in modern markets without women in management. MEI did and was getting the results to show for it.
- There was no idea whatever of the impact of computer technology on consumer electronics, communications, or media.
- Local management was prevented from achieving officer rank, forcing top players to look elsewhere for opportunities and institutionalizing mediocrity at the company's cutting edge—where it met its customers.

Put simply, Matsushita was in no position to deal with competitors like Dell, which surged from nowhere in the mid-nineties to become half Matsushita's size a decade later. Nor could it support

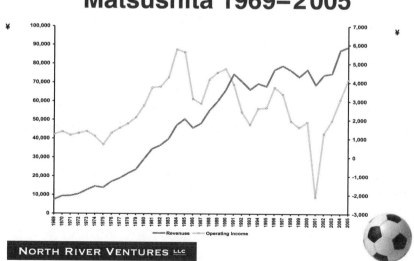

Matsushita 1969–2005

customers like Wal-Mart, which inflated from one and a half times the size of Matsushita to four times the size during the same period. By 1996, Dell and Wal-Mart had models for scaling quickly and profitably, and Matsushita did not.

Matsushita was being hit by better-managed competitors on one side and better-managed customers on the other, an exceptionally nasty position to be in.

In 1996, there was considerable shock in Secaucus when Dell's sales of just one product, a PC, surged past Matsushita's U.S. combined sales of many thousands of products. The logic of what was happening—that simplicity and speed win—was lost on the company. When Sean and I went to Japan in early 1997, no one there seemed aware that this had even happened. I didn't know what was more troubling: shock in the United States, the lack of it in Japan, or perhaps the dichotomy itself. One thing was obvious though: there was no management information flow and therefore no mechanism for making decisions. Rather like the United States on 9/11—even when information was available in time to avert disaster, there was no system for moving this information, drawing conclusions from it, and making decisions. The company was just stumbling along. As we learned more, the fact that it still existed amazed us.

Adding to Matsushita's vulnerability, the company was strung out across several major markets from consumer and professional electronics to white goods, factory automation, avionics, and telecommunications. The company also sold its products in component, product, and complete system form through a variety of divisions and partly owned subsidiaries all with different agendas. Branding and distribution were out of control.

What a small, agile Dell-like competitor could do to any one of these sectors, someone else could do to any of the others: Matsushita was being destroyed in detail.

This chart shows how Kirk pictured the company's situation. He called it the Smile Curve, showing that there was money to be

Value Curve Challenge

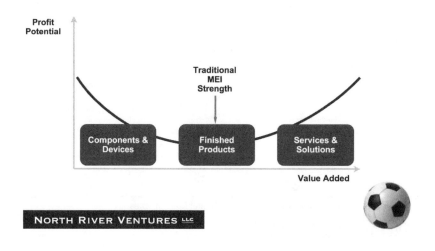

made in two areas where MEI was weakest, components upstream and solutions downstream.[4]

Perhaps more dangerous still to Matsushita was its long-held reliance on entering markets for well-established products, like TVs, and gaining share by making them cheaper and better than anyone else. In Japan, Matsushita was so well known for its wait-until-others-establish-a-market approach that it was called, in a play on Japanese syllables, "Maneshita Electric," or Copycat Electric. While this ceded product introduction leadership to others, it had the merit of selling superior products into established buying patterns and budgets. Matsushita had its own domestic channel of 27,000 National Shops through which to drive sales. For decades, this was an engine of prosperity for the company.

The problem was, traditional Matsushita products in the losing middle of Kirk's Smile Curve had long life cycles and faced only limited shifts in price-performance. A TV, for example, might drop in price by 50 percent over a decade and be replaced by a consumer once every eight to twenty years. Regular model

Matsushita out of Phase

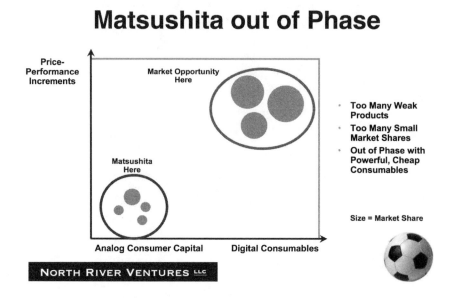

Price-Performance Increments

Market Opportunity Here

- Too Many Weak Products
- Too Many Small Market Shares
- Out of Phase with Powerful, Cheap Consumables

Matsushita Here

Size = Market Share

Analog Consumer Capital   Digital Consumables

NORTH RIVER VENTURES ʟʟᴄ

changes were incremental, and entire production lines could be based on a steady stream of small improvements. The new generation of microprocessor-based products, on the other hand, which include everything from personal computers to digital camcorders, face price-performance shifts of 50 percent every year and many are replaced at least as often. In the digital age, consumer durables are replaced by consumer disposables.

The combined effect of movement on these two axes—price-performance and the shift to consumer disposables—stressed old-line companies like Matsushita beyond their breaking points. There was nothing in MEI's product-driven, incrementalist, Maneshita business model to deal with one of these forces, let alone both.

As Dell showed, others could easily beat Matsushita to market, get ahead of the fast-paced product cycle, and secure the brand high ground years before MEI could get its second-to-market-but-better strategy in gear.

Moreover, Matsushita had a complex structure that pushed authority to make decisions deep into its factories, as far away from customers as possible. Its customer-facing operations were almost without power, but nonetheless were fully accountable, a crippling dysfunction. In addition, the National Shops' ability to deliver profitable sales quickly insulated the company from the demands of world markets. In effect, for many of the company's offerings, the dominance of the National Shop channel at home turned overseas markets into marginal sales opportunities rather than strategic ones. This had the effect of putting the firm increasingly out of synch with its global customers and blinding its operational core to charges going on outside Japan.

By 1995, this stumbling jumble of brands, products, procedures, and companies was under vigorous attack on two fronts: on one front, new competitors from China and South Korea, like Samsung, made products even cheaper and better than Matsushita; on the other front, innovators like Apple and Microsoft quickly established large new markets that MEI had not identified and could not enter.

No one seemed to know what to do. The life of the company was slipping away. One Japanese executive said to me, simply and poignantly, "I have been at Matsushita over thirty years. For many years I have been feeling us get weaker every day." The entire management team was frozen, afraid to do anything. When Sean and I toured the Japanese operation in early 1997 we heard nothing but complaints about what could *not* be done to solve MEI's problems. This was not a happy time.

Compounding the challenge facing Matsushita, management had to deal with a long tradition set by its founder, Konosuke Matsushita, and cemented by him into a voluminous series of business books—a patchwork of personal philosophy, historical examples of how to make decisions, and directions on how to run the company—that leadership found difficult to adapt to modern markets, yet could not put aside for something newer.

Also, Konosuke's *unwritten* traditions—what everyone assumed he would do, even though he was long dead and hardly a single manager had met him, let alone worked with him—continued to hang over the company like a deep fog, obscuring even simple decision making.

The bulk of management and sales were in Japan, where they were insulated from the forces roiling world markets. In response to the global challenges that I put before them, most managers blandly assured me that the company's overseas divisions—which had no power whatever—were responsible for these.

The company was weak and highly vulnerable to predation. As one of the company's senior advisors, it was clear to me how little it would take to send the entire edifice right over a cliff.

I'm often asked, what held the company together for so long? The simple answer is inertia. People kept on doing what they knew how to do and they did it day in and day out, the world over. While the Konosuke bond was wearing thin, people stuck to it. More important, by March 2000, the company had almost $15 billion in cash and a debt/equity ratio of 0.33. Management had ensured, at least, that the firm could weather sizeable storms. This proved a sensible precaution. The storm that hit in the 2001 tech crash was pretty nearly perfect.

When a new generation of management came to the top in the late 1990s, it was faced with the hard fact that failure to reposition the company—quickly—could be fatal. Many had begun to wonder out loud if it wasn't already too late. Kirk Nakamura worried deeply that the firm could be acquired and broken up for its parts. A new sense of urgency was palpable.

What was needed was a new structure capable of profiting from the worldwide power shift to customers engendered by the compressive force of falling information costs. *Panasonic* is about how the new management team adopted such a structure and began the long march back to growth and prosperity.

Kirk Nakamura had urged radical change from his earliest days. For his pains he wound up in the United States. Whether it was to get him out of the way or to propel him to higher rank is unclear. Either way, sending Kirk to the States had unforeseen consequences for MEI and for Japanese industry as a whole.

I know from long experience that most Japanese executives sent to overseas operations, whatever they say about their time there, never bring reforms home to Japan.

Indeed, for several thousand years Japan has dealt with being surrounded by much stronger powers by creating an elaborate set of filters that decouple the country from foreign influence, or at least manage that influence in such a way that Japan benefits without being destabilized. Even second-generation Japanese expatriates, the so-called Nisei, are often filtered out. I was amazed one year when watching a figure skating competition on TV in Japan to see the Japanese-American skater and Olympic Gold Medalist Kristi Yamaguchi's last name written out on the TV screen in Katagana, the script for foreign words.

Ironically, the Matsushita system of foreign postings became the *force motrice* of the reform movement. Unlike many Japanese companies, MEI sends its people overseas for years, often decades, where they become intimately familiar with the workings of the countries they live in and form strong views on what must change for the company to succeed. What the reform did, in essence, was to bring large numbers of these experienced managers home and put them in positions of power from which they could quickly effect change.

Today, when you visit Matsushita, apart from the usual formalities of Japanese graciousness, almost all the inner workings and their descriptions are not much different from what you would see in any advanced company anywhere in the world. Decision making is quick and decisive. It is based on cogent inputs that anyone would recognize. Results are measured in cash and capital efficiencies and, of course, shareholder value.

The advantage is not just what has been done, but what Matsushita knows it can do in the future. MEI today can prioritize and decide based on market realities rather than on its internal issues.

Into the bargain, Matsushita's reforms involved merging a large number of companies over several years and dealing with significant postacquisition challenges. The new company comes with a large M&A expertise and a war chest. In global business, acquisition failure is a big risk and most deals, for reasons I will discuss, destroy value. MEI, by contrast, is emerging from its shakeup looking like Chemical Bank: a serial acquisition machine now calling itself J. P. Morgan Chase.

When Matsushita's repositioning began, no big company in the world, save IBM under Lou Gerstner, had ever contemplated such radical moves. And certainly no Japanese company had done so. Nissan began to reposition itself at about the same time as Matsushita, but to do the job Nissan had to import a foreign CEO, Carlos Ghosn.

What Matsushita contemplated was, for most Japanese companies, way, way outside the box: an all-Japanese effort—no imported management—to overthrow long-established and deeply held traditions and shake up the company from top to bottom. As the eighteenth-century scholar Dr. Johnson so famously retorted when Boswell remarked on the wonder of a woman's preaching at Sunday service, "The wonder was not that it was done well, but that it was done at all."

Matsushita's repositioning has an impact far beyond the company and its shareholders. The wheels came off Japan's business model in the late 1980s, and with Nissan's problems in the 1990s, even Japan's success in automobiles, once unquestioned, looked doubtful. Like it or not, when the world's second-largest economy starts to unwind, we all have a problem. We sell less to Japan than we should. Japan's products move from adding value for us to detracting value, so we stop buying them. The global market shrinks and with it job opportunities for everyone.

Remembering how important Japan was to creating the consumer surpluses that drove worldwide growth in the postwar period, the removal of this value engine from the global stage is no small matter.

A weak Japan creates a power vacuum in Asia that threatens the global balance of power. Japan's allies need a strong Japan to counter a large, growing, but potentially unstable China, and an impoverished and even more unstable North Korea. We all need Japan to have a strong voice, and that voice can be driven only by the standard of living of its people. Continued economic stasis in Japan and the prolonged inability of its leading companies like Matsushita to adapt to the new realities of world markets would have a catastrophic geopolitical effect and might not be recoverable.

But, because Matsushita is the first large Japanese company to restructure on its own terms, it has the potential to reset Japan's competitive position entirely. The type of leadership this takes is unique. Indeed, you could rebuild General Electric six ways to Sunday and whatever you did, my respect for Jack Welch notwithstanding, it would have none of the impact on global stability that the restructuring of Matsushita has had, and will continue to have for many decades.

THE LEGACY OF KONOSUKE MATSUSHITA

To understand just how big the restructuring challenge was for Matsushita, you have to understand something about the company's founder, Konosuke Matsushita, the organization he built, and why he built it that way. This will make it abundantly clear why the structure was so hard to alter.

To most Japanese of a certain generation, Konosuke Matsushita stands for nothing less than the rebuilding of the nation when it lay in ruin and destitution after World War II. Japan is not a small country—economically. But as a Canadian, I know how in a population below a certain size, one or two people can have an outsized effect. Everybody knows who these people are, and they achieve iconic status. In the United States, this is tough to do. Few corporate leaders become household names and those only after powerful and well-orchestrated publicity campaigns. Bill Gates may have celebrity status, but not many can name the head of Wal-Mart, Exxon, or Goldman Sachs even though these companies get lots of news coverage. In Japan, Konosuke Matsushita is an icon.

Konosuke was one of the very few entrepreneurs in history to take a company from seed stage to global empire. Having started, built, and sold my own business, I know how unusual this is. Managers typically come in what you might call generational expertise. There are the visionary founders who often cannot manage anything after sales hit a few million, if that. There are those who can accelerate a company from $10 million to $100 million, and those who have the operational expertise to grow an enterprise through the billion dollars plus mark. Increasingly, there are specialists in the $75 billion and up company. But almost no one can do it all. Konosuke was one who could and he was brought to his knees several times along the way, something that never happened to Bill Gates, Michael Dell, or John D. Rockefeller.

Konosuke founded his company long before the Second World War began. But Japan was destroyed during the war and many Japanese expected that it would never recover. Konosuke Matsushita rebuilt his company and, in doing so, became one of the main architects of Japan's revival. Many people believe, correctly, that modern Japan owes its standard of living to a handful of industrial leaders of which he is one, if not the principal one.

By some measures, Konosuke built more shareholder value in a single lifetime than anyone before him.[5] He was a businessman of exceptional ability and foresight. No Fortune 500 CEO now living can claim to have risen from the streets, struggled for basic literacy, taught himself through years of hard work, built a company from his living room, suffered all the crises of growth, rebuilt the company again from the ashes of a global maelstrom, and piloted it to business superpower status. He has no parallel today.

But his story is little known outside Japan because, except for a single big splash on the cover of *Time* in 1962, Konosuke never sought the limelight. Nor has any Matsushita executive since. In a world of celebrity executives, Konosuke gained none of the worldwide renown of his contemporary Thomas Watson Sr. or of John D. Rockefeller a generation earlier.

Konosuke Matsushita's early life shaped much of the company he built. Born in 1894, the youngest of eight in a prosperous family, he described his first four years as a "peaceful and carefree . . . idyll."[6] But life's hardships came early. His father, a farmer turned speculator, failed in 1898 and had to sell off the family's ancestral home and most of its belongings, a disgrace in a country that values ancestry and the land. Within a couple of years, his oldest brother, who might have made enough money to keep the family going, died and was shortly followed to the grave by another brother and sister. When Konosuke was nine, whatever was left of his family's ability to survive evaporated. His mother removed him from school and put him on a train for Osaka, then a teeming metropolis of just under a million people and the fifteenth-largest city in the world, to live and work in the home of a small-time *hibachi* maker.

During the early years of our marriage, my wife, Verna Mclean, supervised several group homes for teenagers in the charge of the Metropolitan Toronto Children's Aid Society. One of the saddest stories she brought home was the remark of a fourteen-year-old boy about his parents, that "you don't give away something that's valuable." Konosuke was given away, and he knew it. His resentment of his father must have been immeasurable. It is very hard for a boy to accept that his father is a failure, and the contrast with his first few years must have been stark and horrifying. "My mother's anguished face and shoulders drooping with weariness," he wrote in his mid-nineties, "are still a painfully vivid memory. . . . At night after the shop closed and I would go to bed, I could not help thinking of my mother. For four or five nights running I silently sobbed under the covers with what seemed unendurable homesickness. It was a long time before I completely overcame that loneliness."[7] The boy's misery was compounded by bed-wetting. Only three months after Konosuke arrived, the *hibachi* maker left town, and at ten, Konosuke had to find another home and another job, this time at a bicycle shop.

Within a few years what was left of his family collapsed completely. In 1906, two more sisters died. His father, who never returned home or came for his son, yet who never ceased to interfere in his life, and who gambled away what little money he made, also sickened and died. His mother lasted only seven years longer.

You can take it as a given that Konosuke Matsushita grew up a very angry young man. And the fact that he survived this ordeal made him a very tough, very angry young man.

When Konosuke Matsushita started work in the bicycle shop, he started with a lot of negatives: no family support, no education, and no money. He was a small, lonely kid in a big city. Another boy would have become a criminal. With drive, a successful, big-time criminal. Somehow Konosuke kept on track. He wrote years later that he owed much of this to the kindness of the bicycle-shop owner's family to whom management of his life had been outsourced. But no amount of kindness will keep an angry boy on the rails. The fact that he stayed there is quiet testimony to an immense, driving ambition and deep reserves of character.

Left without his family and without an education, Konosuke spent the rest of his life making up for them. His company became his family, a large one that gave him all the trials and more of any family but also satisfaction. To make up for his complete lack of education—he had only three and a half years of schooling—he created, from whole cloth, an entire codified system in tens of volumes on how to run a major corporation. You will find in his works endless details on how to manage people, costs, banks, and distributors, as well as a great deal of personal philosophy on everything from leadership to religion and global politics. Just to read a few pages is to realize that you are staring into the mind of, not just a great industrialist, but also a formidable intellect of the first rank.

The combination of intellect and industrialist is unusual. The effort it takes to build a major empire from scratch requires such single-mindedness that intellectualism is a luxury that even success does not afford. And few intellectuals have what it takes to build a business. Konosuke was different. He became a one-man MBA school and in doing so, ironically, created one of the biggest obstacles to change within the company he built.

Konosuke's combination of a stern pater familias, born from his lack of family, and his strict system of management, born from his lack of education, ossified the company. When the company needed change, it found itself struggling with Konosuke's legacy instead of looking hard at the world around it and adjusting to the rapid shifts in its customers and markets as he had done.

In the United States, the solution to ossification is simple: break it and rebuild. But in Japan, deep respect for a founder means that you have to think your way around his system and step very carefully. If the founder is believed to have said something specific, like the company must be organized in such and such a way, very few succeeding CEOs will defy this injunction, no matter how dire the situation. It is much more likely that the CEO will blame market misfires on a failure to adhere closely enough to a founder's views rather than change these views to suit the new circumstances.

Konosuke's long road to success began in 1910 when he left

the bicycle shop and, after a short period shoveling dry cement, took a job at the inside wiring department of the Osaka Electric Light Company, where he wired everything from small homes and businesses to theaters, mansions, and factories.

Small Beginnings in Osaka

Bicycles, inside wiring, and *hibachi* manufacturing came together in 1917 when Konosuke founded Matsushita Electric where his earliest products were bicycle lamps and dual socket outlets. These two items sprouted over the decades into a company mission to supply everything electric and electronic in as many global markets as possible, with one or two exceptions, like power-generation equipment and mainframe computers.

Starting a business is not easy. I've done it myself. Konosuke and I were not much different in age and we both began in one small room. His was his two-room, 590-square-foot (you read right) tenement house, a crude affair a full-scale model of which you can see today at MEI's House of History in Osaka. Even seeing the model, the true impact is lost until the guide shows you how, as his business grew, Konosuke took sleeping alcoves, stacked them with what look like bunk beds, and turned each bunk into a work space with room enough to sit and work, bent over. He launched the company with ¥100, about five months of his previous salary. Sean White and I started our first company in Toronto in a room of about the same size with C$1,500 each, my share being about one month's income from my previous job. Both "factories" were equally crude. Konosuke's was composed of a few benches and a mortar-and-pestle device for mixing electrical insulator. Ours had two desks we screwed together from plywood and two-by-fours that we cut on site, a single black rotary phone, and two portable typewriters.

In many ways, our motivations were the same. Konosuke went

to his boss at Osaka Electric Light with a new light socket design based on what he had learned from his years installing wiring. When the company turned him down, he quit and went on to make the sockets himself. I had worked for a short time at a bank and then at a newspaper and thought decisions at both needed help. So I left.

Konosuke started with the aid of his new wife, his brother-in-law, and two other assistants. Sean and I had each other to lean on. What we all had in common in 1917 and 1976 was absolutely no idea how to make our products or how to run a business. We all nearly went under almost immediately, an experience that is gut-wrenching. Matsushita Electric was plagued with all the problems of a start-up: poor sales, no capital, questionable products, and what is usually fatal, an entrepreneur without the slightest idea of what he was doing. More to the point, no idea of what he was doing right, or wrong, and no way to tell once he had done it.

But this is where the similarities end. Konosuke came from nothing, had no education, and had nothing to fall back on. Japan was poor, though growing, and the First World War was entering its final cataclysmic stage. Sean and I were both educated young men with few responsibilities and a lifetime to make changes in a large, advanced, rich, and peaceful economy overflowing with opportunity. We both have multiple citizenships and could work anywhere in the industrial world that we wanted to.

Konosuke Matsushita was one tough dude.

Basically, Konosuke did what we all do. He nosed his way around, got his head kicked in a few times, and slowly formulated a working strategy. In his case, he lived to tell about it and to write volumes on what to do and not to do if you are going to try the same thing. What Konosuke learned he turned into the operating philosophy of the company.

His own poverty drove Konosuke to focus on the essential usefulness of his products. He had a knack for seeking out the essence of a thing and reducing his products to a level of simplicity that matched. For example, reasoning that most Japanese homes of his day had one electric circuit, if lucky, he designed a simple light socket/outlet combination that let people use electricity and see at the same time. He designed a battery/lamp combo for bicycles—cars were then practically unknown in Japan—that lasted longer that anyone else's, making it easier for people to get to and from work in darkness.

But all Konosuke's agility did not prevent the company from going through an endless series of crises before the Second World War. In this period, his experience was the polar opposite of his contemporary, Thomas Watson Sr., who built IBM. In his biography of Watson, *The Maverick and His Machine*, Kevin Maney shows how Watson used successive waves of demand for data storage driven by America's late entry into World War I, the relative prosperity of the twenties in the United States, the introduction of Social Security in the thirties, wartime demand in the forties, and the postwar boom of the fifties to constantly propel IBM forward. You can almost imagine Watson using each of these episodes as a spacecraft uses the gravity of a planet to accelerate itself farther toward its destination. His IBM was one of continual prosperity. Even the Great Depression did not stop IBM's growth; it added employees constantly during a period when others shrank or folded.

Konosuke's Japan was nothing like as prosperous as Watson's America, and there was nothing stable about the environment in which Konosuke built his company. He launched his enterprise straight into the global crash of 1920–21, the sharpest and deepest ever. He built Matsushita during one of the most uncertain periods in world history and in one of the most volatile countries of the time. In the late nineteenth and early twentieth centuries, Japan plunged into the same colonial adventurism that plagued Europe until the First World War. Then, like the Germans and Soviets, after the war Japan transformed that adventurism into a military-industrial strategy for swallowing nations whole, while the rest of the world was caught in a prolonged period of economic retreat. Konosuke had to learn his lessons fast and then learn them all over again as his assumptions changed right under his feet in a series of lightning quick events throughout the 1930s that plunged the world into another, even more costly, war.

Once Konosuke got products to sell, and he was a master salesman, he faced regular working-capital crises. His constant nightmare during these difficult times was how to manage growth and working capital. After a period of rapid expansion in 1924–28, when he doubled plant size twice two years running, MEI's growth curve fell off while he battled his way through the thirties. As his company got bigger, the working-capital crises did too. These crises, which as every businessman knows are like returning waves of nausea, got horrible enough that Konosuke was forced to make radical changes in corporate organization. The most profound of these came in 1933 when he created his Division System, which drove the company for nearly three-quarters of a century, only to become the company's primary stumbling block as the twenty-first century began.

Konosuke's Division System

Before 1933, Matsushita was run like most companies of the day: a manufacturing department, a research department, a sales department, and so on, with each functional area responsible for everything. When the company added a new product, manufacturing took it over, lumping it in with everything else. Naturally, as the product base widened—by the early 1930s Matsushita made over three hundred of just about anything electrical that could be made at the time—efforts became diffused, and employees found it harder and harder to keep their eyes on the one person Konosuke believed counted: the customer.

Konosuke was an early adopter of divisionalization, so early that he could be credited with co-inventing the concept with Alfred Sloan at General Motors. He believed that shortening the distance between production and sales made successful and profitable customer relationships. So he took his 1,400 employees and divided them into four divisions with an average of 350 members. Each group had to survive on its own financial resources to ensure maximum independence of decision making and accountability.

In *Beating Japan*, our primary observation was the opposite: that Japanese companies in general were organized to be much too far removed from their overseas customers. All the prescriptions in that book were how to make an organization flat and decentralized enough to harness increased customer market power, exactly what Konosuke intended when he introduced the Division System six decades earlier.

Yet, when I started working with MEI in 1996, the first thing that struck me was how distant its organization was from its customers. Somehow, the Division System that was designed with the sole purpose of moving MEI closer to customers was driving it away from them. I also saw that Matsushita managers talked a good deal, as Konosuke had done, about putting the customer first—Konosuke famously said, "The customer is God"—but did little to ensure that the organization delivered. The company remembered only too well what Konosuke said to do, but had forgotten why he said it. In meeting after meeting it was clear that, no matter how many of Konosuke's tomes on management they read during their careers—and most Matsushita people are deeply familiar with his writings—MEI managers were not at all familiar with *how* he thought and how he reached his conclusions. If this one thing could be reintroduced to the firm's culture, which, Sean and I reasoned simplistically, shouldn't be too difficult, then the possibility of revolutionizing the organization and returning it to growing margins was real. We soon found out how hard this would be.

During the 1930s, Konosuke got his Division System up and running, expanding it in 1935 to nine divisions and four affiliated companies. By the beginning of the Second World War in 1939, he had nearly 7,000 employees and was a power in Japanese industry.

Adding to working-capital stresses came problems training line employees and managers for ever more complex duties, not just in their existing jobs, but in the new ones they would have to take on as the company expanded in both scale and scope. In the mid-1930s, Konosuke added another company hallmark, in-house training. At the time, the idea made sense: the company was growing in a new industry and needed skilled employees with abilities that were previously unknown and so unavailable. This too had unforeseen impacts as the company grew over the decades—it now employs 355,000 worldwide—by making the firm more and more ingrown as its internally centered training had the effect of shutting the company off from the powerful forces reshaping the global economy. When it came time to rebuild Matsushita in 2000, management had to find fresh blood from within a system that had trained itself into autosuffocation.

The Second World War was as dislocating for MEI as for any company anywhere during the period. The Japanese economy was militarized in 1938, and like companies among all the combatant powers, MEI shifted much of its operation from consumer products to industrial war materials, for which, Konosuke complained, it had no experience. Like American companies during and after the war, Matsushita operations followed Japanese armies throughout much of Asia, and the company finished the war with 30,000 employees, five times more than at the outset in 1939[8] and a third more than IBM at the time.[9]

The company by 1945 had several things it did not have in 1939: experience overseas, industrial products, the ability to manage scarcity, and the skills to manage a very large organization. The war transformed Matsushita Electric. In 1939, it was about an entrepreneur, Konosuke Matsushita. In 1945, it was about professional management.

You could make the case that Konosuke, like Thomas Watson Sr., had "a good war" and that of the two companies, Matsushita Electric and IBM, by 1945 Matsushita was much better positioned to become a global powerhouse. But Japan lost, and that is when Konosuke's war really began.

Early in the Occupation, the authorities told MEI to stop production, and with all his top managers, Konosuke was removed from the company. Matsushita Electric was broken up, factories were seized, overseas operations were confiscated, and company assets frozen. MEI's finances, and Konosuke's own, collapsed. Japan entered an economic tailspin until the Korean War began in 1950, kick-starting demand. The five years between were a titanic struggle for Konosuke to pull himself back from the brink. These years were difficult, but he finally won his company back, though Matsushita Electric Works did not reenter the fold until 2004, nearly seventy years after its founding as an MEI "sister" company and sixty years after the Allies severed it from its parent.

For most of us, the events of the first half of the last century are found in history books or old documentaries. The hell of defeat—Japan, perhaps more than Germany, was a heap of rubble—and the Herculean effort it took to rebuild even a house, let alone a 30,000-person enterprise, are hard to grasp. We get off the plane in Tokyo or Frankfurt today and enter a world of modernity and seemingly unbroken prosperity. How hard it was to recover, the level of desperation, the poverty, and the misery of millions of destitute people are unknown. When people say these days, "That is so yesterday," they are not kidding. The staggering amount of information unleashed by the information revolution has pushed recent events into a distant and often-inaccessible past. This was brought home to me a few years ago I went with my son's Boy Scout troop for a tour of West Point put on by the cadets. One cadet was stationed at each statue of a famous general. The cadet standing by Eisenhower could tell us only that Eisenhower was, in fact, a five-star general (he even checked the statue's epaulet to be sure that there were five stars) and the years during which he had attended West Point. Where he had served, when, and what he did after leaving the Army were complete mysteries to a man who was nominally the product of one of the nation's better universities. Cadet after cadet reeled off the same history-free biography of his assigned statue. For the amusement of the other fathers I asked each cadet why West Point was sited where it was. None knew, even though a casual glance up and down the Hudson River from where we were standing could tell a ninth-grade geography student that it blocks access to New York from the north and to the American interior from the south. This ignorance gap is a household phenomenon in America today. Add the fact that we don't spend much time in our schools on Japan's postwar hardships and what Konosuke went through to rebuild his company is lost to us.

Nevertheless, remembering that Konosuke was already middle aged, had been seriously traumatized as a child, had had no more than four years of schooling, and had gone through all the wrenching cycles of start-up, cash burns, gyrating sales, the Depression, and finally the complete destruction of his country brought on by a bunch of irresponsible militarists for whom he must have had little sympathy, the wonder is that in 1950 he had any stomach for another challenge.

That he did, and that he pulled his firm out of the ditch in any shape at all, gave him iconic status. And made changing anything he mandated next to impossible for his successors. Indeed, it took nearly a quarter of a century after his retirement before someone as change-driven as Kirk Nakamura could take the reins.

Following the war, Konosuke's Division System became increasingly sacrosanct. As long as markets for MEI products were growing, which they were for the next four decades, this was fine. But once Konosuke was gone and global markets shifted against Matsushita in the mid-1980s, there was no one to apply his methods, or even who remembered what they were. The company began to drift.

Over time, Konosuke's Division System lead to further diffusion of effort in R&D, marketing, and sales. Konosuke's extraordinary range of overlapping devices, components, systems, brands, and companies could not possibly get the attention they needed. By the time Konosuke passed from the scene, sales success came more by accident than by design.

Moreover, Konosuke's organization encouraged factories to force-feed sales operations around the world with products for which there may have been no market or which were simply misdesigned for that market. By the 1990s, the company had basically stopped dead while markets everywhere were booming. The Division System slowly slipped into a crisis: too many products, many overlapping, sold by too many divisions and affiliates, and most with too little market share to have any market power. The more MEI sold, the weaker it got. Others with better business models were booming; many of MEI's best retail customers were taking 100 percent plus of the profits in MEI's markets, leaving the company to suck air.

Konosuke himself was a relentless eliminator of middlemen. He constantly sought a more efficient means of distribution. So while some of his ideas, like product proliferation, were running out of steam, others, like disintermediation, would come into their own only with the Internet long after he had passed on.

In a world where advantage goes to the speediest—to those companies able to substitute information for other resources faster than their competitors—Matsushita lagged badly. It was ceding advantage to others often without even knowing that it was doing so.

KONOSUKE'S PHILOSOPHY

All of Konosuke's philosophy can be written in a single imperative: "Be a humble merchant."

What he meant by this is that you must design your company and manage its operations to be as close to your customers, and as familiar with their needs, as is the owner of a small store. When you lose that simple proximity, no matter how sophisticated the operation, you lose control of cash flow and market share. Losses will mount and the company will vanish. All Konosuke's initiatives, from the first electric socket through the Division System, the creation of the National Stores, and the dramatic Atami Conference in the mid-sixties where he reshaped his company for a final time, were designed to make the company close enough to its customers to manage all its touch points of cash.

There are two fundamental problems with Konosuke's philosophy:

- It is easier to say than to do, and the gap between say and do widens geometrically with the size of a company.
- How it is implemented changes as fast as the falling cost of information disintermediates markets by increasing the rate of information substitution for other resources.

As Konosuke himself recognized from the very beginning of his company, being a humble merchant really means constant reorganization to keep customer proximity in place. He knew better than anyone that if you are not close enough to your customers to get your lights punched out regularly, you don't know enough about your customers to add value.

But he also found himself caught between the Japanese habit of reverence for the founder—himself—and his own understanding of the need for constant change in the structure of the organization. So long as he was in harness, he leveraged the reverence to make changes as he saw them. Once he was gone, however, founder reverence kicked in and the company stuck like glue to his last set of directives and wouldn't let go. Indeed, it became heresy to suggest changing Konosuke's modus operandi, even though, in his writings, he endlessly urged constant reform and warned against getting stuck in a structure that no longer responded to markets. As a result, Konosuke's philosophy and Matsushita became one and the same. I was in one meeting where I asked an executive why he did certain things and he pointed to his officewide shelf of Konosuke's writings and said, "Because HE said so." End of discussion.

As with everything Japanese, however, things are never this clear-cut. The idea common among non-Japanese that Japan cannot change is an amazing conceit, considering the evident size and modernity of its economy. Moreover, Japan has many historical figures in addition to its business leaders who took risks. Just as Americans look to Washington, Jefferson, Lincoln, and others to inspire them, Japanese look to their own examples. Konosuke's writings are full of historic references designed to inspire his employees to take the risks needed for change. He used one set of three shoguns in particular. These three consolidated Japan during the great nation-building era that swept the world through the sixteenth and seventeenth centuries: Oda Nobunaga, Toyotomi Hideyoshi, and the greatest of them, Ieyasu Tokugawa (the Toranaga of James Clavell's novel *Shogun*). The Tokugawa shogunate lasted from 1600 to 1868. During this time, Japan became a nation-state so highly organized that no foreign power managed to inflict on it the depredations that befell China, Africa, and the Americas. Whatever these shoguns did was tough stuff.

During a critical period in Matsushita's reforms, I used the same three shoguns as examples for management. I remember once being at dinner with Kirk in Osaka and reminding him of the risks that the three took and that he, too, would have to take similar risks. His face showed a clear recognition, almost serenity—hard to imagine in view of how difficult we all knew reform would be, and how much harder it actually became. Kirk repaid my encouragement years later when my wife and I were invited to Shinshin-an, Konosuke's private garden in Kyoto. The manager, Tadahiko Tokuda, asked us to tea in Konosuke's small teahouse. The subtleties of the Japanese tea ceremony are beyond me but the Japanese know tea like the French know wine, and I'm a big fan of both. I was enjoying my tea, not thinking much about the cup, when Tokuda pointed out that I was drinking from the Black Raku Tea Bowl, Konosuke's favorite. I nearly dropped it in surprise. More symbolic still, the bowl was made by Keinyu in his family's traditional style inspired by Sen no Rikyu, Hideyoshi's tea master.

Konosuke himself was not at all religious about how a company should be run. Keep it physically close to customers—something very different from talking about customers and giving them lip service—and reason the company's operations back from that. On the downside, however, the job of reforming MEI was made more difficult for everybody by several of Konosuke's personal behaviors that were a result of his long years of struggle and that, by the late 1960s, he had inculcated deep into the company's collective psyche:

- Keep your head down
- Focus on the business basics
- Waste no time on foolish publicity
- Be modest

In his time, Konosuke had never been rewarded for seeking celebrity status, and he saw no reason why such status was more than a frivolity. The same character traits, when hitched up to founder reverence, prevented the company from seeking celebrity status for its products or its management. This came back to haunt the firm big-time.

Konosuke's behaviors are not surprising in a man of his

background. He was immensely proud, of course, and had plenty of hard edges—he was notorious for his temper and did not tolerate fools—but he was no egotist. He put the company first, second, and third. While he was well known in Japan (it would be hard for him not to be), he was a nonentity outside it. When John Kotter came to write his 1997 biography of Konosuke, *Matsushita Leadership*, he opened the book with wonder at how he had never heard of the man even after eighteen years on the faculty of Harvard Business School. The first he learned of Konosuke Matsushita was when his dean asked him to become the Konosuke Matsushita Professor of Leadership. Konosuke didn't advertise himself, and no one at Matsushita, least of all a CEO, has since. Where Steve Jobs is the face of Apple and is closely identified with its brand architecture and management style, and where Michael Dell is similarly identified with Dell, there is no face of Matsushita, and probably never will be.

By the time I got involved, the sundries of Konosuke's many prescriptions dominated company thinking, even though almost all had been obsolete for decades. The basics had been forgotten, and when they were remembered, were not properly understood.

An excellent example was Konosuke's system of National (and now Panasonic) Shops. He built these following one of his periodic working-capital crises to move the company's National brand products closer to customers through a series of merchant-owned shops selling National-only products. Japan is littered with these shops, most of which are tiny outlets found off main streets and in Japan's neighborhoods. Here, Konosuke reasoned, "humble" merchants could work closely with their neighbors to solve the common problems of household management with everything from National: batteries, clocks, white goods, tools, TVs, and audio products. Proximity to customers came first, and this was his way of doing it. Through the captive National Shop channel, Matsushita could closely manage its customers' experience of its products, the very essence of superior brand management.

Decades later, retail changed. Stores specialized and became larger, and margins eroded. More recently, the Internet arrived and companies started to sell directly to customers with no retail outlet whatever. Still, the National/Panasonic Shops continued on as if nothing had changed. Matsushita felt obliged to support them, even though their time had long gone. The company could not face their replacement with another channel, or even seriously reform them, because they were Konosuke's baby and that made them untouchable even a quarter century after his death.

What was entirely forgotten was why Konosuke had created them in the first place and the speed with which he would have moved to shake things up to get ever closer to his customers in the Internet age. And that, in a sentence, is how Kirk Nakamura saw the firm: in dire need of figuring out what Konosuke would do and doing it. Quickly.

Regional Balance in Japan

To non-Japanese, the people of Japan appear to be a homogeneous whole. The Japanese themselves do a lot to encourage that view, endlessly talking about the uniqueness of their culture, food, language, and so on. But nothing could be farther from reality.

Setting aside the obvious fact that there are large numbers of Koreans, Chinese, and native Ainu, with markedly different traditions from those that we think of as Japanese, as recently as the Tokugawa period the country was deeply divided into regional feudatories. These only momentarily coalesced over the millennia until the great nation-building age that began with the creation of Spain by Ferdinand and Isabella in the late fifteenth century. By the late sixteenth century, Japan, like Spain, France, and Britain, was melding into a unified whole.

But over the several centuries since Spain piloted the model, nation building crossed our planet with varying degrees of success.

Supposedly successful nations like the United Kingdom and the United States went through long periods of discord and violence when they were anything but united. Some, like Spain, still suffer centrifugal pressures.

Equilibrium is not a given for a nation-state, even one composed of people, like the Japanese, who speak a common language.

In Japan's case, pretty much the entire structure and tradition of modern Japan were built in the late sixteenth and early seventeenth centuries by the three powerful leaders Konosuke admired: Nobunaga, Hideyoshi, and Ieyasu. At the completion of their work, which was as bloody and gruesome as nation-state creations tend to be, Japan emerged as a coherent, and coherently managed, country. Its regional feudatories were ruthlessly crushed, though not eliminated as they were in France and Britain. For two and a half centuries, faction seethed quietly, out of sight.

On the surface, the Tokugawa reorganization of Japan was so strong that Ieyasu's immediate successors were able to expel Westerners, something neither China, nor all the inhabitants of the Western Hemisphere, were able to do. Japan's internal coherence was resilient enough to keep the West out right though the centuries of the West's conquests of the Americas, South Asia, Africa, and Australasia. Only fairly late in the colonization process—the mid-nineteenth century—did Japan open up to Western trade and only then after a fifteen-year virtual civil war between resurgent feudatories that culminated in a three-day Gettysburg-like battle near Osaka. Uprisings lasted until 1877. In the event, however, Japan was able to work with the West on its own terms, something no one else managed. In less than forty years after the end of the civil war, a modern Japanese fleet sent just about every ship in the Imperial Russian Navy to the bottom at Tsushima. Japan had arrived.

You would be forgiven for thinking that Japan's deep regional—feudal—differences have long vanished. How, after all, could the

Russians be defeated and, less than half a century after that, Pearl Harbor be attacked by anything less than a thoroughly well-managed and unified nation?

They couldn't, and that is the point. Japan masked the deep differences that long divided it by being well managed.

The first thing a tourist learns about Japan is its powerful regionalism. People are proud of their ancient, local traditions. These run far deeper than regional cuisine and dialects and they tore the country apart as recently as the Second World War, which, arguably, Japan launched in the Pacific when the regional clan that controlled the Imperial Army fell out with the clan that controlled the Navy. The ensuing power struggle, incredibly a hangover from Ieyasu's seizure of control at Sekigahara in 1600, was catastrophic for Japan.

No one is more sensitive to these deep divisions, and the cost of mismanaging them, than the Japanese themselves. Of course, no sane person expects the Japanese to start killing each other in regional strife anytime soon and certainly all Japanese would scoff at the notion. But they also take very seriously the need, call it the obligation, to sew all parts of the country into any large organization. The lesson of the last century and a half is that the nation goes forward either together or not at all.

A major Japanese corporation like Matsushita is therefore careful to ensure that as much of the country as possible shares in its job-creation potential. Doing this, moreover, crafts a company-wide allegiance that effectively replaces the regional allegiances that destroyed the country in living memory.

This effort has proven successful: instead of getting war and destruction, Japan became the world's second-largest economy in only a few decades. Wealth there is remarkably broad-based and this is due in no small part to the regionalism of Japan's leading companies.

Matsushita is no exception. Konosuke was scrupulous in his attention to Japan's regional needs. He made sure that large parts of

Japan shared in his company's prosperity. Loyalty to the company became familial.

Then he went one step further. He harnessed Japan's centrifugal regionalism by planting his partially owned affiliates in those parts of the country where he could capitalize on strong local loyalties. From 1952, when he founded Matsushita Electronics Corporation, through 1979, when he founded Matsushita Battery Industrial, Konosuke leveraged Japan's regional strengths. During a seven-year run from 1966, when he founded Matsue Matsushita, through 1973, when he established Takefu Matsushita, this trend was particularly pronounced.[10] This period coincided with the formative years in the careers of many of today's reformers.

Some of these regional deals had major ramifications on the structure of reform in the 2000–2005 period. In 1955, for example, Konosuke founded Kyushu Matsushita Electric (KME) in Fukuoka, the largest city on the western island of Kyushu. When I first visited KME in 1997, almost all those who worked there—thousands—were local people. Only a few were "outsiders" from other parts of MEI.

Kyushu, through the port of Nagasaki, was for centuries the only trading gateway to the outside world permitted by the Tokugawa shogunate. But Kyushu was also disenfranchised by the Tokugawa, who were easterners, and fumed for two and a half centuries. When Commodore Perry provided the catalyst for shaking up the existing order, the West, led by Kyushu, got rid of the shogunate, restored the emperor, and established industrial Japan. The people of Kyushu are proud of this first-mover tradition. In a sense, they see themselves much as Texans do, as a breed apart, ready to take risks that others would not. They also take very seriously their many centuries of interaction with overseas markets.

During my first visit to KME in early 1997, I explained my thinking on world markets to Hajime Sakai, then CEO, and

Kazuyoshi Fujiyoshi, now CEO of the Panasonic Communications Company (PCC), which inherited most of KME's operations during the 2001 realignment, and returned a year later to find the entire organization restructured. Just like that. Kyushu guys don't fool around.

I remember a discussion at one meeting of how the division of powers in the overall Matsushita organization prevented KME from making cell phones, something that, as it was one of the world's biggest suppliers of telephones, it knew it could do and do well. The division assigned to make cell phones was doing badly. KME management was frustrated beyond measure. Someone finally demanded loudly, "Why don't they let the boys from Kyushu show them how to do it!" That's Japanese regionalism. You mess with it at your peril. No one knew this better than Kirk Nakamura.

When restructuring a company like MEI, Japan's regions must be carefully balanced. While KME lost something in the restructuring, as PCC it gained operations elsewhere in Japan and overseas that fit better with a more rational line of business. In any case, no one can be seen to be an absolute loser except at the margins—there are always operations that must be closed or sold off so that the main balance of the company can be maintained.

Any CEO can immediately see the problem. If you try to rationalize one part of the organization for whatever reason, you risk destroying the fabric not just of the company and its essential loyalties, but of the nation as well. An American CEO like Jack Welch would never have to deal with this: if a line of business doesn't perform, it is sold or shuttered. Choreographed regionalism Japan-style is a part of business management that we don't have to think about. Trying to reform Konosuke's regionalism without disturbing the fabric of the company's, or Japan's, social order became one of Kirk's biggest challenges.

Add in globalization, which is really just a fancy word for free trade in a world of low-cost information on the Internet, and you have a dagger ready to rend Japan's social fabric from top to bottom. If outsourcing to cut costs means the end of a region's role in the company, there will be consequences. We will see later how Matsushita handled globalization by rethinking vertical integration and the nature of value-added in its products. This does not mean that the regionalism at the center of MEI's operation is preserved forever. It means only that it has been dealt with for the moment. As information costs continue to fall, and the organization is stressed again, which is inevitable, a new generation of managers will have to revisit the problem. Probably sooner than later.

Even though Konosuke was the CEO of an information-intense company, we shall see when we look later on at what happened to DEC, Compaq, and Hewlett-Packard, companies whose misadventures made a deep impression on Kirk Nakamura, information intensity does not mean information efficiency. Still less does it allow a CEO to foresee the impact of ever-cheaper information on the structure of a company. Konosuke passed from the scene never realizing the deep inflexibilities of his business model and long before the cost of information went into the free fall that would destroy so many companies worldwide. And very nearly ruined his.

Global Thrust

When Konosuke expanded MEI overseas for the second time after the Occupation returned his company, he more or less ported his regional structure into foreign markets. This made Konosuke's regional balancing act even more difficult to manage, and even more difficult to reform, as the years went on.

Remembering that Konosuke invented the divisional structure at more or less the same time Alfred Sloan did at GM, that he had expanded overseas once already behind the Japanese armies during the war, and that he ended the war with an international company a third larger than IBM, he had every reason to believe that his methods would work. He looked at global markets much the way he looked at Japan and tried to strike a balance everywhere. Compounding this, each of Konosuke's affiliate companies had its own global agenda. In some places these agendas made sense; in others they didn't. Europe is a great example of where regional balance is often a bad idea. France and Germany have long had laws designed to minimize rapid employment growth and structural flexibility. Investing in Ireland and the United Kingdom, by contrast, permits easy access to EU (European Union) markets without the headaches of being forced by government to stand still while markets move ahead of you. Europe's regional complexities are a problem for Matsushita, but everyone else who competes there, including the Europeans themselves, has the same issues.

Konosuke was one of the first to recognize the opportunities in China. He struck up a relationship with Deng Xiaoping in the late 1970s, soon after Mao Tse-tung's death, a relationship from which Matsushita continues to benefit. Konosuke saw the sales potential in modernizing China and early recognized what the change of guard there meant. He also grasped instinctively how regional balance would play a role in securing a strong marketing presence there.

Konosuke's international business model proved successful and grew for more than three decades before it ran out of steam at the end of his life. He had no incentive to change his approach and would have been nuts to consider a risky move that appeared totally unnecessary at the time. Indeed, in his order of priorities, cash management came first and market disintermediation came second. At the half century, when Konosuke began his postwar overseas expansion, there was nothing in the duplication of his regional model internationally that called his priorities into question.

The Glory Years, 1950–1984

By 1950, the Korean War released much of Japanese industry, and with it Matsushita, from the complex system of controls imposed by the MacArthur shogunate. Konosuke reestablished his Division System, rebuilt in Japan, and cut deals in the United States and Europe. He did not, however, have the advantage of being on the side that won the war. Many U.S. companies expanded right behind U.S. forces as MEI had expanded behind Japan's armies. But when the war ended, the U.S. companies kept right on going—Coca-Cola is a famous example—while Japanese companies like MEI lost not only their overseas operations throughout Asia but also many of their domestic ones as well.

Undaunted, Konosuke moved quickly after 1950 to exploit global markets, especially in the First World, and the next quarter century was one of almost continual growth for Matsushita. Sales improvements of 10 to 25 percent a year were not uncommon. Operating profits rose steadily, peaking in 1984 at over 12 percent.

Electric and electronic products of all kinds seemed to explode out from Matsushita during those years. There were TVs and stereos, automotive products, white goods of every type, electric shavers and pencil sharpeners, air conditioners, machine tools for making electric products, batteries and circuit boards, components for industrial use, and office products of all sorts. The range boggles the imagination. These products poured into every corner of the globe. In addition, because Japan had so recently industrialized, Matsushita products had the kind of simple usefulness and reliability that emerging economies need and at prices people there can afford.

Soon, the Panasonic name was everywhere. And respected too. Konosuke's tried-and-true system of waiting for a market to establish itself and then moving in with better-made, easier-to-use, and cheaper versions served the company well.

Things did not go without a hitch, of course. They never do. In the early 1960s Matsushita had one of its periodic working-capital crises, and Konosuke assembled his top management in yet another conference, known in company lore as the Atami Conference of 1964. Here he pronounced yet another revision of his distribution system. At the time, Matsushita took over 200 days to turn a sale into cash, a number that most CEOs would say was recoverable but only at sizeable cost to the company.

Konosuke, however, was seventy, had been to hell and back many times, knew a crisis when he saw one, and knew how to deal with it. What he never managed, however, was to get someone else to do his thinking for him. At an age when he should have had a good half-dozen managers able to identify the problem long before the cash cycle hit 200 days and bring him workable solutions, he did not. This was his greatest weakness. It was here that his lack of education, combined with his interminable energy and the deep stubbornness that had saved Matsushita so many times, created a major character flaw. He was so used to making the really big decisions himself, and so was everyone else, that his company came perilously close to missing out on its best years, the two decades from 1964 to 1984.

The Atami Conference became legendary in the company as Konosuke's last visionary step. There are still a handful of executives who were there as young men and they were deeply marked by the experience. Kirk Nakamura is one of them. To gain inspiration while CEO, Kirk periodically went over to the House of History next to his office, to watch a video of Konosuke's address to the conference.

By the time Konosuke retired from active management in 1977, Panasonic was a household name around the world. When he died in 1989, sales hit $46 billion, an amazing sum for an uneducated man who rose from the streets, and taught himself how to run a company from seed stage to global empire.

The Hard Years, 1985–1999

The post-Konosuke years of 1985–1999 were the most difficult in MEI history since the immediate postwar period. Sales continued to grow, but after the major yen revaluations of the mid-eighties, profits were increasingly hard to come by. Some things worked well for the company. VHS was a big hit, and its Matsushita Communications Industrial subsidiary became Japan's dominant supplier of cell phones and the profit engine of the company. But, as time went on, it became apparent to senior managers that the reliance on only one product at a time for earnings was very unhealthy for a company with such a broad reach. Too many other products either lost money or made too little of it. The harder the company pushed to increase sales, the further away the profitability of 1984 seemed to go. Matsushita was losing its grip, and the great man himself was not there to firm it up again.

During these years, the personal computer and Internet revolutions hit in two strong waves that shifted market power

Matsushita Stumbles

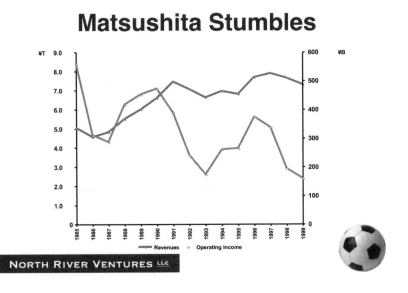

NORTH RIVER VENTURES ᴸᴸᶜ

sharply away from producers like Matsushita and into the hands of their customers. No less a computer powerhouse than Intel had to withdraw its first Pentium processor in 1993 when complaints poured into the company over the Internet, shaking a management that had never dealt directly with the users of its products before. This event signaled to producers everywhere that they could no longer be insulated from the wrath of their customers by their distributors, or in Intel's case, from customers of those like IBM who used Intel chips in their computers. It is from events like these that businesses coined the word "user" to differentiate between their customers, in the sense that Circuit City is Matsushita's customer for plasma displays, and the customers of their customers, the people like you and me who actually use the products and pay for them. Before the Internet, we users had limited recourse to those who made the products we bought. We relied on retailers to take our complaints back to their suppliers, a long and uncertain process. Most of this information was lost: retailers transmit mostly price information, the least useful kind of customer information there is. As the Intel in-cident made clear, from the mid-1990s we could e-mail the CEO of whoever made what we bought and demand satisfaction. MEI was not ready for this.

The Konosuke model provided for that in principle with its humble merchant philosophy. But, in practical terms, it offered nothing because Konosuke introduced his last major organization innovation thirty years before the Pentium. As the Internet disin-termediated market after market, compressing organizations everywhere, MEI pressed on as if nothing had happened. Sooner or later management would have to do something, and the longer it waited to do this the more painful its decisions would be.

R&D Troubles

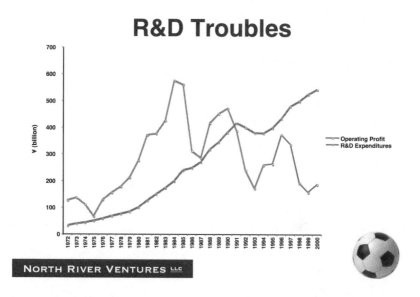

NORTH RIVER VENTURES LLC

By 1987, R&D expenditures were outrunning operating prof-its and the question had to be asked: "What was Matsushita in business for?" If it could not return its R&D costs, then running at twice the percent of sales that they had in Konosuke's day, what was the point? This question would remain unanswered for another thirteen years.

Management was not asleep during this period. Far from it. In 1991, it launched the Breakthrough Plan. This was followed in 1994 by the Revitalization Plan, and in 1997 by the Progress 2000 Plan. In spite of every effort, however, nothing seemed to work, or if it did, did so only momentarily before profits resumed their inevitable slide. The idea that what was needed was a systemic overhaul was a bridge too far. Management looked at the idea with great caution, as it should have. The effort required was greater than anyone anticipated. And it nearly brought the house down.

I got involved with the company toward the end of this period, as Progress 2000 was beginning, when the distance between Matsushita and its customers was at its most extreme, and the centrifugal effect of Konosuke's division and affiliate system had stressed the organization to the limits of its tolerance. Indeed, I said at the time, beyond its tolerance.

Matsushita at the End of the Twentieth Century

By the end of the twentieth century, the system Konosuke built had failed. He had been out of daily management for a generation and no one who was active in the company had worked with him in his prime or understood how he reached decisions.

For example, when I point out to MEI people that almost all of Konosuke's big moves were prompted by a crisis in working capital, this comes as a revelation. For whatever reason, Konosuke never stood up and said, "We are not converting sales into cash fast enough and I propose the following changes to fix this." I am convinced that if he had, his message would not have been muddied over the decades. Management would have been focused relentlessly on improving cash conversion. Constant restructuring would have been a by-product.

In 1998, Sean and I presented to management the Bank of Matsushita chart to drive home Konosuke's cash-management message. Dell was turning a sale into cash in minus-ten days. That is, it was getting paid before it incurred expense. MEI was taking close to three months longer than Dell and was suffering from much lower turns in property, plant, and equipment, and in inventory. In effect, MEI had become a bank, the sole function of which was to finance its inventory. Konosuke would have been horrified; this was his greatest nightmare, something he had struggled against since the earliest days of the company.

The Bank of Matsushita, 1997

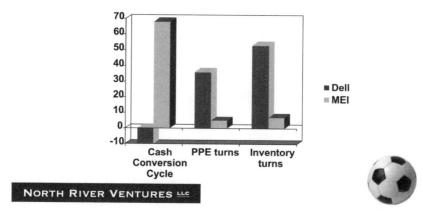

We also showed management in the United States and Japan the Margin Squeeze chart, showing the clear shift in market power to the competition. Matsushita's superior gross margins said that it was the better manufacturer compared to Dell, but its poor net showed, we said, that it was flaming off SG&A and losing all of its upstream advantages and the value of its R&D spending. This balance had to be righted to ensure the company's future.

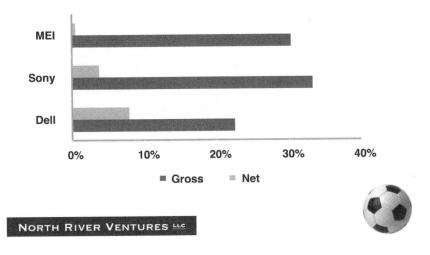

Margin Squeeze, 1997

North River Ventures LLC

We emphasized something else that this chart makes clear: Sony's better performance at the time was better only relative to Matsushita. Compared to Dell, Sony's fundamentals were weak, as became evident in Sony's earnings problems of later years. The real competition therefore was not Sony, we said, but Dell. More to the point, the competition was not Dell itself, but Dell's *system*, just as many decades earlier, the problem for Matsushita's competitors was not Matsushita and its products, but Konosuke's system.

The solution, we reminded management, was to return to Konosuke's basic philosophy, which we summarized as "Use every available means to get closer to your customer."

But this was not going to be easy and it was not going to happen overnight. I prepared a set of data showing the impact of Dell's cash conversion cycle.

This chart showed Matsushita the rate at which Dell had improved its ability to turn a sale into cash. The company's position deteriorated for some time until Michael Dell's decision, Konosuke-style, to restructure distribution in late 1995. He set the clear goal

Dell's Cash Conversion Cycle

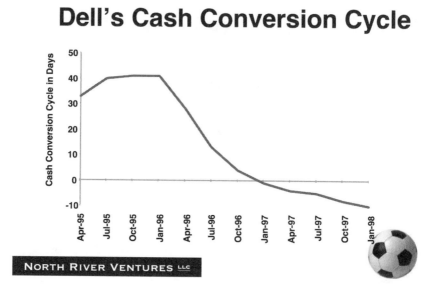

of turning the company into an engine of negative working capital within twelve months by seamlessly integrating distribution into manufacturing. His simple insight that manufacturing should start upstream in Dell's supply chain and end in your home or office revolutionized cash management, just as the Sloan/Konosuke Division System innovations did nearly three-quarters of a century earlier. The problem for competitors like Matsushita, however, was that because they did not, like Dell, make cash cycles their primary measurement of operations, they didn't actually see Michael Dell do this until years after he made his move. I didn't notice myself until early 1998, more than two years after Dell restructured, when Sean sent me some research from Solomon Smith Barney that noted the change.

This time advantage proved crucial for Dell. When mapped onto its competition, which, essentially, is what the Soccer Ball System does, Dell could get a clear picture of who could respond to it and when. Later I will show you how Dell calculates this to its advantage. Since most of Dell's competitors took much longer than Dell to convert a sale into cash when Dell started to integrate distribution into its supply chain, even if these companies did as well as Dell did, it would take them much longer to make the same transition. How much longer? Applying this Soccer Ball Metric to Matsushita showed that the company would not get to where Dell was in the second quarter of 1996 until sometime in 2007. Our question for MEI was, if so, could the company survive until then? No one got this faster than Kirk Nakamura.

These difficulties were compounded by the fact that, as we showed management in the Shift to Growth chart, MEI was in too many large but slow-growing markets, like TVs. Not only was the company's business model obsolete, which would take time to fix, but MEI had no path to growth. For Kirk Nakamura, these were unpleasant findings, but they powered his thinking from then until his retirement in 2006.

Shift to Growth

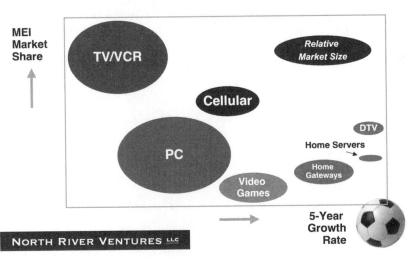

Strategically, the company faced yet a further challenge. The Internet was destroying how everyone thought of "convergence," a pie-in-the-sky market where digitization was supposed to break down barriers between markets for movies, recordings, consumer electronics, computers, and telecommunications, allowing players in each market easy entry into other markets and a strong growth path there. Competitors in each industry assumed that their own abilities would let them clobber incumbents in the other markets. Many believed that their core strengths were a license to buy their way into businesses where they knew nothing. MEI itself bought MCA, though it later dropped the company like a hot potato. Convergence was supposed to make the Shift to Growth chart irrelevant because you just hop, skip, and jump to better market opportunities.

It didn't work out that way. Instead of markets converging on one another, an entirely exogenous force, the Internet, exploded outward, as we showed Kirk in the Internet Model chart in 1996, absorbing other markets and subsuming them. By driving information costs down faster than anyone planned, the Internet was a deflationary force. Markets shrank rather than grew. Convergence did not reduce the risk of being in a PC or a TV prison. It increased this risk, dramatically and quickly. Reform at Matsushita would have to come fast if the company expected to survive this force.

Internet Model

Communications

Computers

Exploding Internet

Consumer Electronics

NORTH RIVER VENTURES LLC

The organization in 2000 was so confusing that no management team, no matter how good, could actually "see" what was going on. Management was like an air traffic control operation with hundreds of planes ready to take off and land but with no radar to see where these planes were. The legacy structure had to be swept aside just for Matsushita even to think about strategic decisions, let alone know what decisions to take. I had been advising the firm for five years at a very high level and even I had no idea which way was up. Everywhere I turned something was misplaced. For customers, the firm was impossible to navigate. Before anything could be done, this had to change.

One of my favorite misalignments was astonishing for its utter pointlessness. Kyushu Matsushita Electric (KME) could make wireless telephones for sale all over the world but not in Japan, and as we saw could not make cell phones for any market. Matsushita Communications Inc. (MCI), a telecommunications infrastructure provider, had the sole right to make cell phones globally, but was incapable of selling anything outside Japan. (See "Some Things Don't Work Out: Cell Phones" in Chapter 3.) The KME folks would have killed to get into the U.S. and European cell phone markets, which were burgeoning. But, so long as MCI, which sold almost nothing there, held the veto, KME was stuck. While the world went through a wireless revolution, Matsushita's organizational constraints kept it outside that business. Regardless of the rationale for this, it was madness. No company can be run this way and no one knew it better than Kirk, who had been on the bleeding edge of MCI's inabilities in the United States, where he watched a market race through a growth curve that MCI (to the astonishment of both of us) refused to serve. And there was nothing he, or anyone, could do about it.

Incredibly, however, by the late 1990s, MCI's business with Japan's leading cellco, NTT DoCoMo, was so great that it accounted for the bulk of MEI's profits. Ironically, while the structure of the group didn't work, and MCI was absent from global markets, its earnings insulated MEI from change.

Atsushi Murayama, a senior managing director at the time and later a top reformer, recalled that at the company's 1999 Top Seminar, an annual offsite meeting for senior executives where I have given lectures since 2003, by chance one of the breakout groups consisted exclusively of all the senior managing directors. "We put aside the theme of the meeting that time and instead just conversed with each other. It was very interesting, since each of the members was experiencing his sense of crisis."[11] After this meeting four others followed. The first of these was on the form group management should take.

When I asked him why the company didn't just break itself up in 2000, he said, "We had a raison d'être that we believed in and we had a concrete proposal for reform and we had much of what we needed in many divisions but they were not so strong." What had held the firm back was that "the company was so obsessed with the past that people were always apprehensive and this weakened their efforts."[12]

"In 1993, Kirk Nakamura could not have done this [restructuring]. We needed another seven years of frustration to get to the point of ignition. These seven years were a necessary precondition."[13]

KIRK NAKAMURA'S EARLY CAREER

Unlike almost any CEO I have known—in fact, unlike every CEO I have ever known—Kirk Nakamura is a highly structured thinker. He thinks in dimensions that others don't see and he has the unusual ability to visualize how, if pieces are put together in a certain way, they will achieve superior performance. For subordinates of such people, this can be unnerving. Most managers prefer a clear goal, like sales up a specified percent. Anyone in the compensation business knows how badly people react to multivariable pay packages designed to cover every aspect of a complex company strategy. Side bets may be great in golf but most people don't like their careers managed that way. A manager like Kirk Nakamura runs the risk of making people nervous; they cannot see the same results he does and have no way to test his hypotheses. Either you trust him, or you don't. Equally, such a manager's ability to generate that trust, long before his actions have delivered proven results that everyone can believe in, is vital to his ability to lead. This, in my view, was Kirk's greatest strength.

For all his ability to think in multiple dimensions, however, Kirk demands simplicity in actions, strategy, and reporting. This makes his thinking all the more difficult to grasp at first because he expects subordinates to reduce what is immensely complex to its simplest elements, act on these successfully, *and* see how they fit into the whole to make the company generate value at accelerated rates. Few people can do this, and the sensation of working blind is unsettling. Once they get it, of course, the process is smoother.

Early in their careers, the Kirk Nakamuras of this world usually run into trouble. What they want to do, what they believe they must do, runs afoul of accepted company norms. They tend to think not only that the company's goals are wrong, but its methods for getting there are wrong too, a double jeopardy. "Since my younger days," Kirk recalled, "I have always thought, 'What should be the new right way of doing business? What should be the right way of organizing?'" Naturally, those in authority want their subordinates to put their heads down and get their backs into understood results, like this month's sales. They don't need their assumptions questioned and they react predictably when they are. "I made my proposals and they were not received well and I was advised to keep my ideas to myself. In those days in Japan, what was expected of a freshman was that he learn about the job. But I was already proposing big things to my superiors and in that sense I was not a normal employee."[14]

Kirk was a young employee at the time of Konosuke's 1964 Atami Conference and was deeply affected by the speed with which the great man moved once he decided that something must be done. Like Konosuke, Kirk thought primarily of sales and customers, rather than of products and manufacturing. In a product/manufacturing-driven company, that was a formula for conflict, which came soon enough. Early on, he recalled, "When I was in charge of sales in Akihabara [the big electronics district in Tokyo], National sales were low and National had the worst market share. The way of thinking was that we sell through other [captive] channels. People in the company were not facing the reality squarely. That's when I thought, if we continue like this, we will be in trouble sooner or later." Since, he said, all divisions thought like this, "the problem was systemic."[15]

In Japan, people are familiar by now with the story of how Kirk as a young sales manager in Nagoya decided that the Konosuke-designed system of sales franchises, each 50 percent owned by MEI and 50 percent owned by an independent franchisee, had to go. Konosuke had commonly used other people's capital to build affiliates, sales operations, and his system of National Stores. He thought this reduced risks on the one hand and bound others into the goals of the business, maximizing sales and profits, on the other. "I thought our retail network must be reorganized," Kirk told me, "and I proposed the integration and the re-organization of the sales companies in Nagoya. My superiors said, 'Go ahead and do it.'" MEI bought out the outside shareholders, the sales companies were merged into a single Nagoya unit, and a new managing director was installed by MEI. "There was," he recalled, "fierce resistance from the 50-percent owners of the sales companies. It was a tough time." This earned Kirk the attention of the board (which in Japan comprises all of a company's senior executives) rather earlier in his career than would normally be considered wise. Worse, that attention was not necessarily favorable. And, because, as the old Japanese expression goes, the nail that sticks up gets hammered down, lots of hammers were getting ready for Kirk Nakamura.

My advice to a young Kirk Nakamura would have been the same advice I've given many in his situation: "You're young. You're talented. Leave, start your own business, and make real money." Kirk almost certainly would have become one of Japan's billionaires. But that was not Kirk's way of thinking. I asked him shortly before he retired what he would advise today, and he said simply, "What I expect of the younger generation is to have clever ideas of what the company should be in the future and they should make concrete proposals and execute those proposals."[16] No talk of entrepreneurial adventurism here. Kirk joined Matsushita and he was going to stick with it. Nevertheless, it was during the Nagoya period that he began walking around with his undated letter of resignation. He was still carrying it decades later when he moved to the United States. "Sure," recalled Bob Greenberg, who now runs the Panasonic branding initiative in North America, "I've seen it. Kirk showed it to me."[17]

Even during the last half year of his presidency, when he had been at the top of the company for almost six years, Kirk alluded to the problems of his younger days when describing to me the risks a young employee should take, saying, "I must add, that kind of person is not liked by everybody, so they must not be afraid."[18]

In Japanese terms, Kirk was something of a high-wire act: he was either going to do something magnificent or fail spectacularly. Human nature being what it is, about this time there were probably people beginning to line up to take bets on which it would be. Some were almost certainly doing more than taking bets and moved early to assure an outcome. Kirk was, from the beginning, a risk taker. In a world flush with private equity like the United States, he would have had some serious seed capital thrown at him. After Nagoya, the signs of an increasingly complex, and somewhat ambivalent, relationship with upper management became more obvious. "Whenever I faced a challenge," he recalled, "I always made proposals to my superiors and they always said, 'Why don't you do it yourself?'" Not exactly supportive, that. And, you could reason that he was being hung out to dry. But he didn't dry.

Then came a shift in how the company managed its restive upstart. "The only exception [to the do-it-yourself injunction] was my posting to the United States. This was *not* my idea. I was in Tokyo when Vice President Sakuma asked me to move to the United States to reform distribution there."

By the time he moved to the States in 1987 to begin his ten-year overseas stint, Kirk had learned several things that became essential to the rebuilding of the company. One of them was how to turn around an operation, something he would do many times. Another was to structure a buyout of affiliates. Both would become critical during his time as CEO when he moved to bring all of MEI's partially owned, publicly traded affiliates and subsidiaries into a single company fold. Another was how to manage hard-to-control events like the forces ricocheting back and forth between the board, himself, and MEI's Nagoya sales affiliates. Kirk ran consumer electronics sales in the United States from 1987 to 1992, moved to the United Kingdom to run Matsushita operations there from 1992 to 1993, and returned to the States to run North American operations in 1993. These ten years would have a big impact on the future shape of Matsushita.

Setting Priorities: Kirk Nakamura's American Experience

Kirk Nakamura knew there were problems in the Matsushita organization since his Nagoya days, but his sense of urgency was exacerbated by his decade in the United States and the United Kingdom. His time there administered a deep shock as he began to realize that American business, especially, was reforming itself at a rapid pace and using information technology to replace large parts of organizations that Japanese businesses considered standard operating procedure. He was confronted with a whole new form of operation exemplified by companies like Southwest Airlines, FedEx, and Wal-Mart that had emerged since the late 1960s to take powerful and destabilizing positions in their industries. Japanese companies were still managing expensive processes that at U.S. companies had simply vanished into the bit stream. Unleashed by President Carter's slashing deregulations of the late 1970s, Americans were disintermediating markets and reaching out to customers at a pace Japanese companies were not designed to do. Kirk realized that you can give a competitor only so much lead before they have redefined your market right out from under you. What he had feared from his Akihabara days was happening before his eyes.

You can think of this like the classic Coke versus Pepsi competition being replaced by Coke versus customized sodas made to your precise tastes in the container of your choice wherever you are. Soon "Coke is it" becomes "Coke, it isn't." Cans 0, customers 1. If you are designed to sell cans, no matter how well, and if you don't see the disintermediating and decentralizing shifts in the market because your organization is not designed to let you "see" the shift through its operating fundamentals, you are toast. Kirk got this immediately.

Where MEI was optimized for supplying TVs to retailers, for example, and might be optimized to do this better than anyone, none of this mattered once Dell had made retail obsolete. How was MEI to deal with that? There was nothing at all in Konosuke's Division System that coped with the elimination of everything the system was designed to serve. For all the value of my Soccer Ball System, which was not fully developed until early 2001, my major contribution to Kirk's reforms in the late 1990s was to point out that Konosuke designed his Division System—and everything else—to disintermediate markets and increase cash velocity. If MEI could focus on Konosuke's market disintermediation and forget his Division System, at whatever the cost, it would reenergize its own innate ability to create value. The antidote to the Dells of the world was, of all people, Konosuke himself.

Being sent to the United States, as Kirk said, "was *not* my idea."[19] I am convinced that moving Kirk to the States was a test. He was a risk taker and sending him here would determine once and for all if he really had something to offer. The United States was a notoriously difficult market to manage, and full of pitfalls for the untutored. And Kirk was certainly untutored. If he failed, he would be out of the way for good. If he succeeded, he could legitimately be considered for the presidency. MEI itself hung in the balance.

The United States was Kirk's first experience managing non-Japanese, and it must have been a jolt—at least as much of a jolt as it would be for a Westerner to wind up managing a Japanese business unit with an entrenched culture that there are only limited ways of changing. In addition, Kirk is often described as shy, which is not true, but his essential simplicity—he would not know how to make a red-carpet entrance if you paid him—comes off that way. Unlike many other Japanese, whose natural garrulousness fits in well with Americans, regardless of language barrier, Kirk's reserve added to his communications challenge and probably made everything he wanted to communicate that much more difficult for him.

But it is the measure of the man that he learned to communicate in English effectively and quickly. Interestingly, he took Harrison Ford, his favorite English-language actor, as his example of how to speak English. Kirk chose well: Ford's diction is immaculate and his accent exceptionally balanced. Today, Kirk can say what he wants in English, no matter how complex, in a remarkably compressed time. More compressed than anyone I know, and I am far from alone in this observation.

In my meetings with him, he always manages to communicate what would take most people an hour in less than a minute or two. Plus another couple of minutes for clarification, if he feels the need. Cyril Wood, now head of Panasonic United Kingdom, told me that he thought Kirk was the best communicator he had ever met.[20] Coming from an Englishman whose command of his language is precise—you can hear the commas—and who speaks no Japanese at all, this shows Kirk's ability to overcome language barriers in spite of his reserve.

Indeed, Kirk tends to speak English the way Japanese should be spoken in its politest form: with long pauses between sentences, even phrases. You must wait to be sure he has finished saying what is on his mind, pause a second or two, and then say your piece, briefly. I cannot imagine how this must have gone over as he struggled to deal with his new charges in New Jersey, where speaking fast—think *The Sopranos*—is a blood sport. "One thing I do," he told me when I asked him about this, "is to stand on equal footing with people, at the same ego level."[21] This is putting it mildly. To me he once referred to himself as "*watakushi wa*," the most polite form of address possible and I was stunned. There is no way in English to relate what this means.

None of this is to say that Kirk cannot be as voluble as any American. Privately, he has a big laugh and likes nothing better than the company of good friends. Equally, however, tales of his anger when subordinates frustrate his intentions are legion. But you can't just slide into a new job in a foreign country where you don't speak the language, and from which you can legitimately expect to be propelled to the top job, by gyrating wildly between quietude and bad temperedness. You will command precisely zip respect and get nothing done.

What must have become evident quickly, moreover, was that where he could realistically think of being CEO at some point, none of those non-Japanese who worked for him overseas could ever aspire to the top job. They were permanently locked out of Japanese senior management, and their attitudes toward their work, and to him, would reflect that. This had a deep impact on his thinking and how he moved to reposition the firm. I understand this issue better than most. Three and a half decades ago, when I joined the Canadian bank my father and grandfather worked for in London, I found myself investigating a suspected fraud of about $25 million, large for the time. It turned out to be maladministration, not malfeasance. Sales had grown fast over the previous five years, and operations had not caught up. But, because none of the English employees had a hope of moving up to the head office in Canada, there was no benefit to them to solving problems, so no one did. They did their jobs—rather, they got through the day—and went home. I recommended to management that it change this. Otherwise it risked institutionalizing mediocrity forever. And the next time it saw $25 million missing, it might not be so lucky.

Canadian banks in those days, like Matsushita in Japan today, had a culture of loyalty through trial by fire. Home country staff stick to the flag like Roman Legionnaires to their Eagles, regardless of what is going on around them, however bad. Overseas staff have no reason to do this if they can't call one of the Eagles their own or aspire to the purple.

In the United States, Kirk faced language problems, the uncertain fit of his own style, and an ingrained local culture that rewarded the minimum, not the maximum. These were things he never forgot and they marked him deeply when he became CEO.

On top of all this, he had to deal with judgment challenges: how do you assess your people's character when your cultural frame of reference is so different? Sure enough, this came to haunt him when an executive he had promoted was caught with his hand in the till. But, as I know from my own experience, it is the rare manager that hasn't had to face this one down, usually several times, even with every cultural advantage.

Before Kirk asked Sean and me to advise him at Panasonic North America, he read *Beating Japan*, where we explained that Japanese firms separated authority—usually in Japan—from accountability—usually placed on a foreign salesperson who didn't speak Japanese, had no pull with *honsha*, and had probably never even been to Japan. These structures, we said, were too difficult for foreign employees to understand, let alone influence, and would be impossible for customers to leverage to their own advantage. And if customers cannot leverage an organization to get what they want, they will find someone else whom they can influence. The wider the gap, the less the ability of management to respond to shifting markets. We went one step further, saying that if this gap was wide enough, information could not cross it, ever, making the inability to respond to customers absolute.

Iron Laws of Information	Impact on Markets
1. The cost of information is *always* falling	1. Implodes layers of distribution as it drives out costs
2. Cheap information *always* chases out expensive information	2. Makes markets increasingly chaotic and less manageable
3. Customers *always* appropriate market power proportional to the speed at which information costs fall	3. Puts a premium on speed of operations
4. Disorder in cyberspace *always* increases	4. Favors topologically flat, customer-facing organizations designed to profit from disorder
5. Value added *always* flows to the least regulated market	5. Devalues vertical integration, puts premium on intellectual property
6. These laws *always* operate simultaneously	6. Puts a premium on service embedded in products to create large and multidimensional customer service envelopes

In *Beating Japan*, we codified the Iron Laws of Information in cheeky reference to Ferdinand Lassalle's nineteenth-century Iron Law of Wages.[22] You will see in them some basic principles of economics (2nd Law) and physics (4th Law).

We recommended four strategies for countering the Iron Laws in *Beating Japan* that later evolved into the Soccer Ball System and which Kirk used to begin restructuring his U.S. operations:

1. Decentralize
2. Disintegrate vertically
3. Flatten the organization
4. Sell service, not products

You can see already the hollow, or soccer ball, look of the resulting structure. Kirk took these concepts seriously. What he liked about them was how they fit into a systematic diagnosis with a clear set of prescriptions that were neither fuzzy nor vague. He told *Asahi Shimbun* reporter Takao Tsumuji in early 2005 that he had three heavily marked copies of *Beating Japan*: one by his desk in Osaka, one at home, and one in his office in Tokyo. Tsumuji was doing a profile of Kirk and his reforms for the paper and had come to New York to visit me because, Tsumuji said, Kirk had told him that to understand what Matsushita had done, he must meet me in person and learn about my system.[23]

On arriving from the United Kingdom as CEO of MEI's North American operations in 1993, Kirk moved quickly. Critically, he had the assistance of Dick Kraft, then president of Panasonic North America. Dick had decades of experience in the U.S. consumer electronics business, joining Matsushita from Quasar when Matsushita acquired Quasar in 1974. In a precursor to his relationships with his executives once he became CEO of MEI, Kirk relied on Kraft for the firm grounding in U.S. markets and business practices that he needed if he were to make changes.

By the time Sean and I got seriously involved with Matsushita in mid-1996, Kirk had digested *Beating Japan* and put in place a new management system based on:

- *Small*, self-standing Unit Companies capable of quick market response;
- *Simple* processes for designing, making, and delivering products and supporting customers;
- *Speed* for turning customer information into products and services faster than competitors;
- *Strategies* that enable Matsushita to see customer trends ahead of the competition and leverage these into value added sales quickly and effectively; and
- *Smile*—a high level of customer service.

This encapsulated Kirk's early rethinking of Konosuke's 1933 Division System. He would introduce these same tenets in his first Management Conference speech as CEO four years later.[24]

His self-standing Unit Companies of 1994, under the top item, "small," became the model for the entire enterprise in 2000 as Domain Companies. His reasoning for this structure, he told me at the time, was the emphasis in *Beating Japan* on moving authority and accountability closer together. Kraft recalled, when I was preparing this book, that Panasonic North America at the time had ten thousand SKUs that were being force-fed through two major divisions, one for consumer products and one for industrial products. "The thinking was simple," he said. "The fundamental idea was that we wanted to get the vitality of getting management closer to customers."[25]

As Konosuke's Divisions had, Kirk's Unit Companies gave his top managers ownership of well-defined product areas and made them responsible for the results in their units. "Like building a Boeing 747," Kraft remembered, "the company had to be broken down into smaller pieces." Until that time, top managers of sales company operations in the United States, or anywhere in the world for that matter, were caught between force-feeding by factories that had only limited knowledge of markets, and their own shifting customer requirements.

Arthur Matsumoto put together the first two Unit Companies to manage products that fell outside the mainstream of Panasonic sales at that time. The first Unit Company covered a miscellaneous range of MEW products, from Kenmore vacuum cleaners for Sears, food service business, hotel business, OEM products for other brands, home and building ventilation, and pencil sharpeners (an incredible 700,000 units a year), to shavers, massage chairs, power tools, kiosk businesses, and lighting. Arthur recalled that Kirk pushed to get all these products broken into smaller Unit Companies but many did not have volumes large enough to be handled this way. The second was a new venture for MEI, a systems company that sold to Las Vegas casinos and to theme parks. The whole process of unitization for all markets took about six months.[26]

Dick Kraft told me that from this process, Kirk "learned how the business worked and how you could be successful in a country in which you find unfettered worldwide competition, something you didn't get in Japan. He learned that you can have a company with fewer people, that you can lay off people, and how, as a CEO, to deal with competition, personnel, and government." Kirk recalled, "I think, when I look back at my own history, without my experience in the United States, I could never have taken this role or undertaken reforms. In the traditional Japanese business community, a company president traditionally has to say 'yes' or 'no' to staff proposals. Now, however [following the reforms], he is required to stand at the forefront and lead."[27]

Kirk asked Sean and me to advise him during this critical period of what became the core of his later reform. We had before us an organization as dysfunctional as its parent but which he felt he could restructure successfully. Dick recalled, "Kirk and I used to talk all the time about how Japan was following the same route as the United States, but was about twenty years behind." In other words, Kirk was operating in a market that, for Japanese decision makers at headquarters, didn't exist yet.

An industrial group, for example, made fax machines, and, as Kraft recalled his conversation with Kirk, "there was nothing in the industrial company to allow us to gracefully hand over this product to another [Matsushita] company strong in consumer products." Cell phones were plagued by the same problem: they were made by a Matsushita industrial company that sold mainly infrastructure to common carriers. Kraft felt that cell phones should have been made by part of the company with mainly consumer expertise. The result was production, sales, and branding all running at cross-purposes. The problem in cell phones was never solved and, in the event, came back to bite Matsushita hard. So hard that I will devote an entire chapter to it.

He and Kirk both realized, Kraft said, that to grow the company Kirk would have to:

- Get better product/customer alignment in the organization;
- Harvest the profits in systems, where the real money was increasingly being made; and
- Have a single global brand that was simple and easy to understand.

Progress was painfully slow in the 1996–97 period and we all had to face the fact that nothing much could be done to a U.S.–based sales company that had no real impact on the operations of the corporation. Time and again we reached dead ends that could be reformed only from the center. When Kirk returned to Japan in 1997, he had a precise idea of what had to be done if the company was to survive and the determination to see it through.

In the next chapter, I will describe the experiments in organization and decision making that Kirk undertook in the United States. Most, if not all, of these are now part of MEI standard operating procedure. Getting there was not simple. Some things worked and some did not. The latter had to be changed radically.

Several of Kirk's U.S. initiatives survive today in their original form, like the ToughBook personal computer company. Others, like global branding experts Landor, whom I introduced to him, became progenitors of global initiatives. Still others, like the organization structure of the company, were piloted when we worked together in the United States. Many of his customer service initiatives, like the restructuring of call centers, the Internet sites worldwide, and the Panasonic Centers, stem from this time.

For much of the Japanese press, where Kirk has been lionized in recent years, this period is blank. Yet this was when Kirk did all his planning.

At the same time as Kirk was reorganizing his U.S. operations, other Matsushita executives reached similar conclusions. A couple of them had tried reforms of their own with equally frustrating results: nothing could be done anywhere unless the whole company was remade from the ground up. At this early stage, they had to arrange a set of priorities for MEI and figure out what came first. With such a confusing structure, this was not simple. A surprisingly clear consensus was reached more quickly than I, in all my years of working with the Japanese, expected.

Kirk had moved from one sales operation to another, from domestic to overseas, where he spent the next ten years. Before becoming CEO, he held only briefly a line position as head of the Panasonic AVC Company, Matsushita's largest by sales, and so came to the top job with very little experience of anything *other* than customers, especially overseas customers in critical United States and European markets.

When he became CEO, Kirk Nakamura was both customer-savvy and global in his thinking. He had broken lots of glass and knew the risks he was taking. But the trials of the 2001 tech crash would make everything he had seen and done pale in comparison.

As I have said, you could reasonably look at Kirk's transfer to the United States as an attempt to throw him into the deep end. If he was in over his head, bye-bye to a problem. If he swam, all well and good. In the event, something else happened entirely. "I think this was the moment, when I was responsible for an entire sales company, that I came up with my own way of thinking." His ideas had matured. He was forty-eight.

The Digital Revolution: The Template for Reform

When Kirk asked Sean and me to work with him at Matsushita's U.S. operations in mid-1996, he had already begun the process of reform based on what he read in *Beating Japan*, and he asked us to tell him two things:

1.   What to expect in Matsushita's markets.
2.   What Matsushita should do about it.

This request is the essence of Kirk's style: ask a very simple question with immensely complex implications. Regardless, your answer better be as clear as his question.

The result was *The Digital Revolution*, a 128-page booklet published in November 1996 and printed in a slim 5.5″ by 8″ (14cm by 20cm) format so that it would fit in any briefcase and could be referred to easily. We called it somewhat irreverently "The Little White Book" and it quickly gained "must read" status and became a reference point for years afterward. The format became so popular that a decade later, some PNA executives keep copies at their desks for their teams. Kirk made it the basis for his Matsushita-wide reforms four years later.

The Digital Revolution essentially made four points:

1. The falling cost of information was creating consumer surpluses that were shifting the balance of power in global markets from producers like Matsushita to their customers.
2. Smart companies like Dell were coming up with new business models to harness this shift.
3. Others were doing nothing, risked being run over, and Matsushita was one of them.
4. Time was of the essence: decisions today have to be made in Moore Time on the Moore Curve, the rate at which computer-price performance increases.

The Digital Revolution concluded that, as a result of the power shift in markets, all profits were going to companies that controlled the sales process, as Dell and Wal-Mart did. Structurally, Matsushita was not designed to do this. Its entire emphasis, in spite of all Konosuke's injunctions to the opposite, was on making products. How these were sold appeared immaterial in the company's decision making.

We gave a painful example, noting that the average U.S. corporation loses half its customers every five years.[28] Sixty to 80 percent of those lost customers report that they are satisfied or very satisfied just prior to defecting.[29] The defection comes as a surprise.

For many years, we said, a Panasonic factory automation customer, whose CEO we advised, invited its customers, the press, and Wall Street analysts to tour its facilities and see how its wonderful Panasert machines were adding value. The company bragged about falling inventory turns, high yield rates, and improved customer service levels. One day, the Panasert machines were gone, replaced by a company neither we, nor anyone else, had ever heard of.

This Matsushita customer had decided that the simplest way to further cut inventories and improve cash flow and quality was to allow the people on the line the flexibility to redesign the line at will. Matsushita, along with several others, was invited to install test lines that would run in competition with each other, allowing the workers to decide which worked best. Matsushita declined and the business was lost. All of the high-technology analysts on Wall Street, some of America's leading technology journalists, and many blue-chip customers were immediately signaled that the name Panasonic now meant second best.

What caused the loss of this business was Matsushita's inability to fully integrate its operations into those of its customers, to make Matsushita's lines of communication transparent. Matsushita could prevent this, and cut costs, by extending its customer service envelope, integrating itself into customer processes and procedures, and making it more difficult for them to defect.

The Digital Revolution had a call to action designed to get Matsushita people to readdress their founder's basic principles. This became central to Kirk's own thinking and to the methods he used to get buy-in from the rank and file who had been so steeped in company tradition. We asked, what would a young Konosuke, perhaps a thirty-five-year-old Nisei here in the United States, do in a market such as ours? The answer, we said, was clear:

> Konosuke would do *anything* to shorten the distance between himself and his customers. He would waste no time in turning the Internet into a giant National Store with sensational levels of customer service. He would use the latest information systems to ensure minimum inventories, optimal cash flows and the fastest possible response times. He would be in his customers' factories re-organizing their production lines himself. He would be driving his MIS suppliers to ever more sophisticated systems for ensuring his own customers' growth and profitability.[30]

We said that to survive in today's fast-moving markets, Matsushita would have to take the risks that Konosuke would have expected. To compete in Moore Time, Matsushita would have to remake itself to tolerate high speeds. Failure meant disaster. Short lines of communication with customers and within the company are the furnaces of value creation in Moore Time. Matsushita must, therefore, make sure that its lines are always shorter than those of the competition. This would enable it to move faster, respond more quickly, and gain market share profitably. *A firm designed so that information cannot move from customers to decision makers and back in Moore Time is a sinkhole for corporate value.* Therefore, Matsushita's entire focus, we said, must be to *shorten all its lines of communication until they are transparent to its customers.*

The problem with this was that Matsushita's organization was big, bureaucratic, and layered with companies and divisions. In the information universe, however, we warned, customer demand explodes outward, and away from suppliers, rather like Hubble's Law, which says that galaxies move away from ours faster the farther away they are from us.[31] The market analogy is that customers move away from producers faster the more layers of distribution (distance) that producers put between them.

We further pointed out that mass markets exist because high information costs keep individuals silent. Once information costs fall far enough, consumers have the technology to make themselves heard, one by one. A mass market of 300 million faceless consumers is one thing. A market of 300 million empowered individuals talking back on the Internet is quite another. Harnessing these immense forces takes a corporate commitment of unheard-of vitality and endurance.

Traditionally, we said, retailers acted as informed buyers on behalf of their customers. When Konosuke Matsushita founded Matsushita, he could depend on this channel to provide him with the information he needed to direct his product decisions. Indeed, most of his early decisions, and often his mistakes, were based on relations with a handful of people who resold his products to others. The problem, of course, is that even category killers broker much of the flow of information from customers to producers. The most successful retailers don't overinterpret what they get from customers for their suppliers; they simply pass it on. As these retailers seize control of the sales process, build their brands, and maximize profits, suppliers basically get information that is no better than data generated at the point of sale. The only information that flows reliably through retailers to producers is about price: customers want to spend less. The only ones benefiting from the revolution in retail are the retailers.

Suppliers that do not communicate *directly* with consumers, therefore, suffer severe consequences. They are last to hear about market trends. In a classic example, in the early 1990s, consumers suddenly switched from dot matrix to ink-jet printers, whipsawing companies like Matsushita that were selling the old technology. The failure of Matsushita's factories to communicate directly with their customers cost the company hundreds of millions of dollars in lost sales. This put unnecessary strain on other parts of the company.

Suppliers without direct customer contact are forced to fight in the marketplace with two blunt weapons: price and product proliferation. In an effort to avoid price cuts, ill-informed suppliers resort to frenzied new product introductions. Inevitably, they must then turn to price cuts to clear out inventories of unwanted products. The net effect is to depress earnings and sales growth.

In many ways, we said, change in OEM (original equipment manufacturer) markets had gone in the opposite direction.

Traditionally, manufacturers did not communicate "soft" information about their products and customers to suppliers. They drew up specifications for components, and put them out to bid. Suppliers were interchangeable, like the parts they provided.

Successful OEMs today, by contrast, have reduced the number of suppliers they use, and work much more closely with them. Frequently, component manufacturers are brought into the product design process, and are privy to far more information than they would have received in the past. At the time of *The Digital Revolution* this change was most pronounced in the auto industry, but it has since spread to most manufacturing sectors.

Information technology makes these close bonds work on a daily basis, allowing manufacturers to integrate suppliers into their order entry and factory automation systems. OEMs using IT in this way benefit from supplier expertise. They lower their development costs, improve manufacturability, and raise system-level quality. Suppliers that can adapt will do well. They can differentiate themselves on something other than price. In particular, they lower the cost of doing business for their customers, which is very different from lowering the price of their products. Consequently, they raise costs to their customers of switching suppliers. OEMs tightly bound to their suppliers cannot simply go out to bid to shave costs. Manufacturers and OEMs must work together.

You can see from both of these cases that information technology is more important than products. In fact it is usually the sole differentiating factor, and this finding came to dominate Kirk Nakamura's thinking about the future direction of Matsushita.

This finding lead to another that impacted Kirk's thinking: that IT effectively wraps products in a service envelope, forming a product-service hybrid. You cannot tell where a product ends and a service begins, but there is no getting away from the fact that one-dimensional, all-product businesses cannot compete in markets where products and services are deeply embedded in one another. For traditional manufacturer MEI, this was no easy thing to grasp. Service was taken to mean after-sales service for repairs and warranty fulfillment, a cost line. The idea that embedding a thing with a relationship of some sort could cut costs, improve working capital, increase OFCF (operating free cash flow), and grow market share was foreign to a factory-driven company where people frequently told us, "We make things."

What makes product-service integration even more difficult to grasp is that, much as Lisa Randall describes branes in her fine book, *Warped Passages*,[32] the service dimensions of a product are not uniform. They can be defined many ways depending on product and packaging. Dell's integrated manufacturing/distribution system is as much a product as it is a service, as we pointed out in 1996, but so is, in a very different sense, Apple's iPod/iLife hybrid. Teams stuck in a plant far removed from global markets cannot see these branes unless they have powerful IT systems that give them a window into daily market conditions for their products. *The Digital Revolution* said that Matsushita's U.S. operations had no way of doing this, which in turn meant that Japan didn't either.

The Digital Revolution outlined our basic philosophy for dealing with these challenges: "A customer's entire experience of Matsushita defines quality. [The company] must raise the switching costs to its customers, building a wide range of soft benefits into its processes in order to sell on something other than price."[33] *The Digital Revolution* then made several recommendations for what Matsushita's U.S. operations could do to take advantage of changing markets:

1. Shorten internal lines of communication to make them more transparent and responsive to customers.
    *   Flatten management.
    *   Decentralize into the field, putting management closer to major accounts.
2. Shorten external lines of communications.
    *   Extend service cycles and drive more in-depth customer relations.
    *   Integrate company operations with those of customers to raise the costs to customers of switching suppliers.
    *   Sell more systems and fewer components to increase value added to customers.
    *   Introduce major account management systems.
    *   Create C-level to C-level communications.

- Make sure that the relationship has a real earnings impact for customers, making it strategic to them.
- Build a customer care network.
- Established a database of all customers, what they buy and when, that can be mined to focus company energies on the most profitable, fastest-growing opportunities.
- Reform call centers to drive information directly from customers into Matsushita's design and manufacturing centers worldwide in real time.
- Use call centers to talk to customers after they have bought products to see how they like products, get feedback, and drive product and process improvement.
- Establish a direct sales channel Dell-style for consumer products.
- Get control of brand and actively manage the customers' day-to-day experience of Panasonic.

To do this, we said, Matsushita must make three changes:

1. Extend service cycles toward infinity. *The shorter product cycles become in Moore Time, the longer customer relationships must become for a producer to succeed.* If product cycles are shortened and service cycles shortened also, collapse is inevitable.
2. Unit Companies must adopt a strategy of forward integration into their customers. Each sale must be followed by a well-defined service envelope that nurtures customers for the next sale.
3. Sell systems, not components.

The only way to grow and profit in compressed Moore Time product cycles is to build long-term customer relationships that neutralize its impact. I call this the Rule of Inverse Service Cycles. It says that *value is added in the sales process, not in products.*

Rule of Inverse Service Cycles

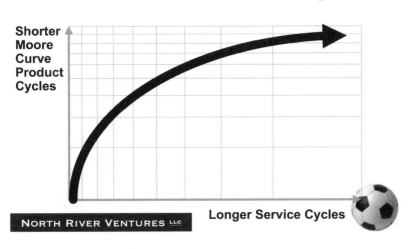

NORTH RIVER VENTURES ᴸᴸᶜ

The problem with our recommendations was immediately apparent, and was designed to be. Very little of what we recommended could be done without major reform at the center of the company. Take something as simple as a major account program. As a customer like Wal-Mart becomes global and makes global decisions, a U.S. sales force with no leverage in the rest of the company can offer little. Indeed, as we made clear in *The Digital Revolution*, Wal-Mart was becoming a brand umbrella under which brands like Panasonic would have to take shelter in order to survive. To maintain any leverage whatever with Wal-Mart, Matsushita would have to offer highly differentiable products, and something new—services.

For example, the success of the Wal-Mart system was based on inventory reduction. This allowed the company to dominate the market with its "Everyday Low Prices" strategy. Any supplier that had the logistical prowess to further reduce Wal-Mart inventories while minimizing stock outages would be a winner. The risks to not doing this were clear, even in 1996. That was the year Wal-Mart began a major initiative in inventory reduction, cutting twenty days off its inventory by 2001, fueling substantial growth. Clearly a company that did not have inventory management built into its sales offering would be left holding the short end of the stick: price discounts or nothing. Our message for Kirk was not complicated: Get Matsushita in position to get important accounts on a growth track and make sure you are seen by them as central to their working-capital management or watch all Matsushita's growth and profit opportunities go out the window. But Kirk's conundrum was, as we knew full well, what exactly do I do about this when I'm sitting in Secaucus, New Jersey? Answer: not a lot.

Our brand recommendation raised even more complex issues. Matsushita did not track its biggest customers globally, making it impossible for the company to gauge how a customer problem in one area affected the same customer in another. Since it was never clear just what Matsushita's customer exposure was, the Panasonic brand could not be managed except in the most abstract sense. Indeed, we said that we were not even sure that Panasonic was a brand, in the proper sense of the word. This made the company highly vulnerable to competitors.

In addition, since Panasonic North America was selling products from Matsushita's large array of companies and divisions with unrelated ideas as to what brand meant, how could the question even be addressed? And what was the price of not addressing it? Sooner or later, whoever ran Matsushita would have to deal with this. Or Matsushita would go out of business.

On just about every recommendation, the measures actually available to Kirk were limited. But they were just as limited to everyone else in the company. Some were beginning to see this and Kirk soon gave us an opportunity to meet them.

With the delivery of our assessment, Kirk set up a wide-ranging set of six task forces to review all aspects of the operation:

1. Brand image
2. System sales

3.   Business structure transformation
4.   Direct sales
5.   Customer satisfaction
6.   Unit Company realignment

He asked me to meet with all of the task forces, give advice, and let him know their progress and my frank view of their competence. With these task forces he was able to grasp quickly what would work and what would not on a corporate level. In a precursor to the restructuring of the parent company, to accelerate processes and accelerate them accurately, he assigned top executives to double up on their line responsibilities and personally sponsor each task force. To make sure everyone got the message and to show he would not lead from behind, Kirk sponsored the task force he deemed most critical to success, the Brand Image Task Force.

Like the Unit Companies, these task forces would have long-lasting effects, providing a dress rehearsal for the eventual reorganization of MEI. The Brand Image Task Force was transformed directly from PNA into Matsushita's global *Panasonic Ideas For Life* brandline created by Landor, a company I introduced to Kirk in 1997. In 2001, Matsushita used this brand vehicle to merge its subsidiaries, a reform priority.

Kirk asked Sean and me to take *The Digital Revolution* on a *tour d'horizons* of Japan in January 1997, a trip I will talk about next. For now, however, what jumped out at us was the range of responses to *The Digital Revolution* in Japan. Everywhere, we were greeted with interest. But several executives, notably Hajime Sakai and Kazuyoshi Fujiyoshi introduced earlier in this book, questioned us closely. During the next few years they went to great lengths to restructure their own operations, only to run into the same walls that Kirk had: the structural problems were not peripheral; they were systemic and could be solved only through a root-and-branch reconstruction of the company. Their work proved critical, because when push came to shove in 2000–2001, Sakai and Fujiyoshi proved formidable allies who would play a large role in Kirk's reforms.

The issue of top managers proved irksome during the task force phase and gave Kirk a taste of what he would find as his responsibilities increased. At several senior management meetings, he asked executives to commit to changes and some were reluctant, pushing him back with vague excuses cloaked in specious reasoning about why things could not be done the way he wanted. His frustration mounted as he grew more and more annoyed at their unwillingness, or inability, to get the job done. I remember being astonished at how much pushback people thought they could get away with. Eventually he let his anger show, on one occasion turning to me after someone's equivocation, demanding, "Mr. McInerney. As the company's advisor, what do you recommend?" I said something like, "Cut 50 percent," and he turned in a flash to the group and said, "We will do it." I don't think I made any friends that day.

Kirk learned a lot about how to identify the managers he would need, which ones would jump at opportunities, which ones would need pushing but, if pushed, would shine, and which ones needed to retire with as much grace as they could muster.

Just at this time, with his task forces working away, Kirk went into something of a funk. Sales did not reach his target for the quarter, and his neck went out (Matsushita's cash flow and Kirk's neck are tightly synchronized) and he was sidelined in considerable pain. This incident gave me insight into the extraordinarily deep relationship he fosters with his subordinates. People seemed to feel that their own futures were in serious jeopardy if he didn't get well. A real sense of gloom descended on Secaucus. Sort of a "what will happen to us all if he can't carry on" mood. This ability to engender powerful personal attachments across large numbers of people is uncommon in leaders. Most make their mark by example, shrewd direction, and good management of people and resources. Few add personal affection into the mix. Kirk did. And in a language in which he was not even slightly comfortable.

When U.S. sales rebounded in the spring of 1997, Kirk too rebounded, *con gusto*. When I went into his office to congratulate him, he was walking several inches above the floor, neck pain and all. With the rebound, he knew that he was almost certain to be recalled to Japan to take on a much bigger job that would put him in direct line for the presidency of the company. Sure enough, in May 1997, Kirk went back to Japan to run the AVC Company, Matsushita's largest division by sales. The first phase of our work together was over.

This incident returned to me in late 2005, near the end of our working relationship, when the unthinkable happened and a couple of long-discontinued Matsushita products, kerosene heaters, failed and two people in Japan died of carbon monoxide poisoning. I was in the country at the time this crisis hit, researching *Panasonic*, and didn't take the matter at all seriously. People die from misusing kerosene heaters all the time in the United States and the public is regularly warned on the evening news by fire commissioners and TV reporters of the dangers of using them in unventilated rooms. To me, it was just self-evident misuse of a product. Which shows how little, even after three decades of advising Japanese companies, I really understood about how Japan responds to events like these.

All eyes immediately turned to Kirk because, in Japanese tradition, he should be held to account and should resign in atonement. Never mind that the company had not made the heaters for a decade. Never mind that it had launched a nationwide recall—152,000 of these heaters were sold during the life of the product—and that Matsushita had offered a sizeable bounty to anyone returning one. Never mind that it had redirected its entire Christmas season advertising budget to the recall, putting its own top and bottom lines—and management's highly publicized commitments to shareholders—in jeopardy. The heaters failed, people died, and the CEO should apologize in the time-honored way.

What took me aback was the same "what will happen to us all if he can't carry on" frame of mind that I saw in Secaucus in 1996. The distress in the company was palpable; you could cut it with a knife. Everyone I met was, there is only one way to describe it, completely freaked out. I thought all their reactions overblown. As it happened, in early December, Joe Shohtoku, a recently retired senior executive and one of the principal architects of MEI's restructuring, took me out to a dinner he had promised a month earlier but had to delay because of the funeral of a teacher from his youth to whom he owed a great deal. Since Joe had retired, our meeting was not official, we had none of the usual minders present, and he could speak his mind openly. He told me that Kirk's e-mails to his inner circle had suddenly become darker in tone over the previous twenty-four hours and he felt certain that Kirk would go, probably within a couple of days at most. To say Joe was sick about this would be putting it mildly. He saw years of hard work going up in smoke; Kirk's disgrace would deprive the whole top team's efforts over so many years of much of its credibility. Though he didn't say so—he didn't have to—no one, no matter how close to Kirk, was prepared to broach the subject. The team Kirk had relied on for so many risky moves could take him only so far. In this decision, Kirk was alone and hourly more tormented by the deaths of his customers and the damage to the company's brands.

Joe's comments drove the point home. Kirk's forced departure would indelibly besmirch everything everyone had worked so hard to achieve. He would be remembered in Japan as a great, re-forming CEO who resigned in scandal. For a Japanese man with his combination of pride and modesty, this would be mortifying in a way no American CEO could imagine. I was his advisor of longest standing, I was an outsider, and I was in Japan. The job of speaking to Kirk was mine.

Even after ten years of working with Kirk, I was not sure how to speak to a traditional Japanese man about something so deeply Japanese without making a hash of it. But if Kirk could somehow come to see a way to handle the crisis, his mood would change immediately, as it had in 1997. He wouldn't walk on air as he had done then—two people had died—but he would turn to the problem decisively and get it behind the company, no matter what.

The next morning, a Saturday, I e-mailed Kirk reminding him of how Johnson & Johnson handled the Tylenol scare in 1982 when someone put cyanide in J&J's market-leading Tylenol capsules, killing seven people in the Chicago area. Even though J&J withdrew 31 million bottles of Tylenol in what should have been a brand fiasco, within two years the Tylenol brand was back, bigger than ever. I followed this with a second e-mail, laying out an action plan to get Matsushita back onto high ground by leading an industry-government initiative to educate the public on the safe use of kerosene heaters. He quickly e-mailed back thanking me for "sharing this very difficult situation with us Matsushita people." I've learned over the years to distinguish e-mails and letters from his hand and those he asks his longtime secretary, Hank Osawa, to prepare. This one was pure Kirk. Moreover, personally thanking an outsider for joining Konosuke's people in its time of need is an expression of gratitude that is, in Japanese terms, extremely deep.

The following Wednesday I went in to see him for a long-arranged meeting. On my way in, I told his personal translator, Makoto Nishikawa, who has overseen the translation of my management presentations in Osaka for years, that I was thinking of speaking forcefully on the subject of Kirk's resignation but wanted his opinion first. Nishikawa, on whose advice I've learned to rely, said simply, "You know Kirk and only you can decide what is right." In English, go for it.

Kirk looked stressed almost beyond measure. The first thing he did was to thank me for the reference to Tylenol. It had helped him see that the brand could be rebuilt quickly with the right effort. Kirk typically puts long pauses in his thoughts and you must always wait to be sure he has finished what he wants to say. This time I jumped in, telling him as emphatically as I could that, as traditional a Japanese as he might be, if he had "even the slightest thought of resigning, this is not the time nor the issue." I told him that he had to remember that he was the CEO of a global company and he had global responsibilities. Japan was only part of the operation. There would be a time for retirement but this was not it. Just as in 1997, he was transformed. His face relaxed. The pressure was still there. Two customers were dead and nothing would take that away. But you could see his strength return. Nishikawa was about to translate for me and Kirk waved him off, saying to me, "I will get this problem solved. Then I will return to making Matsushita a growth company."

Kirk's remarkable ability to engender personal attachments had an outsized impact throughout this crisis. Thousands of employees voluntarily fanned out across Japan, hunting down kerosene heaters one by one, standing on street corners to hand out flyers warning the public, and going door-to-door. One of those who worked closest to me in recent years, Nick Akamatsu, told me that he was leaving the next day to spend two weeks far from home to chase down heaters and get them out of circulation. I asked him if this wouldn't be hard on his wife and two young children so close to the holiday season. "Yes," he said, "but I feel that this is where I should be during this time. Most of my major work for the year is pretty much over and I can easily do both jobs." Simple, unaffected, and, I thought, uncommon in my part of the world.

But the kerosene heater crisis was well into the future when Kirk left the United States for Japan in May 1997 and the life-long salesman took on a line responsibility for the first time. Once back in Japan, however, Kirk had the same problem Fujiyoshi and Sakai did: no matter how senior he now was, there was a real limit to what he could do within the structure of the company. *The Digital Revolution* of MEI would have to wait for another three years.

But when it came in 2000, it had been coiled up with the one or two extra twists that unleashed it with an extreme force.

Going to Osaka Castle

One of the most remarkable things Kirk ever asked me to do was to visit Japan with Sean in early 1997 to tour the company, giving seminars on *The Digital Revolution*. This may look simple enough: give the same seminar two or three times a day for two weeks. What's so hard about that?

It was not hard. It was dangerous.

First, we were not being asked to talk about Matsushita in the United States, except in the shallowest possible interpretation of our mission. What Kirk was asking us to do—without actually saying so—was reminiscent of a scene in the novel *Shogun* where the Englishman Blackthorne escorts the shogun hopeful Toranaga unarmed into Osaka Castle and gets him out again, alive. We were to go to Japan and tell everyone in clear and firm tones the direction in which Kirk would take the company when he became CEO. But not to say that, exactly.

Second, he sent us with two of his own people as minders, Shin Maegami, who was still learning to master English, and David Chapin, who had learned Japanese as a child in Japan but who considered his fluency imperfect. In other words, we were being sent without Matsushita's usual flotilla of expert translators and corporate communications managers, leaving plenty of room for miscalculation. Especially for a man hoping to lead the company one day.

Third, we spent endless hours over dinners taking in copious drafts of sake with all the leading executives, few of whom spoke a word of English. If the possibility of misunderstanding in the seminars was great, once we'd all had lots to drink it was incalculable.

Fourth, we knew Kirk only slightly at this stage, having worked with him for just over six months, and Matsushita not at all. We could have made fools of ourselves, and Kirk, without even trying.

Kirk trusted his career to us. I thought he was crazy. But it worked.

There were moments, however. One executive spent an evening regaling us with tales of a CD he had just made, his latest. Then about all the other ones. Our message was falling on infertile ground. Another wanted to see what these *gaijin* were really made of so he invited us to dinner and served a live fish. Actually, a dying fish that the chef had quickly cut open to breathe its last at the table. Our host happily poured beer in the fish's mouth to make its last seconds more interesting for everyone. Sean and I have worked together for decades and didn't succeed in business without knowing that looking up in surprise, or looking up at all, would have cost us much face and scuttled Kirk's message. So, without a word we took our chopsticks and dove in, expressing great satisfaction. The executive's face had to be seen to be believed.

In another memorable meeting it fell to Sean to give the seminar. We were delivering them in turn and his turn was up. The meeting began late in the day. We were ushered into a small seminar room in the main consumer electronics labs under Yoshitomi Nagaoka. The first sign of trouble was that Nagaoka-san brought in a big team. The second was that the room was hot and unventilated. The third, and real killer, was that Nagaoka is a heavy smoker and his entire team decided it was good form to light up with the boss. The room turned blue. Sean, increasingly unsteady on his feet as he spoke for the next ninety minutes, slowly turned a ghastly shade of gray. By the end of the hour he collapsed into his chair. I took all the questions.

The point of this episode is Kirk's remarkable ability to take the measure of someone quickly, even of those he doesn't know very well, communicate what he wants, and get it done. He should reasonably have expected that, however well we worked with him in Secaucus, New Jersey, once let loose in Japan we would make every cultural faux pas possible and mess up royally. The fact is that he never said to me or to Sean that he wanted to be *shacho*, or that our mission was to make sure that there would be no surprises once he got the job. It would have been an exceptional breach of protocol for him to do so. Nevertheless, it was quite clear to us what we were there to do, and we were fully conscious of how risky the proposition was at every moment during the trip. Somehow, with the help of David Chapin and Shin Maegami, we knew where the line was and stuck to it.

This story is also typical of Kirk's management style. In interview after interview for this book, and in my experiences with many MEI managers over the years, versions of it are told over and over. Kirk quickly identifies the people who can do the job, gives them often-unexpected assignments that they consider way over the top, and expects results. This style was core to Matsushita's ability to reform; it enabled Kirk to bring powerful and decisive managers to the fore quickly. And when his restructuring ran into the tech crash of 2001 and nearly destroyed the company, these managers—whom you will meet in this book—saved the day.

Returning from our January 1997 visit to Matsushita's Japanese operations, Sean and I reported to Kirk our conclusions. The company had:

- A powerful market presence.
- A complex structure.
- Confusing division and affiliate mandates with:
    - All the problems of the Divisional System.
    - None of the benefits.

It was also:

- Excessively multilayered.
- Unsure what "service" meant.
- In need of a new mission statement.

None of this was lost on certain officers of the company. Masayuki, or Mike, Matsushita, now vice chairman, had asked us the killer question, "Why do Japanese car makers succeed when we do not?" Atsushi Murayama, now president of Kansai Airport and a chief architect of reform when it finally happened, told me in an interview for this book, "I knew for ten years that we had to reorganize. But I thought that we could not, and this led to a lot of frustration."[34]

In May 1997, our work with Kirk was over. We were invited to his farewell reception and were taken aback to find ourselves the only outsiders there. When I went up to shake his hand and take my leave, I learned why. Kirk had a surprise in store. He asked me if we would support him in his new role in Japan. The next phase had already begun. But Murayama's frustration would last a while longer.

CHAPTER TWO

THE SOCCER BALL COMPANY

MATSUSHITA AND THE CHALLENGE OF THE INTERNET AGE

AT THE END OF CHAPTER ONE WE SAW THAT IN THE INTERNET AGE the falling cost of information gives customers unprecedented power over producers like Matsushita; how when information costs begin to fall along the Moore Curve—the rate at which computer price-performance increases—these shifts in market power happen at speeds that challenge any management's ability to make decisions fast enough. We saw that new business models, like Dell's, were harnessing these forces. We also saw that many misread so-called convergence. Great names like Kodak, Hewlett-Packard, Sony, the entire recording industry, and then Microsoft suddenly looked like they were standing still, and had to undertake disruptive overhauls. Even Dell, after a decade on top, is being overtaken by events. In Chapter Two, we will see what companies must do about collapsing information costs and how they can profit from them. We will review the Soccer Ball System that MEI used to return to its highest levels of profit in fifteen years.

In the Internet Age, *a company's survival depends on the speed at which it substitutes information for other resources like land, labor, and capital.* Quickly and the firm prospers. Slowly and it dies.

High rates of information substitution make a firm look rather like a soccer ball with all assets and operations on the surface, where they touch customers. These assets and operations are held together by advanced communication technology. Indeed, if the rate of information substitution lags, internal communications usually fail long before products do. You see this every day when companies with excellent products are swept aside because of failures in other parts of the operation like customer service and working-capital management. Think of once great names like DEC and Compaq, or the Bell System.

When companies habituated to the slower price-performance shifts of, say, traditional TVs, as Matsushita was, hit the digital age where computer technology drives prices through the floor every day, unit sales must go up exponentially just to keep sales even. Profits often go right out the door. This can happen overnight, stunning management unready for it.

In addition, as we saw in Chapter One, very low information costs unfold new dimensions along which traditional products compete. Apple's iPod, for example, combines hardware, the iPod, with an Internet-based service, iTunes, and content on MP3 files of many types. IBM does the same thing. And so does Southwest Airlines. By operating on all three dimensions, these companies create customer service envelopes much larger than anyone operating along just one dimension. Companies caught competing on only one of these dimensions, like the entire consumer electronics and world recording industries, are at a serious disadvantage. Those that move rapidly along multiple dimensions grow fast and throw off large amounts of shareholder value.

With shifts of market power from producers to consumers *and* new product dimensions opening rapidly, maintaining a brand, let alone trying to build it, can be a hapless task.

To harness these forces and profit from them, companies have to have a new structure that is unlike anything known in history. This structure has to be a super-efficient transmitter of information and an exceptionally efficient user of cash and capital, and to do so must be topologically as flat as possible.

Regardless of size, the most efficient users of cash and capital in their markets are operating free cash flow vacuums, sucking up all the OFCF in their markets. Companies that don't get such a structure in place can be overtaken quickly by companies that are much smaller and do have such a structure, a major risk to giants like Matsushita. In addition, companies that try to scale fast without highly efficient cash and capital usually bleed cash.

These forces divide markets into absolute winners and losers, making markets unstable and treacherous to manage. The issue facing a traditional Japanese company like Matsushita was how to manage these forces, gain significant market share, and create a platform for enduring profitability. All at the same time.

This would become for MEI rather like changing the fuselage, engines, seating arrangements, and galleys of a passenger plane in midflight, all without disturbing the passengers.

This chapter will outline the drivers of modern corporations like Dell and Wal-Mart. It will show that the basis of competition has changed and that new business models are taking all the growth and profits in their markets, leaving older model companies, like Matsushita at the end of the twentieth century, struggling for what is left over. Modern companies had more customer information than Matsushita had, and they could act on it more quickly. Management faced a hard choice: the slow but steady dissolution of the firm or radical change.

THE ORIGINS OF SOCCER BALL MANAGEMENT

The principal idea behind Soccer Ball Management is not new. In 1967, a high school friend, and now author, Michael Barnholden, urged me to read Marshall McLuhan's new book *Understanding Media*. This was the second volume in a two-part series (the first volume, *The Gutenberg Galaxy*, was published in 1962 by the University of Toronto).

McLuhan's central idea was simple: Take a message, say the daily news, send it over various kinds of media from word-of-mouth to newspaper to TV, and the impact of the medium will change the message itself. So: same story, change the medium, and get a different story. Whence McLuhan's famous dictum: "The medium *is* the message."

We see McLuhan's information alchemy every day when a director turns a top-selling book into a movie. No matter how "true" to the text, the impact of the big screen changes the story, often making it unrecognizable.

McLuhan's biggest, and to me most provocative, example was the European Reformation. McLuhan pointed out that when moveable type transformed the Bible from handwritten manuscripts copied laboriously over decades to easily printed books, the entire power structure of society shifted. The Europe of the Treaty of Westphalia looked nothing like the Europe of Henry Tudor. Human behavior changed in ways that contemporaries did not anticipate and could not manage, something that is familiar to most CEOs in the Internet Age.

What Marshall McLuhan pointed out, however—and this is a challenge to today's CEOs—is that organizations from different media eras, or different points on the information costs curve, coexist. "An age in rapid transformation is one which exists on the frontier between two cultures and between conflicting technologies. Every moment of its consciousness is an act of translation of each of these cultures into the other. Today we live on the frontier between five centuries of mechanism and the new electronics, between the homogeneous and the simultaneous. It is painful but fruitful."[1] McLuhan's frontier is where occurs what Kirk Nakamura's favorite economist, Joseph Schumpeter, called "creative destruction."

For quite some time after the Reformation began, print-age organizations and manuscript-age organizations existed side by side, staring at each other across a great ideological divide, and fought each other ferociously, without really understanding each other's premises. McLuhan's observations about shifting behavior are crucial: I work daily with CEOs who live, as it were, in a manuscript age and who cannot see the same choices as CEOs in the same market who live, as it were, in a print age. If you cannot see it, you can't make decisions about it. The result is a set of management behaviors that are not only mutually incompatible but also mutually incomprehensible.

All through the late 1980s and 1990s, Matsushita lived on McLuhan's "frontier between two cultures." It was like many companies today that make decisions as if it is still the 1970s, at a point on the information cost curve far removed from the Internet Age. Kind of like *That '70s Show*, only it isn't funny. They see nothing wrong with their methods because their internal information velocities let them see nothing else. You experience the same thing when visiting the Uffizi museum in Florence where fifteenth-century paintings hang side by side, some with perspective and some without. The effect is jarring: the old and the new both think they are new. Matsushita was a painting without perspective in a perspective-driven world. Kirk Nakamura referred to this problem endlessly in his early management speeches as CEO.

Translate this Uffizi Effect into a world where information costs were falling along the Moore Curve—a world where computer processor price-performance doubles every eighteen months—and this effect isn't jarring; it's horrifying. We are talking about a lot of lost jobs and value meltdowns in very short periods. That in essence is what I saw when I first advised Matsushita: the old world inside the company and a whole new world outside it. The meltdown risk grew daily.

This is why, for example, a perfectly well-trained CEO like Carly Fiorina can make decisions so unlike those of Michael Dell or Steve Jobs, even though they are in the same industry. These managers live in different worlds with different dimensions and different decision matrices. Yet they compete against each other. It is almost as if businesses from different centuries were trying to compete for the same contemporary customer. Intuitively it is not hard to see who will come out on top. But measuring the cross-century differences, and giving management data on which to transform itself, is what CEOs need to understand the dimensions of the alternate universe of their competitors and what they have to do to take market share. The number of CEOs who get this is tiny. I've spent many long hours trying to help CEOs in Japan, Canada, the United States, and Europe understand the impact of McLuhan's frontiers on their decision making. I think that the reason Kirk Nakamura grasped this issue was the cultural shock of finding himself in the West. It opened his mind to things that many of his U.S. contemporaries still don't understand.

McLuhan showed that, writ large over the centuries, changes in communication media have social and economic impacts. Moveable type not only spawned the European Reformation, it also created the United States and the modern corporation, with results that much of the rest of the world is only now beginning to realize.

When I entered the University of Toronto in 1969, I was invited to sit in on McLuhan's graduate seminar, and had a chance to see the great man in action. The problem I had—everyone had—was that McLuhan, for all his fame at the time, was a wretched communicator. He was a terrible writer—like Marx he overwrote to the point of being incomprehensible—and his spoken words were often an obtuse and incoherent jumble. Learning from him was a trial.

The essentials, however, were incisive. I noted that each of McLuhan's media ages also coterminated with major shifts in organization design, not least in business. So, change the media and you change organizations. On this point I owe much to the work of Harold Innis. Innis taught economics at the University of Toronto, knew McLuhan, and greatly influenced him. Indeed, McLuhan wrote that both *The Gutenberg Galaxy* and *Understanding Media* were footnotes to Innis's *Empire and Communications*, making *Panasonic* a footnote to a footnote.

Innis published *Empire and Communications* in 1950. His thesis was that different empires (read businesses) from the Egyptian to the British were held together by different communications technologies. The efficiency of each communication technology determined the physical shape of the empire. Papyrus, Innis wrote, enabled one kind of empire, Egypt, and paper enabled another, Islam. The medium dictated the structure of the organization. Most CEOs see what Innis meant every day: print supports only hierarchical organizations while the Internet enables "flat" organizations. What I took from Innis and McLuhan in the 1960s, however, was that each of their media ages was actually a shift in the speed with which information moved. Moveable type is faster than handwritten manuscripts or word of mouth, and electronic media are infinitely faster again. I had the first of my post-McLuhan principles: *The velocity of information is the message*.

In its simplest form, the Soccer Ball structure is just the fastest way to move information within a company and between a company and its suppliers and customers.

Based on my new principle that information velocity is destiny, I determined to write the next chapter in McLuhan's book. Sean White, whom I met at the university and with whom I've been in business ever since, brought an essential piece to the analysis. In the early 1980s, he pointed out that *faster information is cheaper information*. The flip side of ever-increasing information velocity, he said, is accelerated drops in the cost of information. By creating an identity between information velocity and information costs, Sean made information velocities *measurable*, and therefore meaningful to decision makers. The Soccer Ball System in its detailed form shows managers how to take these measurements and turn them into actions that grow shareholder value.

This is my fourth major work on McLuhan's core principle. The first three, with Sean White, are:

- *Beating Japan* (Dutton 1993), which describes the impact of falling information costs on whole nations.
- *The Total Quality Corporation* (Dutton 1995), which describes the impact of falling information costs on production quality and the environment.
- *FutureWealth* (St. Martin's 2000), which describes the impact of falling information costs on wealth creation.

Falling Information Cost and Wealth Creation

Add faster, cheaper information to a product and consumers get more for less, creating a consumer surplus that they can spend on other goods and services, thus growing the economy. Ever-cheaper information, therefore, is the *force motrice* of wealth creation. *All wealth is created when the cost of information falls.*

But by giving consumers more money to spend, consumer surpluses shift market power from producers to consumers. If the rate of information substitution is low, as it has been for most of history, this process is imperceptible. History records the slow change in civil organization from the Sumerian city-state to the empires of late antiquity and on through the emerging structures of China, Japan, and pre-Reformation Europe. If the rate of information substitution accelerates suddenly, however, it causes social, political, and commercial disruptions as the European Reformation did in the sixteenth century, with a onetime drop in the cost of information initiated by moveable type.

No European organization of *any type* survived the Reformation unchanged. Think about that for a second and ask why surviving the current free fall in information costs brought on by the

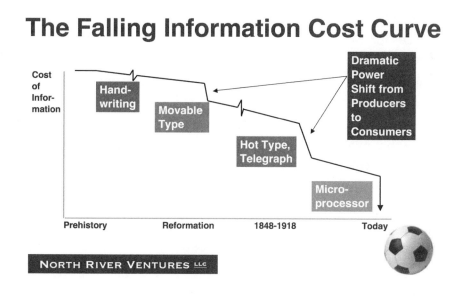

The Falling Information Cost Curve

computer age should be any easier to manage. Then ask why your company should do any better today than those medieval organizations that cruised into the Reformation blind and were crushed by it. As every country that went through the Reformation found, each point on the information cost curve requires different organizational structures. A business design that works selling mainframes, for example, is unlikely to work selling personal computers, as IBM found out to its cost and Dell to its profit, even though both sell computers. IBM and Dell sat on either side of McLuhan's "frontier between two cultures," as the old organization (IBM) tried to compete with the new (Dell), and failed. This is the Uffizi Effect on steroids.

Even small consumer surpluses driven by falling information costs can have dramatic effects if they are *widespread* enough. The combination of information and grasses unleashed the agricultural revolution, creating large amounts of wealth, changing human organization forever by driving the development of both accounting and writing and the early city-states of the Middle East and Asia.

If information costs rise, as they did in the Dark Ages, wealth is destroyed. Even if they decline at a *relatively* slow rate, as they did with the Soviet Union, wealth is still destroyed. And this relative relationship is what kills so many companies. They think that because they are running the latest in information technology, they are fast enough to add value, when, in fact, they are destroying it.

The challenge for Matsushita, in a nutshell, was how to generate information velocities high enough to get ahead of falling information costs. What Sean and I found early on was that management was deeply divided, with parts sitting on either side of McLuhan's frontier.

Falling Information Cost and Management

My first Navigation Rule for modern management is, therefore: *The cost of information is always falling.* Since there are almost daily announcements doubling the power of previous generations of microprocessors and associated hardware and software: *Information costs are in a complete free fall.*

Because each information cost/velocity revolution requires a revolution in management no less dramatic than the Reformation, to profit from the free fall, management needs what Trotsky called a permanent revolution, a process of change that keeps rolling along.

Getting ahead of the information cost curve is a daily event.

Yet, even though it should be self-evident that how you manage fast-falling information cost is the key to your survival, managers only rarely grasp this and often seem mystified as to why their operations are no longer generating the wealth they once did. But, just as Konosuke wrote, if you are not part of the wealth generation process, you have no function in the market and will soon cease to exist.

In *Beating Japan*, Sean White and I observed that only organizations designed along specific lines have internal velocities fast enough to turn customer input into value fast enough to get ahead of the falling information cost curve, harness its centrifugal forces, and generate enduring shareholder value. These must, as I said earlier, be "hollow," being:

- Vertically and horizontally disintegrated
- Decentralized
- Flat, with no more than four management layers
- Designed to deliver customer service

This is a service-driven structure with all of its operations on the "surface" where they interact with customers. We did not at the time have the data to measure this relative hollowness and therefore operational speed.

When we wrote *Beating Japan*, moreover, no single company met all four criteria, though many met one, and sometimes two, of them. Today many companies meet all four criteria. Some have come from nowhere to be world beaters, and most important, all have survived recent years of economic underperformance and fiscal mismanagement with flying colors. Cisco, still relatively small in terms of sales, became the 11th most valuable company in the world. Dell rose to 36th, far outranking Ford (212th) and GM (189th).[2]

As more companies began to fit our mold, it became easier to see which metrics to look at to determine their relative internal velocities. Take Dell. In 1997, Dell was 204 days of sales—over half a year—behind the number two PC maker, IBM.[3] Dell ended 1998 less than two weeks of sales behind IBM. By year-end 1999, Dell was 169 days of sales *ahead* of IBM. In only twenty-four months, Dell improved its relative position by more than a year. It is an astonishing achievement which powered Dell successfully for a decade, and from which IBM learned, under Lou Gerstner, stunning most of IBM's competition.

In contrast with Dell, Hewlett-Packard had all the right products to dominate the fast-growing PC market, but not the organization to deliver them. H-P fell from 24th most valuable company to 50th in only one year, 1999, and this during one of the biggest growth opportunities in the company's history—it was the second-fastest growing PC supplier in 1998 after Dell; its printers were in offices and homes the world over. But H-P just couldn't turn these benefits into shareholder value because its operating velocity wasn't high enough, and six years later H-P remained in 50th position, significantly underperforming the S&P 500. Its CEO was fired and replaced by Mark Hurd, an operations expert who moved quickly to turn the company around.

If history is any guide, however, companies do not transform themselves; newcomers create all the value. Matsushita and IBM may prove to be the exceptions. Put the lessons of these two together and CEOs like Mark Hurd have a roadmap for the revitalization of very large organizations. *Panasonic* is this roadmap.

Critically, as the H-P example shows, problems do not come from lack of product, information, or technological prowess; they come from management's failure to identify information velocity as the centerpiece of operations and then to move fast enough to get ahead of the curve. The Matsushita team had to identify information velocity as the company's value creation priority and then figure out how to accelerate this across a wide array of products and geographies. We shall see next, however, that time itself is a complicating factor in how this is done.

Management Decisions in Moore Time

Information velocities increase in Moore Time. Moore Time is a concept I created in the middle of the last decade to explain how fast decisions must be made when computer price-performance improves along the Moore Curve. Moore Time is a measure of time on the Moore Curve. *To keep ahead of the information velocity curve, therefore, management decisions must be made in Moore Time.*

The Moore Curve is not just an interesting metric for the computer business. Moore Time forces companies in many industries to live within ever-shorter product cycles and ever-shorter cycles of customer attention. Thus it is a brand nightmare.

For most, Moore Time means rushing new products to market while shelves are still brimming with "old" new products that must be sold off quickly in a series of fire sales. Competing this way is expensive—and wasteful. *Managing in Moore Time is essentially a problem of managing inventories and receivables, and therefore, of working capital.*

We have just come a long way: McLuhan's "the medium is the message" is now "working capital is destiny." And it's all about the same thing, managing the velocity and cost of information. What has changed is that what McLuhan wrote more than forty years ago, and Innis fifteen years before him, cannot be translated into useful management tools. But everyone in the world who has so much as picked up an accounting text knows what working capital is and so can use the lessons in *Panasonic.*

Soccer Ball Management is all about setting working-capital goals aggressive enough to force to the surface all the touch points of cash in the system. Understanding the relationship between cash touch points and Moore Time is the essence of the Soccer Ball System. Moore Time has a massive impact on how fast a company can turn a sale into cash. Miscalculate Moore Time and cash gets sucked out of the company, not into it.

The great genius of Sam Walton, and later of Michael Dell and John Chambers, was figuring out how to cross McLuhan's frontier, getting around the "old" new product problem with innovative distribution strategies that slashed inventories, while the competition stayed behind. That too was the genius of Konosuke in his day and the genius that Matsushita's reformers sought to rediscover in the company's DNA.

Fundamentally, the problem of Moore Time is that most companies graft what they take to be modern manufacturing techniques to legacy distribution systems.

This mismatch results in companies designed to push ever more of the latest products and services into an obsolete sales and distribution system that is layered with pools of inventory and cash wait states. Production velocity goes up, and information velocity goes down. Sales stagnate, and profits go through the floor. For manufacturers, competing in Moore Time is not about the speed of production or of product introduction, though many, especially Asian companies, think it is. It is about integrating manufacturing, service creation, and distribution into customers in one seamless flow designed to move the latest goods to market without leaving pools of inventory to be flamed off every time there is a new generation on the Moore Curve. Service companies do something similar. Think of phone companies trying to use advanced routing systems to move modern services over outmoded, low-capacity copper wiring to homes and offices. General Motors has the same problem with its dealerships.

While value can be created in Moore Time—like the Internet Bubble—it can also be taken away in Moore Time—the dot-com collapse.

The Big Bang chart shows this cycle repeated over the last half century as a series of explosive, Reformation-like events ripped into industry after industry. Note that:

- Each order of magnitude improvement in Moore Curve price-performance unleashes an order of magnitude increase in the number of computerized products. To get ahead of this, your organization must go into tomorrow's markets with tomorrow's organization.

- Toys are now more powerful and far more abundant than the PCs of only a few years ago.
- No company that was able to dominate one segment of the Moore Curve was able to dominate the subsequent one. Many have simply disappeared. This is Microsoft's challenge today.
- Each order of magnitude increase in the number and power of devices places extreme pressure on business organizations. Many organizations are stressed beyond their breaking points.

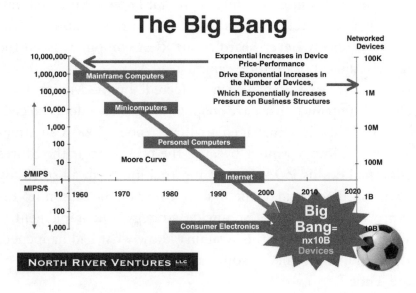

- Early on, mainframes existed at a ratio of one for hundreds of thousands, even millions of consumers. Today, every man, woman, and child in the consuming world can have the power of many mainframes on many different devices, most of which are consumables.

- Thus, we are fast moving from a world of hundreds of millions of devices to tens of billions, all of which are networked at high speed.
- The next massive discontinuity is with us now: IBM's recently announced 500 GHz processor means that within the decade we will see audiovisual devices of unimagined power in our pockets.[4] Business models must be designed today to tolerate the forces that will be unleashed.

None of this is news in the computer business, where whole generations of once proud names have been swept aside. RCA was NBC's computer of choice on the night of the 1960 U.S. presidential election. It performed magnificently, precisely predicting the outcome in one of the closest U.S. federal elections in history, the final results of which were not known until well into the following day. Yet, today, most people in the computer business have probably never heard of an RCA computer. Even the computer industry, therefore, can misread Moore Time.

Market after market has been "infected" by the Moore Time problem. Companies that have adapted to this have done exceedingly well. Wal-Mart managed to turn a poor 2004 Christmas selling season into a winner because the president of the Stores Division had on his PDA enough information from all stores by 8:00 A.M. on Black Friday, the first morning of the season, to restructure the company's systemwide strategy and implement it within five days.[5] Most firms wouldn't know what had happened, good or bad, until the season was over. That's the impact of Moore Time.

The IT Wal-Mart uses is prodigious but the time to cash benefits that give the company the scale economies on which it keeps growing at $300+ billion in revenues are even more so.

Like it or not, businesses must have Moore Time information velocities, or die. The "or die" part of this proposition has come to haunt industries from telecommunications to computers, and many of the icons of the high-tech age are gone. When I started working with Matsushita, the company looked like it was about to share the same fate. The concept of Moore Time was unknown and the company and its IT were structured for a different era. One of those who saw this clearly was Kirk Nakamura. He became increasingly alarmed as history moved on and MEI did not.

Moore Time has several far-reaching impacts.

- Product cycles implode.
- The power shift from producers to customers accelerates rapidly.
- Disintermediation, already a problem as customers use their market power to demand direct relationships with suppliers over the Internet, becomes more accentuated.
- Global brands become more difficult to manage than they are today.

Combined, these impacts mean that a company that cannot operate in Moore Time will not just underperform the market; it will vanish. This troubled Kirk. He did not want Matsushita to be the next Pan Am.

The Soccer Ball: A Structure for Modern Companies

As Wal-Mart does, top-grade companies use very high velocities of information to turn customer information into cash fast, generating outstanding returns for shareholders. Everything—everything—about the modern corporation depends on speed and that depends on IT. Size, scope, products, and technology are all helpful but never determinative. High-velocity companies are like vacuum pumps: *irrespective of their size, they suck all the profits out of their markets*.

What does all this have to do with a soccer ball? Firms that have high enough velocities of information to tolerate the compressive forces of falling information costs actually look like soccer balls using, as I have said, IT to put all their assets and operations on the surface, where they touch customers. Everything else is someone else's business. This shape leaves very little on the inside to hinder the flow of information, allowing Soccer Balls to do a lot more with a lot less.

This structure is strong, yet flexible, and most important, is topologically flat and capable of great speed. Soccer Balls are highly efficient users of cash and capital resources and they usually inflate by taking in over 100 percent of the operating free cash flow in their markets, leaving losses for everyone else. This makes them not just tough competitors, but lethal competitors, as many of the world's airlines are finding out.

Their customer-facing, cash- and capital-efficient structure brings to Soccer Balls large amounts of proprietary information on customers that they can leverage into superior products and services and ultimately into brand superiority, the ability to affect outcomes in their markets.

What keeps the air pressure in the Soccer Ball higher than that outside, and maintains its strong but flexible structure, is the Internet. The Internet allows a company to connect so seamlessly to customers, suppliers, and even to itself, that it can be decentralized enough and flat enough to tolerate free-falling information costs. Soccer Balls also have great margins and growth, and always generate value faster than their competitors. The Soccer Ball is a structure shared successfully across industry lines by companies as different as we have seen as Dell, Apple, Southwest Airlines, and Wal-Mart.

The opposite of a high-velocity Soccer Ball is a low-velocity Lead Ball, a company so dense in assets and operations that it cannot turn customer information into sales quickly. Kirk, whose understanding of soccer is better than mine and whose care over mixed metaphors is even more acute, calls them Shot Put Balls.[6]

Cute analogies perhaps, but shot takes energy to put and most people know that lead is so heavy that even X-rays cannot penetrate it. Customers won't do any better.

Where Soccer Balls struggle twenty-four hours a day daily to serve their customers better, Lead Balls must struggle instead with their own mass. This distinction leads down two completely different decision trees.

When information costs go into a free fall, Soccer Balls create value and jobs. Lead Balls destroy both.

Early Versions of the Soccer Ball System

Sean White and I began developing the operational details of the Soccer Ball System in the late eighties when a senior Canadian government official came to New York to ask us for help. Canada wanted policies designed to position Canadian companies at the top of the world's high-tech pecking order. A few months later, NEC—one of the world's biggest makers of computers, ICs, and telecommunications products—came to New York to ask us what to do about persistent market share problems in NEC's telecommunications division.

We told NEC and the Canadian government that, to get ahead of the falling cost of information and stay there, companies must be designed from the ground up to substitute information for other resources, like land, labor, and capital, *faster* than the velocity of information increases. Their velocities of information must be designed to profit from this rate of substitution. Anyone who cannot do this falls behind the curve and disappears.

It was at that time that we put together our first Soccer Ball–like recommendations—that to tolerate the pressures of modern markets, successful organizations must be topologically flat and designed to deliver customer service. From the earliest days of the Soccer Ball Management System, it was apparent that a structure like this would be both strong and flexible. But tough to manage.

You can think of managing a Soccer Ball as being a bit like flying a stealth aircraft: Without all the information systems that constantly alter its airfoil, a stealth plane cannot fly. With them, however, stealth is astonishingly effective. CEOs who don't understand this lose "air superiority" (read "brand superiority") in their markets. Like stealth victims, most don't know what hit them.

Each Soccer Ball is organized not just to keep ahead of the falling information cost curve, but also to keep ahead of a curve that is incredibly steep. *Soccer Balls are designed to tolerate high speeds*; their managements know that you don't fly through the sound barrier in a plane made of plywood and canvas.

Our early model, however, had problems. It had a four-layer limit to management that didn't work. Even with fourteen direct reports per manager, four layers limited companies to about 40,000 employees. At $250,000 in sales per employee, these companies couldn't grow past $10 billion in sales per year. How could I explain that Wal-Mart, then a $139 billion company, was growing at 20 percent year after year?

This problem is solved because *the Soccer Ball structure uncouples the number of organization layers from the number of employees and sales per employee*.

Dell, for example, achieves sales of $850,000 plus per employee because the core of the company is an intranet, not people or assets. A typical consumer electronics competitor, by contrast, might get sales of only $250,000 to $300,000 per employee. Moreover, as I showed earlier, Dell's gross margins, which were in the 18 percent range, were well below the mid-30 percent of consumer electronics companies. Yet Dell's net outshone all of them.

While consumer electronics companies flame off their high gross margins on SG&A expenses and large inventory buffers, Dell reduced much of its SG&A and almost all its inventories to the cost of communicating over the Internet. Doing this, Dell dematerialized inventory on its own shelves, those of its suppliers and dealers (now eliminated entirely), the inventory in its pipeline, and its spare parts stock as well. All the while the company grew faster than its competitors, as did all the firms that supply it. And they all made more money into the bargain.

Dell and Wal-Mart are functionally identical. So are Southwest Airlines, IBM, and Cisco. All comprise simply a bunch of customer-facing operations connected to a server over the Internet. You will see this phenomenon time and again. Top companies *all* look like hollowed-out Soccer Balls regardless of industry and location, which means that the lessons of one industry can be easily translated into another.

Conceivably, with the Internet rather than people at the core of its operation Dell, like Wal-Mart, could grow many times over. Its ability to dematerialize production, distribution, and corporate staff may allow it to grow larger than companies still several times its own size. And faster. Exactly what large companies like Matsushita need to do.

What is fascinating to me, as McLuhan observed of his "frontiers," is how many CEOs cannot see this Uffizi Effect. These managers still live in the 1970s and make decisions as if nothing about running a business has changed. They have no sense of how much power customers have appropriated, let alone what to do about it. Customer market power appropriation also places immense pressures on national economies and on national leaders who think they are still in the 1970s. Nowhere is this clearer than in France and Germany. Both suffered prolonged stagnation because they did not liberalize their economies fast enough to profit from increasing information velocities. France, for example, likes to insist that the rest of the world go back a few decades so France's so-called national champions can compete on an equal footing. Almost no Eurozone manager would implement the Soccer Ball System, because it exists in an alternate universe outside the manager's perception. That Japan in general and Matsushita in particular bridged the Uffizi Effect, and Europe did not, has far-reaching implications that will impact Europe for the next half century.

The Soccer Ball System rewrites *Das Kapital* to say that *revolution is not a shift from capital to labor*, however, *but from producer to customer*. While there isn't a capitalist among us who would agree with Marx's assertion that the tensions between capital and labor will inevitably result in revolution, there isn't a capitalist among us who would deny that there has been a revolutionary shift in power from producers to customers. And a hell of a lot of tension.

Soccer Ball Metrics

Because the Soccer Ball System connects all aspects of operations to customers directly and increases information velocity between them, it governs everything you do: organization, operations, brand, finance, human resources, and customer service.

The first thing to grasp about the Soccer Ball System is that there is nothing new in its fundamentals. All it says is that smart managers focus on three things:

- Working capital,
- Balance sheets, and
- IT tools for gaining superior results in both.

Soccer Balls have:

- A velocity of cash (days of inventory plus days of sales in accounts receivable minus days of cost of goods sold in accounts payable) of five days or better, and
- A velocity of capital (operating income over enterprise value) in excess of 20 percent.

The first is a working-capital measure commonly called a cash conversion cycle. This number is easy to track and tells more about the internal health of a company than any gauge I can think of. The second is simply the degree of efficiency of total capital employed. These numbers give a clear indication of how well management uses the two most important resources available: cash and invested capital. Work both these numbers well and your company will perform excellently regardless of most other factors.

Laid out this way, the system is disarmingly simple. To run a company, management needs a couple of measures that it can read quickly and understand. If you look a little deeper, however, you find that there is an unlimited set of operational impacts to these two measures. Accelerating cash conversion means ever-tightening inventories, and it doesn't take much experience to know that doing this will force to the surface fundamental questions about structure and cash management everywhere in the company every minute of the day, 24/7. The theory is simple, but as *Panasonic* shows, the execution is complex. Do it right, however, and you create discontinuities in your market that allow you to extract disproportionate amounts of value.

How Soccer Balls Create Value

Companies that turn sales into cash quickly must have first-class operations, high velocities of information, and therefore top-graded management. This means that they take better advantage of growth markets than their competitors and are less vulnerable to downturns. These firms are highly tuned, IT-based engines of negative working capital. Lead Balls are poorly tuned heat sinks for cash.

You can see from the Soccer Balls Create Value graph how Dell and Wal-Mart rewrote the rules in the unlike industries of retail and manufacturing between 1996 and 2003. The two decided at

Soccer Balls Create Value

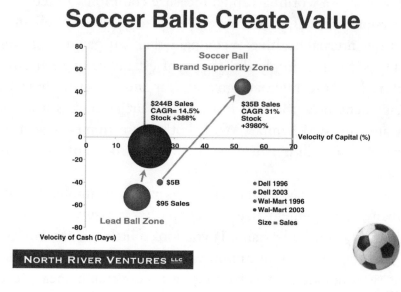

more or less the same time to revolutionize their distribution, coring themselves out so they could scale quickly and profitably, regardless of size.

Both firms put distance between themselves and their competitors. They followed the Iron Laws of Information Sean and I wrote about in *Beating Japan*, disintermediating and flattening themselves to extract large amounts of value in their markets. Because most competitors at the time did not use Soccer Ball Metrics to track each other, they saw only the results—market share—and assumed that these must come from good sales and marketing. This was incorrect: the closer Dell and Wal-Mart came to negative working capital, the more leverage they got out of their sales and marketing. This is a subtle but telling distinction and neither firm has made any secret of it as press on their management shows. As a result, there is nothing particularly inspiring about Wal-Mart's ads (or Dell's)—just a clear and repeated commitment to everyday low prices. In effect, Wal-Mart's velocity of cash became its brand pillar, enabling the "Everyday Low Prices" brandline to work. This simple observation became central to Kirk Nakamura's push for an

IT revolution at Matsushita. As he told his team in early 2004, "The key is cash velocity."[7]

Failure to drive cash velocity has devastating consequences. In February 1998, Dell got paid ten days *before* incurring expense. Compaq took a full five weeks longer to turn a sale into cash and DEC, which Compaq had just offered to buy, took nine weeks longer. What made these numbers so alarming was that, when I calculated how long it would take DEC to get to Dell's minus ten days, the answer came out to six years. Thus, DEC's nine weeks of relative cash inefficiency put it six years behind Dell in Moore Time. Compaq acquired DEC and its cash inefficiency, moving itself into a value stall from which it could not recover. After acquiring DEC, Compaq fell about a decade behind Dell in Moore Time—which is why the company had to put out a for sale sign a couple of years later. *Velocity of cash is, therefore, an exact measure of ability to compete in Moore Time.* Later, I will show how these data impacted Matsushita.

	1999	Internet Sale
Lead time, order-to-manufacture	10 days, minimum	3 days
Shipping time, normal	11 days, average	1–8 days
Shipping time, premium	n/a	1–4 days
Elapsed time, order-to-delivery	Up to 8 weeks	4–11 days

In 1999, General Motors made this calculation, showing how the Internet could give it nearly seven weeks in cash and eliminate the staggering number of cars in its pipeline.[8]

GM was unable to benefit from its own data and is still locked into an unsustainable and obsolete distribution model. By mid–2006, GM's inventory days had risen to 84 overall and for some models ran as high as 153.[9] That's five and a half months! Clearly it is essential to look at the data behind the Soccer Ball Metrics to first diagnose the problems and then generate workable solutions.

Soccer Ball Diagnostics

We can learn a lot from Soccer Ball Metrics. I use them first to look into a company's operations and determine about its attitude to customers and its ability to generate operating sources of free cash flow. Between these two, I then lay out all the elements that are not working or that work well and can be leveraged successfully. Often companies have hidden assets that they can better use, saving them time and money.

In a low cost of information environment, the closer you get to negative working capital, the better. This means turning sales into cash fast. As a rule, companies that do not turn sales into cash quickly don't do anything very well; they are too operationally deficient. You can be certain that they have systemic problems with OFCF generation. My beginning point when I see this is Charles Mumford and Eugene Comiskey's excellent *Creative Cash Flow Reporting* (Wiley 2005).

I look at inventory days first because they reveal operational issues that most people wouldn't notice. Anything over thirty days on a consolidated basis suggests deep problems with the supply chain, manufacturing, and outbound logistics, three big areas. It also suggests a low level of integration with customer operations, usually too low to add value. This in turn means the company is competing on price: it is selling its products at a discount rather than itself at a premium. You can look at this in one of several ways:

- Management doesn't know enough about its customers to show them how its own systems can reduce inventory days for both companies to create a working-capital win-win. This means that the CFO, MIS, and account management teams don't talk to each other very often. Look at your own data and then ask some questions. You will be blown away, believe me.
- The company has lost so much market power that it is suffering inventory blowback. Its customers are cutting their inventories at the company's expense and management is learning to live with inventory bloat, never a good sign. GM's data said clearly and publicly as far back as 1999 that it would have to tear itself to pieces to reorganize. *Wall Street Journal* readers got the news seven years later. You may be missing your own warning signs and losing large amounts of value.
- Management doesn't have control of operations or any idea of how to get control, or even what operations to control. This is ugly, the unk-unk problem, the unknown unknowns that mean you have no idea about what you don't know.

Then I look at receivable days. Again, anything over thirty days suggests problems in account management and also in billing operations and after-sales support. You will also find a systemic inability to support customer values directly, like selling on price when your customer needs better working capital, so that there are fundamental operational mismatches. Expect to find that:

- Account management teams are weak. In some companies I find no account management teams, just product or service sales teams. These companies are forced to take the worst terms because they offer very little.

- C-level conversations with customers don't exist, or exist on an unproductive basis. One company I know suffered enormously in the tech crash of 2001. It had more golf outings for customers than Michelle Wie has daily practice shots. But when I recommended that their talking points should be all about generating customer OFCF, I was told that their customers wanted to talk only about the company's products and prices. Right.
- Top management doesn't have the skills to sell into customer value sets. I find this problem all the time. Selling cash flow and showing a customer how to get closer to negative working capital is something managers know nothing about and they could not say how their own products and services do this.

The third element of cash velocity is days in payables. Inefficient management commonly masks poor inventory and receivable data by stringing out suppliers. This makes working capital look good without fixing the problem. In fact, it makes the problem worse: it cannot possibly be good for a company to suck all the cash out of its supply chain. This just makes the system weaker, not stronger, and increases the likelihood of predation and/or collapse. Soccer Ball–managed companies work on the assumption that the working-capital health of the entire system is essential. Lead Balls don't care and probably don't know that they should care.

Finally, I look at velocity of capital. You must examine these data carefully.

- Nokia, for example, has great capital velocity and so-so cash velocity. This means that it is what Michael Dell calls a "pool of cash" waiting to be siphoned off by a competitor with superior working-capital management.

- Apple, by contrast, has great cash velocity but so-so capital velocity, positioning it to strike hard with innovative products (as it did), and to do so repeatedly and with impunity.
- Many companies improve cash velocity at the expense of capital velocity, especially when they start off from a poor working-capital management position. This indicates real problems pulling it all together.
- Companies that do both very well achieve brand superiority, the ability to affect outcomes in their markets. They are hard to displace from this position because of their operational virtuosity.

So, you can tell a lot about a company from its Soccer Ball Metrics. At the end of the day a company with good metrics has superior control over the touch points of cash in its system. A company with poor metrics has less control, or no control. And superior control over touch points of cash also means bringing in large amounts of information on customer needs and preferences that can be leveraged profitably. Wal-Mart's understanding of its customers is legendary and gives the firm a proprietary advantage that covers the bulk of its operations, globally. This means that it can compete from more parts of the enterprise than can others. But there is nothing Wal-Mart does that is secret or even slightly mysterious to outsiders. It just drives itself constantly closer to negative working capital with better inventory management systems. This has allowed a $300+ billion enterprise to keep scaling profitably since its earliest days as a small shop in Bentonville, Arkansas.

The Soccer Ball Zone System

To help companies navigate their futures, I lay them out in my Zone System to see how they stack up. Though I don't show it

The Zone System

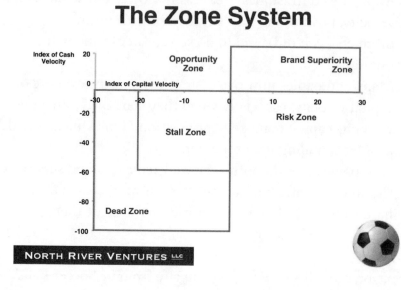

here, I use an algorithm based on my Soccer Ball Metrics to grade company management A, B, C, and so on. Changes in grade standings are excellent predictors of stock market values, and I track these on my web site, www.northriver.com. Grades also predict which mergers will be accretive and which won't be. Most mergers are between Dead and Stall Zone companies with poor-to-failing management grades. And most fail as a result.

The Dead Zone

The Dead Zone is the breakers yard of the modern corporation. Companies are here because they have lost control and have little internal cohesion. I advise CEOs in the Dead Zone to set very aggressive goals in inventories and receivables and to drive these personally. Everything else, I tell them, should be delegated. They will not have time, for at least a year, to deal with new products or top line initiatives of any kind. I go so far as to tell them that any top line initiative taken while in the Dead Zone could kill off the company, just as Compaq's acquisition of DEC forced it to sell itself to H-P. Executing a merger when in the Dead Zone is a premeditated form of market exit.

Dead Zone companies often have dead corporate cultures: people with no initiative and no hope, who plan at best to hang on to their jobs. At one Dead Zone company I advised, managers told me flat out that they knew that none of them would last five minutes at GE and that their company would never hire the best. But they knew that to keep their jobs all they had to do was not rock the boat.

In companies like this, even the best CEOs have a hard time pushing for change. The inertia is just too great.

The Stall Zone

The Stall Zone is the hardest to manage of all the zones because it is the place where management's internal consistency is most tested. For incrementalists—managers who make a career out of tweaking a number here and there to get to their usually conservative goals—the Stall Zone is home. Here they can keep operations on a more or less even keel, so long as no Performance Zone Soccer Ball enters their markets.

Stall Zone companies can usually turn in respectable performance for prolonged periods, making shareholders content, if not happy, and most important, allowing management to keep its job and all the perks that go with it. For most executives, it is only human to want to be in the Stall Zone and to proceed no further. This zone does not require them to break the mold Lou Gerstner–style, and, while they work hard, of course, their lack of imagination is not penalized. They work for their salaries, and shareholders take the hit on value.

It is so hard to cross the Stall Zone that the biggest risk to firms in this zone is that they will fall back into the Dead Zone. Time and again I find companies whose management just doesn't have the stuff to make the transition. I have been forced to conclude that, no matter how hard it is to do, getting from the Dead Zone to the Stall Zone is a just small part of what it takes to get to the Performance Zone. Stall Zone companies have yet to make the biggest decisions in their histories. If a company decides to get inventory days from a Stall Zone thirty to a Performance Zone three, for example, its entire supply chain will have to be replaced as will most of its customer interfaces. That, of course, is everything.

The Risk Zone

CEOs in the Risk Zone need to think of one thing only. Their combination of high velocity of capital and low velocity of cash is an unmistakable signal to predators that they are easy, profitable hits. This zone is for Michael Dell's "pools of cash." These pools spin off lots of operating earnings but do not have the operating strength to compete with Performance Zone companies. This makes them attractive objects of predation to companies whose first-class control of the touch points of cash gives them superior information about customers and markets.

Risk Zone companies can survive for extended periods, however, especially if they have a proprietary lead in their markets. But once their sector becomes commoditized, they quickly become victims of companies with higher velocities of cash. Dell and Wal-Mart both made their mark by spotting Risk Zone companies and dismembering them. Nokia recently found itself in the Risk Zone, under easy attack from fast-rising Samsung, among others. Management promptly went into a crisis and Nokia had to work its way out of a tight spot. Not everyone is so lucky.

Companies like Apple look at the Risk Zone in the right way. They first tighten up operations to gain top-grade velocities of cash, putting themselves into the Opportunity Zone from where they can attack in their chosen markets. This makes these companies much less vulnerable to predation when they are at their weakest: launching untried products into untried markets, something that regularly sinks Risk Zone and Stall Zone companies.

CEOs of Risk Zone companies should focus on a single solution: gain control of all the touch points of cash in the supply chain and eliminate every cash wait state imaginable.

The Opportunity Zone

Opportunity Zone CEOs need to think of operating earnings to the exclusion of all else. They already have strong operations; they're just not making enough money. The good news for these CEOs is that they don't have to spend their way to success through large R&D or SG&A budgets. In fact, most should be looking for R&D cuts because the name of the game for high cash-velocity companies with a ton of customer information is not absolute R&D expenditures, but the *efficiency* of those expenditures. The same can be said of SG&A.

Time and again I see CEOs who get better and better velocities of cash but are unable to turn the profit corner because they are overspending. Typically these companies are not turning their customer information to profit, and need to ask hard questions about what they are doing with all the customer information they are getting. Companies like Wal-Mart try not to let a single piece of customer information go to waste. The trick in the Opportunity Zone is to recognize that you are in it and then focus on earnings.

Opportunity Zone companies can also launch new products more safely than most outside the Performance Zone. Apple was a classic. It used its Opportunity Zone position to clobber the competition with iPod and iTunes, soaking up OFCF and growth, a nice double play. Apple was even able to define the iTunes/iPod market to its own specs, turning a commodity MP3 format into a proprietary lake. This would be like Microsoft using an open source operating system to wipe its competition from the market. Competitors with weak operations try to counterattack the Apples of the world with products, which is impossible.

Smart CEOs get to the Opportunity Zone first. There, time is on their side. They have the market high ground, as it were, and can carefully survey the competition to see where they should hit it. And when they hit, they hit very hard indeed.

The Performance Zone

Performance Zone Soccer Balls, and those very close to The Zone, share one important result: they gain brand superiority and impact their markets.

The crisis in modern management is among firms failing to get into this position. I see an increasing number of problems among firms that cannot get into The Zone. Interestingly, many of these are in major account management.

The reason for this, I believe, is that the MIS needed to put companies in the Performance Zone gives them superior control over information about their customers. Indeed, it is amazing how different customer information is between those companies in The Zone and those outside. This use of IT-managed customer information often allows Performance Zone Soccer Balls to inflate themselves on *all* the operating free cash flow in their markets.

Soccer Ball Prescriptions

To get to the Performance Zone, I tell CEOs to set their working-capital goals as inputs to the system. Most pay little or no attention to working-capital data, assuming they are outputs of other actions. This is wrong.

Once inputs have been set, at say thirty days for inventories, receivables, and payables, giving a velocity of cash of thirty days, and a velocity of capital of 5 percent, I have the CEOs set the date by which the company will reach these targets. From this date management must reason back through all the issues that must be tackled to get it there. A lot comes to the surface. Often this is a seemingly endless list of inefficiencies. I suggest grouping these under root causes—there are usually four or five, all big— and eliminating them one at a time, a process that can take a year and sometimes two.

While this phase is under way, management must start on the next phase, turning a sale into cash in twenty days, with following phases of ten and five days. Similarly, management must start ratcheting the velocity of capital up to 20 percent, with the entire process to be completed over twenty-four months. What happens during this time is that the company discovers that there is little that it does today that will remain after two years. Large parts of the operation must go or be reshaped. Many new capabilities must be added. All the while the touch points of cash in the system, many of which management didn't know existed, begin to light up, some fast. Management begins to see, usually for the first time, what its customers' needs are and learns to sell into these.

Setting working-capital goals like this and ratcheting them tighter over time is fruitful—it is cash driven, after all—but it is not easy. One client told me that it was the hardest thing the company had ever done. But its stock is worth thirty-five times what it was.

The result of the Soccer Ball process is a company that is aligned parallel to its customers. In business-to-business markets, for example, this means R&D to R&D, manufacturing/operations to manufacturing/operations, sales and marketing to sales and marketing, and so on. The old company lined up at 90 degrees to its customers, where sales and marketing alone touched specific parts of the customer organization and the rest of both enterprises were hidden from each other. By contrast the Soccer Ball is a highly productive, everything-on-the-surface system that leverages to all aspects of a company's operation with its customers all at once. It also forces those who oversee the operation from end to end—the C-level managers—to be fully accountable for all aspects of their customers' operations. It requires them to know where they are adding value for their customers, especially cash flow, and how to add more of it.

The system works no matter to whom you are selling, whether an industrial company or an individual consumer. Businesses that bring more of their operations to bear on their customers gain more market share more profitably than others. Kirk Nakamura knew that Matsushita had to be reshaped to do this.

Soccer Ball Metrics and Moore Time

The Moore Time challenge is that *for lack of a month, you can lose a Moore Time decade*. Thus, small relative variances in information velocity translate into disproportionate differences in market share. But when told they need to put huge efforts into a move that will gain only a few *calendar* months, most management teams don't see the payoff and won't put in the time. Inertia takes over. Management just doesn't adapt.

Let me show you how this works in practical terms.

You saw before how in early 1998, I advised my clients that if Compaq improved as rapidly as had Dell, it would take Compaq three full years from its then current position to catch up to Dell. Compaq went the other way, falling so far behind in Moore Time that it would have taken nine years to get to where Dell was nine years previously. Compaq's position was not recoverable. As I wrote in my *North River Advisor* at the time, market exit was certain. In the late 1990s, Matsushita looked more like DEC than Compaq, let alone Dell, and no one grasped how dangerous this situation was more clearly than Kirk Nakamura. He understood immediately that if a company structured like Dell used its Moore Time advantage to turn an integrated distribution system on any major part of MEI, the whole company would crumble.

To understand Dell's thinking, let us look at how Dell calculates its Moore Time advantages. The next chart compares Dell's velocity of cash to a range of consumer electronics and PC suppliers during the critical 1996–2000 period.

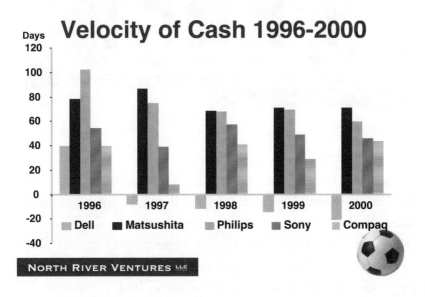

The first thing you see is that Philips's cash velocity improved quite a bit during this time and Compaq's, as noted, was getting worse. Sony and Matsushita were not doing much of anything.

But to Dell, the absolute measures on this chart don't show their real value for management decision making. When I recast these data on the next chart to show *relative positions*, they show Dell's time advantages. Compaq, which was even with Dell in 1996, saw its relative position worsen each year afterward. Sony's position, too, worsened dramatically. And for all its hard work to reduce its cash velocity from 102 days to 60, Philips's position was much worse, relative to Dell's, than five years previously.

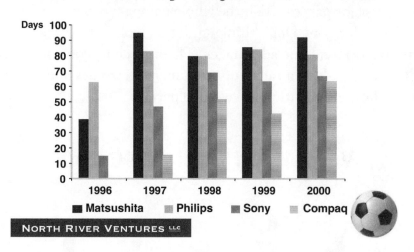

Cash Velocity Days Behind Dell

Every single company on these charts, *no matter how much it improved in absolute terms*, found itself markedly worse off with respect to Dell at the end of the period.

Mapped onto the "Dell Curve," the rate at which Dell improved its cash velocity during the first five years after its decision to do so, these relative data show Dell's *ten-year* Moore Time advantage. Using the Dell Curve as a best-in-breed benchmark, it should have taken the best-performing company on my charts—Compaq—six years to get to where Dell was in its February 2000 fiscal year. It should have taken Philips a full five years—until 2005—to get to where Dell was in May–June 1996, nearly a decade behind. Indeed, following the Dell Curve, the *very best these companies could expect by 2005 was to be arrayed where Dell was somewhere between April and December of 1996.* To Michael Dell, this meant that the field was his for the taking.

Anyone operating with these principles, as Apple does today, can assure themselves that under the most favorable circumstances competitors will be *unable to respond for between five and ten years*, an insuperable advantage, and hugely tempting.

My Navigation Rule here is that it is not enough to improve cash velocity. Relative cash velocity is what matters. I told Matsushita that to prosper, it must understand the basic principle of modern manufacturing: *To manage the sales process profitably, you must integrate distribution seamlessly into production well enough to generate a high cash velocity.* Your production systems must end, not on your shipping bays, but in your customer's home, office, or factory. Moreover, to compete with a Soccer Ball by driving down COGS while still flaming off SG&A would be futile because gross margin pressures always hurt a Lead Ball more as it has so few other ways to profit.

Indeed, compared to a Soccer Ball's integrated manufacturing model, one could say that its competition exists only to flame off inventory at fire sale prices. Another way of saying this is that Lead Balls are not manufacturers; *they are banks specializing in*

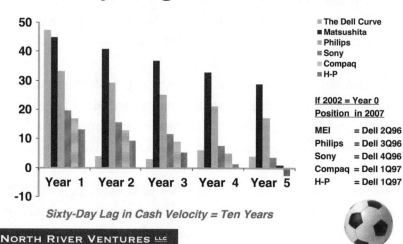

Competing in Moore Time

- The Dell Curve
- Matsushita
- Philips
- Sony
- Compaq
- H-P

If 2002 = Year 0
Position in 2007

MEI	= Dell 2Q96
Philips	= Dell 3Q96
Sony	= Dell 4Q96
Compaq	= Dell 1Q97
H-P	= Dell 1Q97

Sixty-Day Lag in Cash Velocity = Ten Years

NORTH RIVER VENTURES LLC

inventory finance. And, like the Bank of Matsushita chart I showed the company in 1998, poorly run banks at that. Nothing troubled Kirk Nakamura more.

Emergence of Market Dyads

Markets everywhere are being divided into dyads: Performance Zone predators with high-grade Soccer Ball Metrics and low-grade prey. Industrial polymorphism like this is unstable. Top predators do more for less. Their cash and capital efficiencies allow them to turn customer information into cash faster than do their competitors.

Prey companies end up sucking air, not cash. They must struggle with their own mass in a way that top-grade companies do not, increasing the risk to their shareholders. But it also increases the risks to others of doing business with them, sometimes unacceptably. This bifurcation of markets affects low-grade companies doubly:

- They must transform themselves into high-grade, cash- and capital-efficient operations.
- They must minimize the profit risk of selling to low-grade, cash- and capital-inefficient customers.

The middle ground in business is vanishing. Incrementalism—the idea that fixing a few numbers can generate enduring growth and profitability, or solve major problems at the center of a business model—is bankrupt. Modern business is increasingly binary: you win or you lose. The gray zones that allowed so many companies to saunter casually through a market year after year have disappeared. For Matsushita, this signaled the end of its Maneshita days. It had to make painful choices that only a few of its top managers at the time could understand.

To see the urgency of its decisions, let's look again at what Wal-Mart and Dell did to their competitors.

Dell improved its velocities of both capital and cash efficiency each year between 1996 and 2001. By the time Lead Ball Compaq was forced to exit, Dell was outperforming it in every respect: sales, profits, market share, and shareholder value. Even after the market decline of 2000, Dell's advantage for the long-term investor remained unquestioned. Moreover, Dell's market share continued to grow for another five years even as market researchers published data showing declining markets for personal computers.

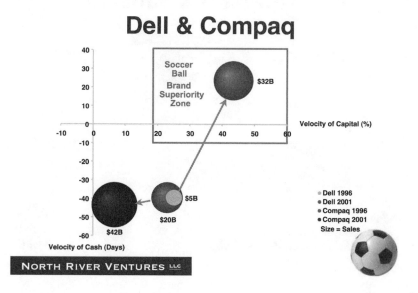

Dell achieved brand superiority. It so dominated its market for a decade that it affected outcomes for all its competitors. In the competitive and mature commodity market for personal computers, Dell became a dominator.

Only Soccer Balls like this can ever achieve brand superiority.

What is astonishing, especially in view of the chart above, is why Compaq never responded to Dell. The chart shows that management took the company in entirely the opposite direction, becoming worse off on both axes each year, and stayed on this course until forced in September 2000 to put itself on the block.

I have long been puzzled about why this should be so: CEOs do not voluntarily move away from the value-creation sweet spot on which their company depends for survival. No one wants their options to be under water. Unless, as I said earlier, their operational design prevents them from seeing the sweet spot, as it did for Compaq and Kmart.

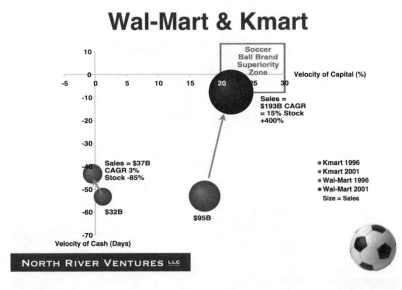

On this chart you can see that Wal-Mart, like Dell, improved its capital efficiency and cash efficiency each year and crushed its competitors. Wal-Mart now outsells its next eight competitors combined and sets growth records for a firm of its size. The company that should have been Wal-Mart's arch competitor, Kmart, moved in the opposite direction, taking itself out of the play. Kmart's management simply didn't grasp the power of Soccer Ball Management and measured performance against the wrong criteria.

Dyads are increasingly common, and the stock market is making clear distinctions between them. Those companies that understand the value of the Soccer Ball structure and the simplicity of its capital and cash metrics know how these metrics translate into growth and shareholder value. Dell and Wal-Mart created vast numbers of new jobs throughout their entire supply chains. Compaq and Kmart, by contrast, were clear underperformers.

One of my clients, a large European company, found that the three Soccer Balls in one of its sectors had inhaled $43.5 billion of operating free cash flow in the preceding four years and the remaining seven Lead Balls, including itself, shared minus $1 billion in OFCF. I advised the CEO of the division that he must either restructure, as Matsushita was doing, or exit. Reasoning that he could not handle the stress of restructuring and did not want to preside over an exit, he resigned shortly afterward and the division was broken up a few months later. This says it all. Soccer Balls don't just compete. They kill.

For Kirk Nakamura and his top team, these data indicated that a one-way shift in global manufacturing was well under way. They showed that if Matsushita was on the wrong side of the shift it could be forced to exit in Moore Time. In other words, very fast. The shock to Japan would have been unimaginable. But it was just as clear that many in Matsushita, maybe most, hadn't gotten the news. Getting it to them was one thing. But getting them to act on it, let alone quickly, would be quite another. Ironically, Matsushita was helped by a lot of bad news.

There Is Always a Warning

Because Soccer Balls and Lead Balls coexist on either side of McLuhan's frontier, there is always a warning. My favorite example of management's failure to read these warnings is the War of the Spanish Succession. Fought 300 years ago, it has consequences we read about in the newspapers every day. The short of the story is this. Around 1700, the French "Sun King" Louis XIV, already with holdings in North America, the Caribbean, and India, had a chance to put his son on the throne of Spain. In a single move he would have bagged all of Spain's holdings in America, Asia, India, and North Africa, giving him control of basically the whole world, making France the first superpower. In the Americas alone he would have had everything from the Arctic Ocean to Tierra del Fuego. Louis was going for the megamerger of the early eighteenth century.

Had it worked, I would be writing *Panasonic* in French.

But it didn't. Listening to his own ego and a lot of bad financial advice, Louis, like so many Lead Ball CEOs, launched a war to corner the world that bankrupted France. Within fifty years of his death, in the Seven Years War, France lost its remaining possessions in North America, India, and much of the Caribbean. In another generation, the monarchy itself was swept away in the French Revolution. Napoleon tried to win back France's once-leading position and he lost too. Today's president of France has roughly the power of a state governor in the United States. Maybe.

Louis and Napoleon were both defeated by the superior financial tool of a much smaller power: the Bank of England, which made Britain the first Soccer Ball. Founded in 1694, seven years *before* the war that killed off Louis' megamerger ambitions, the bank created liquidity by allowing Britain to harness its future earnings for war better than any contemporary financial mechanism. Indeed, it had been only a century since Philip II of Spain regularly bankrupted his merchant class in order to finance the imperial expansion that so attracted Louis.

The writing had been on the wall for France for seven years when the war started in 1701, just as it had been for Compaq and Kmart. Louis (read management) did not respond to what were by then well-publicized, and well-understood, financial moves by the British (the Wal-Mart of the day). Nor did France make any serious move to respond throughout the *115 years* of wars that followed. Which is why Soccer Balls can count on no one responding to their initiatives for a long, long time. English today is the lingua franca of much of the world.

This is not hindsight. The tools of the Bank of England were there for Louis to use; his failure to use them was his alone. IBM's early attitude to the personal computer was not much different and it nearly cost IBM the company. It took a decade and hundreds of thousands of jobs to turn IBM around. In his great work on the history of capitalism, *Civilisation matérielle, économie et capitalisme*, Fernand Braudel made an interesting case out of the Louis XIV example.[10] He pointed out that while Louis' miscalculation was pivotal, it was one in a series of French miscalculations dating back centuries and that would last well into the twentieth. Braudel taught that there are many chances to win and many to lose. The preconditions for capitalism developed many times in China, India, and the Muslim world, but were ignored almost everywhere. Braudel tracked the fits and starts with which modern economies emerged, describing as Sean White and I did in *Beating Japan* why some systems work and others do not. Braudel concluded his three-volume study saying that everything—political, economic, and social—has to pop at once for a capitalism to emerge, and it has to keep popping at once for it to succeed. In Britain, everything came to fruition in parallel and in France in serial. Parallel won.

Few CEOs today would deny Braudel's assertion that most market failures are serial in nature. Like France, however, collapse is not foreordained, but it can be programmed into the organization. The risk of management failure is exacerbated by something Braudel did not understand and that Harold Innis implicitly did: the increasing velocity of information.

As information velocities increase, errors cascade ever more quickly, making decisions ever harder to make and the cost of errors even greater. In Moore Time, CEOs bet the bank constantly.

Steve Jobs would probably say that Apple makes Thomas Watson Sr.–type decisions quarterly, even monthly, rather than once a decade.

There are other implications as well. Matsushita made its Maneshita name by waiting patiently for others to develop a technology and establish a market and then moving in with better-made, cheaper versions that took market share. Today, that would be like Louis waiting for England to establish that the Bank of England works well and then launching a cheaper, simpler way of harnessing the nation's future earnings, a perfectly sensible strategy in a slower age. France actually tried, got it half right, and wound up with the Enron of the day, John Law's Compagnie des Indes, one of the biggest frauds until our time.[11]

CHAPTER THREE

BRINGING MATSUSHITA FORWARD

GIVING MATSUSHITA A VEHICLE FLEXIBLE BUT STRONG ENOUGH TO profit and grow in modern markets was not easy: Konosuke's structure went one way, and the needs of modern markets went another. Unless these differences could be resolved simply and quickly, Matsushita's culture would not change, and the company, already loosely constructed, would disintegrate. To Kirk Nakamura and a handful of managers, there was no choice. The decision was binary: live or die.

In the United States, binary decisions are daily facts of life. Japan, by contrast, prizes blended decisions, harmonizations that often seek to combine mutually exclusive ends, even mutually exclusive means. These harmonizations are attempts to balance competing interests and usually result in an unproductive stasis. The flexibility so evident to outsiders in Japan's success in building the world's second-largest economy usually comes from a series of small, catalytic decisions, often unremarkable in themselves, that change completely the overall tone of the thing to be harmonized. Progress is made. You can see the impact of stasis in the prolonged economic stall that bedeviled the country from 1990 until quite recently. Equally, you can see the impact of catalysis in Japan's financial reforms, essential to moving the economy back onto a growth curve.

For Matsushita, however, time was running out and traditional methods were not an option. What made it possible, though not easy, for Matsushita to make binary decisions in an environment that avoided them like the plague, were three things. First, Kirk Nakamura had long recognized core structural problems in his company and had spent enough time outside Japan to grasp the essentials of what could be done if the company tried. Second, and no less important, a close reading of the founder's philosophy and actions during his lifetime showed that he would not have shied away from the decisions management had to take, and indeed, that he would have done pretty much the same thing. Third, a market collapse in 2001 administered such a severe shock that it forced everyone in the company to question the system at the same time.

The marriage of a homegrown CEO to the founding principles of his company is all-important in a tradition-dominated country like Japan. No CEO can just walk into a Japanese company and make changes U.S.-style. The trick in a founder-dominated company like Matsushita is to reinterpret the founder's thinking for today's realities. To non-Japanese CEOs used to tossing out the old with a sharp knife, trying to rework a founder's philosophy sounds like a waste of time. But it is what made the restructuring of Matsushita unique. In this chapter you will learn that, to paraphrase the physicist Richard Feynman, if you think you understand corporate culture problems, you don't.

The core of the solution for MEI was that, regardless of anything else he did, Konosuke was a pioneer at disintermediating markets. He reorganized the firm several times to do this. His number-one operating principle was that the structure that brought all the elements of the company closer to its customers, a structure that today we call "flat," would gain the most market share and profit. And nothing drove him to action faster than degeneration in MEI's working capital. You would think that Konosuke's relentless focus on disintermediation, flatter organizations, and working capital would be a green light to advanced applications of the Internet to corporate structure, Dell-style.

But all three of these central business principles had been forgotten over decades of increasing focus on product proliferation and manufacturing at the expense of everything. Before Kirk Nakamura, you will rarely see any of Konosuke's main beliefs mentioned in association with Konosuke by anyone at Matsushita. Unless I had read him myself, I would not have known that he had such doctrines, let alone that line management ignored them for decades.

By contrast, the bulk of Konosuke's business prescriptions, which he derived from his essentials, and which traditionalists followed to the letter, were outmoded formulas for an untimely corporate death. He would have recognized this instantly—he was that kind of man—but without him, no one moved, and Japanese stasis kicked in. By the time I got involved in 1996, catalysis was no longer an option: it would take far too long.

Clearly, interpreting Konosuke the right way meant the difference between life and death for MEI. Doing this helped Kirk Nakamura get so many people in so many parts of the company moving forward.

You can see MEI's core challenge in the following chart. In 1996, both Wal-Mart and Dell made strategic decisions to improve radically their cash and capital velocities. For both the result was a powerful growth curve and surges in shareholder value over the next decade. MEI, which sells to one and competes with the other, was faced with a business model for which it had no antidote. It was moving off in the wrong direction, away from value creation. These data suggest that the company may not have

Central Strategic Problem, 2000

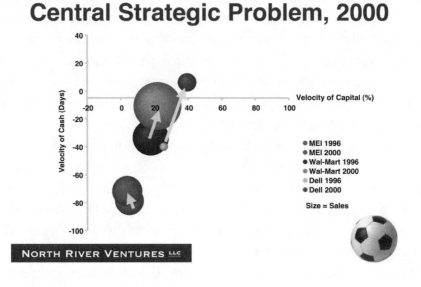

recognized—it would scarcely be the only firm to do so—how dangerous the situation was.

Wal-Mart's dramatic seizure of market power left its suppliers with little leverage and under price pressure. Dell's integrated manufacturing/distribution model drained cash flow from its competitors and their sales channels, depriving them of the oxygen of business. You can see from the following chart why it took so long for Matsushita to get the message.

In 1996, Dell was still tiny by comparison to many Japanese firms, and though Wal-Mart was large, its performance was not outstanding. There was nothing about either company that would signal alarm on the other side of the Pacific. The speed with which Wal-Mart and Dell subsequently moved would have taken a long time to register in Tokyo and Osaka. In addition, as Sean White and I observed in *Beating Japan*, the reporting structures of most Japanese companies were not then designed to detect what Dell and Wal-Mart were doing, even though Wal-Mart was already a giant. In this respect, Matsushita was no different. As

Japan 1996

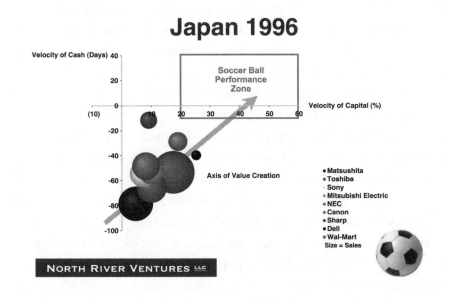

Kirk Nakamura told his managers in March 2001, "Some in our company have not even noticed that such [old] models no longer make sense in a rapidly transforming marketplace."[1]

What set Kirk apart was that from his U.S. vantage point as head of Panasonic North America, he was all too aware of the problem and could see that without fast—very fast—action, Matsushita could, in his words, "go straight over the precipice."[2] When, immediately after he took over, the company was hit hard with the tech crash, suffering both sales and profit reversals of historic proportions, the strength of the Wal-Mart and Dell implementation of the Soccer Ball System became clear. Dell's sales dropped just over half a percent and its operating margin remained better than MEI's had been since 1990, over a decade before. Wal-Mart had no tech crash: its sales went *up* 13 percent, and though its operating profits decreased by a third, like Dell, its margins were way better than MEI's had been for most of the previous decade.

The Dell/Wal-Mart early implementation of the cash and capital efficiencies of the Soccer Ball System had downside benefits

that protected these companies in ways that were unthinkable in
the past. Everyone else was taking a beating. Denser structures enter weakening markets while struggling with their own mass and
almost always suffer larger reversals than their Soccer Ball competitors. Because Soccer Balls have better control of all the touch
points of cash in their systems, they know more about their customers and their own operations, and can move more quickly than
competitors to respond to softening conditions, mitigating downturns. For Matsushita, long used to cycles induced by changing
foreign exchange rates and the vagaries of large parts of the global
economy, a structure that muted the impact of poor market environments is every bit as important as one that allows it to capture
growth opportunities. Kirk put it this way: "We cannot be perfectly confident that we can adapt to such changes. We should always be developing an agile management structure that can move
lightly and responsively, like a soccer ball."[3]

The next chapter will look at Kirk Nakamura's core challenge
of matching Konosuke Matsushita's traditional ideas with the realities of the Soccer Ball Structure.

THE MATSUSHITA REFORMS

When Kirk Nakamura became the head of Matsushita in June
2000, he knew that he had very little time, probably no more than
five years, to do way more than Lou Gerstner had done in ten
years at IBM, but with a bigger and much more complex company.
In addition, where IBM still had the sales DNA instilled in it by
Thomas Watson Sr. in 1914 and Gerstner the personal blessing of
Thomas Watson Jr.—Watson, by chance a neighbor of Gerstner's,
had turned up in the back seat of Gerstner's company car one
morning when Gerstner was on the way to work, to tell him how
angry he was about what had happened to "my company"[4]—Kirk,
by contrast, had to work with a company that had forgotten its

organizational DNA—close with the customer at all costs—and had been on a course to implosion for fifteen years. Gerstner had the approval of impatient shareholders; Kirk had the doubts of most everyone outside the company, especially the Japanese press. While their attacks on his ability stung, he learned to use them to goad his managements on to great achievements.

Gerstner could bring in anyone he chose. Shareholders wanted major improvements and wanted a clean sweep. He had the mandate of Heaven, as it were, and worked in a culture that expected him to bring in a powerful team, get rid of the deadwood, and shake the place up from stem to stern. Kirk had to play the hand dealt to him: either he had talent on the MEI bench or he did not. As for outsiders, I'm as close as it gets and I played no role whatever in the running of the company or in advising his Japanese teams as I had advised his American teams in 1996–97. In fact, it's safe to say that apart from a few senior executives, very few people in the company knew of the template Sean and I had laid out for Kirk during his U.S. period, let alone the rationale behind most of Kirk's decisions. Indeed, as the price of accession, Kirk had to accept some on his top team that he didn't want. The amazing thing is that, while there were resignations, of course, no outsiders came in and some of those Kirk would have preferred not to have in his top team turned into pillars of reform, accumulating expertise central to Matsushita's change and growth.

While Gerstner's moves at IBM were well publicized worldwide in both the business and nonbusiness media and Gerstner himself came from the big-name consulting firm McKinsey by way of RJR where he was CEO, Kirk had to be discreet. Most of what Kirk did has never been publicized outside Japan. He is the polar opposite of the celebrity CEO, using none of the leverage of the global media. It is possible that he was playing safe. Carly Fiorina, the CEO of Hewlett-Packard during much of the time Kirk ran Matsushita, played to the media and lost her job with publicity to match. But playing to the house is not Kirk's style and he did not try to change this just to get the job done. He let his actions speak louder than his words. For example, a rave-up in the web publication *Supply Chain Digest* marvels at the lengths to which Matsushita's root-and-branch reforms went, but has a top Panasonic North America executive referring only to the initiatives of "Panasonic's CEO."[5] Can you imagine Jack Welch sitting still for "GE's CEO?" I don't think so.

Another major concern was that whatever direction the company chose, the fabric of Matsushita had to be tough enough and agile enough to handle less than 100 ¥/$.[6] You can see from this graph that MEI's big growth and profit problems coincided with a sharp revaluation of the yen in the mid-eighties. The company never adjusted structurally to this.

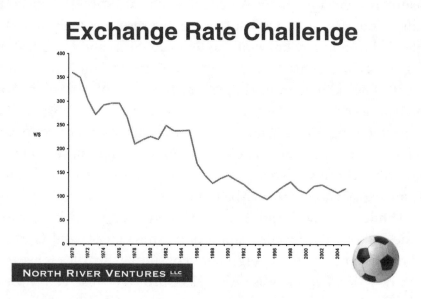

As a result, management could make cosmetic moves, even some fairly radical ones, but unless the company was restructured root and branch, exchange rate shifts that were out of the company's control could always come back to bite it.

The method Kirk Nakamura chose to unveil most of his strategic moves was also unusual. He did them all at once, in a series of announcements over a few short months. In fact, it is a mistake to call them a set; they are more like a torrent, a furious storm that seems almost incoherent when you first review them. He pressed these through quickly, pushing out unwanted managers as he did so, and forcing others to adapt fast, often against their will.

The best way to think of what Kirk did when he gained the top office is to imagine a three-dimensional matrix on a global scale in which *each element* in the matrix had to be replaced *at the same time* just to begin the process of coring out the company and bringing its value-creating DNA to the surface of the Soccer Ball. The entire physical structure had to be moved while keeping customers and making the business more profitable. Everything was done in parallel, nothing in serial. He called this his Schumpeterian "deconstruct" phase. Then, he redirected the operation, before the deconstruct part was completed, to a growth curve—which he called his "create" phase.

The move from deconstruct to create was like making several hundred thousand sedate drivers used to the comforts of automatic transmission shift gears, not just manually, but by throwing the clutch and the gas to the floor at the same time to downshift at redline into a curve. A very short changeover for sure, and unnerving, even sickening, if you are not used to it. Once you are, it's time to rock and roll.

Added to this, Kirk began his redline racing changes in the last half of 2000, just as the high-tech bubble burst, rapidly deflating MEI sales, sending the firm into the red, and creating a crisis of confidence in his leadership. Exacerbating these difficulties, the countercyclical strength of the diverse parts of Matsushita that had balanced downturns in one area with upturns in another had come unstuck years before, putting pressure on management to come up with a solution. At the time he described this to his team in stark terms. "We are in a critical situation, having nowhere to fall back to. If we cannot achieve a quick rebound, Matsushita will become history."[7] In the United States we are used to dire talk, for sure. But in Japan, Kirk's message had a whole different level of urgency. Remember the Japanese reverence for ancestry and Konosuke's lifelong anguish after his father's speculation debts lost the family its birthright. For Kirk to tell his people that they were about to do the same thing, collectively, invoked a sense of crisis that we can't grasp. If your boss gave you the same talk, you would probably dust off the résumé, call the headhunter, and say, *sayonara*. The Japanese do not think that way. Their first instinct is to stand and fight. Anyway, the economy was in such rotten shape and private equity in such short supply that there were few alternatives even if your résumé fairly sparkled.

In an immensely tricky maneuver, Kirk moved in the middle of this crisis across dozens of fronts at once, forcing simultaneous changes in every aspect of operations:

- Design from scratch an organization structure to bring the company closer to customers than the obsolete Division System.
- Get every division to launch a set of new products with immediate growth and profit potential.
- Move the company out of old products, exiting markets, and closing operations.
- Manage the first three moves without killing sales, or the company's brands.
- Get the company to move fast, something it has not done since its founder's exit a quarter century before.
- Adapt large parts of the firm to designing, making, and selling high enough volumes of digital products, like DVD players, to counteract fast-falling prices for these products.
- Reposition a work force from old markets, like TVs, to new ones, like plasma displays, where everything they have ever learned is completely useless.

- Make the lines of business fully accountable for their sales and cash flow performance.
- Introduce service as part of all product sales.
- Merge the company's partly owned affiliates in order to eliminate market overlap, product duplication, and conflicting brand messages.
- Rebuild the Panasonic brand worldwide after decades of neglect.
- Restructure all of Matsushita's domestic sales operations, including its unique but weakening system of captive retailers, the revenue heart of the company.
- Rebuild flagging morale and the "stagnated corporate culture."[8]
- Replace a "we make everything" philosophy with a "we lead our markets or exit" philosophy.
- Replace a "sales at all costs" philosophy with a "cash at all costs" and restructure all operations, whatever their function, to generate operating sources of cash.
- Focus everyone on share price, unusual for a Japanese company.
- Reverse the company's polarity from factory-to-customer to customer-to-factory.
- Replace an outmoded dependence on vertical integration with a more flexible black box plus outsourcing structure.
- Replace conveyor manufacturing lines with high-yield, flexible cell manufacturing.
- Eliminate bureaucratic and unproductive headquarters operations.
- Make time-to-global market a priority, replacing the old "Japan first and then, if it works, launch elsewhere" philosophy that treated foreign geographies as incremental opportunities rather than as major ones.
- Replace the "we copy others at lower cost once the market is established and we can count on large orders"

philosophy with a "we disrupt markets everywhere to take profits first" approach.

- Redesign the company's cost accounting to force senior management to take clear responsibility for global results.
- Make the lines of business responsible for all their investments (these had previously been subsidized by head office).
- Alter management compensation to reflect the core Soccer Ball cash and capital efficiencies that drive profits and value.
- Introduce integrated manufacturing/sales, Dell-style, to a company traditionally dependent on distributors for much of its sales.
- Rip up the MIS structure and replace it with one designed to speed up customer feedback, minimize inventories, and better control touch points of cash and the supply chain.
- Ensure that the company can profit at low yen/dollar exchange rates.
- Hardest of all, move the company close to negative working capital without extending payables unrealistically and depriving the supply chain of cash.
- Do all of the above globally.

This is no short list. Most CEOs worth their salt could do this. But they would take a good ten years, probably more, and would do it on a smaller and simpler company than Matsushita. Much smaller and much simpler. Moreover, Kirk laid out the entire path in his first policy speech on becoming CEO, implemented most of it in twenty-four months, throughout the tech crash of 2001 with not a hint of backpedaling, and followed up with three years of course corrections.

"What encouraged me most," Kirk recalled of this difficult moment, "was our founder's statement that anything but management's philosophy must be changed according to the changing times. That's management, and I'm sure that if Konosuke

Matsushita were still alive now, he would continuously reinvent the company and make the most use of information technology to do it."[9] In a sense, therefore, Kirk sought both inspiration and benediction from Konosuke, without having the advantage of Konosuke showing up in Kirk's car one morning to give it to him in person as Thomas Watson Jr. did for Lou Gerstner.

If you had asked me before he began if it could be done, I would have said, of course not. In fact, Sean and I often spoke privately, before Kirk became CEO, of the hopelessness of ever bringing MEI into the modern world, no matter what Kirk may have wanted. Lots of people talk the talk but few ever walk it. So many changes in parallel are either lunacy or impossible. But they were made.

Describing so many parallel moves in a two-dimensional book is a challenge. So I will split Matsushita's reforms into several parts. I will start with MEI's sales and profit bridge, which itself has multiple elements, each of which had to work for Kirk to pull the whole thing off. It will be clear, moreover, that the bridge would not work without the structural reforms, and the structural reforms would not work without the bridge. Kirk finessed this by personally directing parts of both. Once you review his bridge and understand its time constraints, I will introduce members of the management team. Then I will show you how the reform program was organized and follow with an examination of reforms one by one so you can see the inner workings of the clock, as it were.

Once the foundation of the firm is out of the way and you have seen the challenge, the people, and what they did, I will examine Matsushita's new brand platform, with which I was intimately involved, and then the new product philosophy Kirk introduced, how he managed to outgrow markets and bring the company to operating profit growth for the first time in three decades. I will wrap up the description of Kirk's reforms with a discussion of the company's focus on environmentalism as good business, a concept

Sean and I influenced, and the impact of this greening of Matsushita on its profit outlook.

One of the keys to how this book actually got written is a coincidence. Kirk told me that "one of the biggest headaches of running a sales company was working-capital management,"[10] and he became increasingly focused on it. Over the years during which I advised him, I refined my Soccer Ball System by using the mechanics of working capital to see how these might be better managed for greater shareholder returns. Kirk's need for precise management tools and my system came together—collided, practically—when, just as Kirk became CEO, in my August 2000 *North River Advisor*, I introduced the Soccer Ball System with an analysis of Cisco. In his Top Seminar a few weeks later, he told senior managers, "For our company to survive, we must implement a flat, weblike structure in which all company employees at all levels are in direct contact with customers."[11] In March 2001, I was able to produce the precise metrics of the Soccer Ball System that guide complex decision making. Regardless of timing, MEI in 2000, it must be obvious by now, was the worst possible case on which to implement my system. It would have been far, far easier to use it on a green field project, a company built from the ground up, like Wal-Mart. But even start-ups stumble on their way to scale and value creation, often realizing only well into the process how they create value. Matsushita was, without doubt, the most difficult place to start, and certainly the largest, which only made the challenge more daunting. But start Kirk did.

The V Product Sales Bridge

Central to Matsushita's sales problem in the years leading up to Kirk's accession was that as operating profits had continued to slide, R&D expenses continued to rise. By 2000, MEI was spending 2.7 times its operating profit on R&D, and the downward slide showed no end. The company was getting less and less benefit from its R&D all the time. In fact, the more it spent the worse things got. Management had to come up with a new sales bridge strategy to drive value back into R&D and reinvigorate sales and profitability.

A normal sales bridge looks like the chart below.

The Sales Bridge

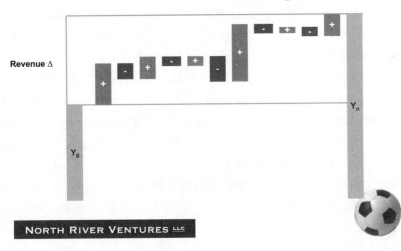

NORTH RIVER VENTURES LLC

You can see that a company must more than compensate for its declining products with winning ones in order to grow revenues. The same is true for profits or cash flow. This depiction does not show Matsushita's underlying problem, however.

For starters, a company with 1.2 million product models[12] shown in a chart like this reveals nothing about the essential challenges and still less about how they can, or should, be managed.

Harder for competitors to see too, luckily for the company, by the end of the twentieth century, Matsushita relied mainly on established markets, many of which were for analog products like televisions that were mature or declining. The company's Niagara Falls approach to product proliferation meant that what looked like reduced risk over a broad portfolio was more like an excessively diversified collection of dogs, all of which were declining at once. The evident need for change only raised deeper questions about what the company was trying to sell and to whom. In 2000, management reversed one of Konosuke's central thrusts: make everything electrical and electronic for everyone. The new focus would be on V (for Victory) Products that Kirk described this way:

"The only criteria for selection of V Products is that they must be able to capture the number one share of a major market as well as contribute significantly to profits. The purpose of these products is to foster rapid V-shaped [MEI-speak for fast] recovery of market share or attain an unrivalled share of the market."[13]

MEI recast its sales bridge with V Products on the one side and legacy products on the other—the V-shaped recovery in the chart—showing that there was a hole at the center of the MEI business model. V Products are in markets where Moore Curve price-performance is strongly deflationary. For sales to increase, unit volumes must go through the roof. DVD players are an excellent

The Matsushita Sales Bridge

Revenue Δ

Goal:
1. Drive Up Sales in "V Products" Fast Enough to *Far Outrun* Sales Declines in Legacy Products
2. Do it *Fast*
3. Do it *Profitably*
4. Do It in *All Major Markets* Worldwide

Y_0 Y_n

NORTH RIVER VENTURES LLC

example. Launched a decade ago for hundreds of dollars a machine, Wal-Mart recently sold them for well under fifty. Just to keep revenues even when prices drop to one-tenth or less of their former levels means selling ten times the volume. For Matsushita, faced with increasingly cheap products from low-cost countries like China, the answer to this problem could not be more cheap products that compete on price. The company saw immediately that it would have to reset the competitive clock and win back differential advantage.

Without a supercharged drive in new markets, or in well-differentiated new products in existing markets, the company was doomed. In fast-deflating markets for digital products, however, there was no way management could launch a product or two, no matter how well they did it, and hope to grow itself out of a legacy trap so big. Even a few very successful launches would have a limited impact on the top line.

By 2000, it was clear as a bell to any sentient Matsushita manager that the V Product effort would have to be companywide, concerted (not easy when sales are $72 billion, let alone with so

Matsushita Bridge Challenge

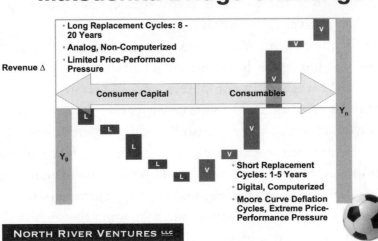

many markets to move at once), and very hard hitting. Just how
hard hitting becomes clear when you see Matsushita's legacy trap
in the preceding chart, which shows that V markets have nothing
in common with legacy markets.

The relationship between plasma TVs and analog TVs, for example, is like the relationship between cars and horses. They have
little in common except that they are methods of transportation.
Every last piece of expertise and many facilities that were world
beating on the horse side of the line were completely useless on
the car side. This meant all the people and all the company's operations, worldwide, would have to transform themselves at
speed. This is where the Moore Time rubber meets the road. Remembering the introductory sections on Konosuke, his system,
his teaching methods, and his business philosophy, such a transformation would be difficult, Moore Time notwithstanding. A
reasonable person could easily conclude that it was impossible.
When Lou Gerstner came in to IBM, the company, as we saw, at
least had a lot of its major account sales DNA, driven into it by
Thomas Watson Sr. in 1914, intact. It had been in the fast-
changing computer business for decades. Matsushita had neither
of these advantages. None of its DNA, no matter how advantageous or well preserved, was of any use. Whatever the company
had learned over the previous eighty-three years was valueless
there. Not relatively. Absolutely.

Also, it was clear to Matsushita management in 2000 that no
one who was big in the horse business had ever made it in automobiles. IBM was still in computers, and all Gerstner had to do
was refire its engines. But to get out of its own legacy trap, Matsushita would have to show industry-leading expertise in both the
old and the new at the same time, bifurcating its efforts when bifurcation was death. Matsushita would have to manage its legacy
business down with great care, making sure customers were not
left in the lurch, and as it turned out, managing the secular shifts
away from legacy products in different countries at different

rates. So, while there might one day be a global demand for plasma displays that moved ahead in all developed economies at more or less the same pace, in the early years, when Matsushita was still struggling with the legacy trap and the huge amounts of cash it can suck out of a company, different markets moved at different paces, increasing risks for the overall operation and making simultaneous global product launches difficult.

The V Product mandate emphasizes both number one ranking and industry-leading profits. The genius of the system was that how to do this was left up to people at the lowest level of the firm, empowering them as they had not been before (and in Japan would not have been) to think way outside the box, and, as the sections following show, to come up with really useful products (apologies to Thomas the Tank Engine for this, but, like Andrew Lloyd-Webber, I couldn't resist) that would command a premium and gain top market share fast.

V Products look great on paper and you can put all the strategy behind them you like. But there are some things that can never be anticipated. By 2000, Matsushita still counted on its home market for about 53 percent of sales. But Japan's economy had been in stasis for a decade and was not going to be Matsushita's long-term engine of V Product growth. There might be a fast replacement cycle for some things, of course, but without Japan on the move again, the long term there looked marginal. Sales in China were moving quickly but Matsushita's sales in the United States had not risen in line with the boom of the 1990s and were nothing like proportional to U.S. GDP. So, with both Japan and the U.S. markets weak, the big economies of Europe on go-slow, and a China that might or might not be the engine of growth, Matsushita could no longer balance downturns in one geography with an upturn in another. The company would have to plot its sales strategy carefully. V Products would have to be very, very good and sales even better.

Inherent in the V Product strategy and the corporate realignment needed to pull it off were, in the words of top reformer

Kazuyoshi Fujiyoshi, two things. First, "a shift from what was optimal for one group to what was optimal for the whole company." Second, "with the Soccer Ball approach we shifted from pushing sales growth to pushing free cash flow."[14] Then, just as the V Product program got under way, Matsushita was slapped sideways by the tech crash of 2001 and began to bleed red ink for the first time in its history. Before we turn to this, we must look at the structure MEI put in place to manage its operations.

Reenergizing Top Management

If Matsushita was going to change all at once—the company, remember, was larger and more complex than IBM when Gerstner took over—it needed an extremely effective top team. Excellent would not be good enough. Only exceptional would do. And what Kirk Nakamura did not know, though Sean and I did, was that in 2000 the Internet Bubble was about to burst. We had written about the coming telecommunications crash for a decade and knew exactly how it would happen, and precisely when, but we did not foresee its devastating impact on adjacent markets like consumer electronics. In the event, Matsushita would have to rip itself to pieces and rebuild itself on the fly in the middle of one of the most traumatic events of the information age.

This would test any management, but Matsushita's went into this double crisis with major handicaps.

Unlike U.S. companies, where outsiders are common, especially during reorganizations, Matsushita relies almost exclusively on homegrown management. There are one or two outsiders, but they are not on the company's inside track and have never contended for its top job. In addition, the company does not hire MBAs (though it does send some promising young managers to MBA schools) so there are no professional managers in the company's top ranks and very few in middle management. It is fair to say that there is something of an anti-professional culture in the company: its best and brightest are the graduates of top Japanese universities. But they come from faculties like economics and engineering. What they learn about business, the company teaches them. A culture like this can quickly become inbred and short-sighted, which is what happened.

Also lacking was the regular cycling in and out of managers from other companies. In North America, we expect managers to have long résumés full of expertise from a range of companies. In my venture capital partnerships, someone who came to us from a company like Matsushita with two decades of experience would not get much of a hearing. But someone who has built a line of business at several firms would. Without a flow of new blood in and out of the company, Matsushita was unable to call on trained expertise to fix its problems. This made it hard for the firm to understand how varying corporate cultures worldwide overcome organizational and other challenges. Its management bench is entirely self-taught.

On the other hand, unlike many other large Japanese firms, the company is not the exclusive pasture of graduates of Tokyo University, or *todai*. Officers of the company come from a range of schools, giving it, by Japanese standards, considerable flexibility. The tight bonds that *todai* people take with them into their companies, to the exclusion of non-*todai*, and that they maintain for decades even after they retire, don't exist in Matsushita, or at least to nothing like the same degree. Moreover, MEI takes in graduates from a range of disciplines, further diluting the influence of any one school.

American and European readers may think that this is not such a big deal. But they don't understand how deeply Japanese university relationships run. First, these relationships are built into the language. Japanese allows six conjugations of every verb case. That means six ways of saying "he went," so you can imagine English broken up into: "he went," "he wenta," "he wentiss," and so on, each communicating a level of social relationship too complex to explain here. The short of it is that graduates of the same college, in the same year, speak to each other on a level of equality unknown in almost *any* other social relationship. Think about that for a second—if only to imagine running a meeting—and you see the advantage of not crowding your organization with grads from one school. At the same time, these college bonds are lifelong and invoke significant obligations: the graduate of a school is honor-bound to assist another in finding a home in his or her company. To resist this force, you have to institutionalize a decentralized hiring policy against one of the dominant strengths of Japanese society. Which is exactly what Konosuke did.

Because MEI is decentralized, it is, in my view, much easier for MEI people to work with non-Japanese. This many sound a bit extreme, but I have seen how dysfunctional a *todai*-driven company can be. Sean White and I were once asked to help a company with strong *todai* bonds. So strong, in fact, that the only way to figure out what was going on was to engage all the managers in casual conversation about the glories of university days—drinking and other more delightful pastimes—simply to find out where they went to school, without appearing nosey. We took this information back to our hotel, laid it out on the company organization chart, and drew red lines between the *todai* grads to see what the *real* reporting structure was and whose views to value and whose to disregard. Worked like a charm. But what customer will go to these lengths? So Matsushita's catholic hiring strategy is, in Japanese terms, a real advantage.

Also, there is in Japan an enormous distinction between founder-built firms like Matsushita, Sony, Toyota, and Honda on the one hand and, on the other, firms that descend from ancient samurai clans that survived the end of feudalism in the latter half of the nineteenth century by reemploying their capital in business. Founder-built firms have altogether more freedom of action because their founders broke tradition—often lots of them—to build their companies. Countering this is the fact that, as we have seen, founders are revered in Japan in a way that is hard for us to imagine. Bell, du Pont de Nemours, and Edison are the stuff of our history books, not our reverence. Even Bill Gates, who may be respected, even feared, will never get the reverence Matsushita people give to Konosuke. And Gates would not expect it.

At the same time, however, in spite of Konosuke's regionalism, there is a decided emphasis at Matsushita on the *kansai*, or western zone of Japan. It was here that the firm was built and from where the bulk of MEI executives seem to come, especially before the reforms.

In addition, Matsushita's factory-centric structure and management philosophy made Konosuke's customer-first values impossible in practice. "If you work in the market," Kirk told me, "you can clearly understand this. But management tucked away in factories did not understand, and I was very irritated by this lack of understanding."[15]

Another clear trend is the deficiency of women in management. Many of those you do meet have been promoted by Kirk personally, brought into the company by him, or hired at his express request. Apart from Kirk himself, and one or two of his team members, the need for more women is not something you hear much talked about, even though the risks of not having them at all levels of decision making increases the risk of product failure and sales failure enormously. Fixing this will be a huge challenge for Matsushita, a subject I will address later in this book.

MEI does one thing that is not all that common among Japanese firms: it sends people overseas for extended periods, often decades. This proved to be Kirk's ace in the hole and requires some explanation.

Japan has a very tight culture. By that I do not mean that it is impervious to foreign influence, because that manifestly is not the case. The culture's permeability runs the other way too: we don't print sushi in italics, because we eat so much of it the word is about as foreign as pizza. But Japan has a formal social order, part of which is encoded in its education system. Getting a child a job in a top company means getting the child into a top Japanese university, which means getting into a top high school and so on all the way back to preschool. A parent's priority, therefore, is to make sure the child is positioned on the first rung of this ladder and to keep the child—especially boys—moving up. Once a child falls off by spending time overseas, there is no getting back on.

For many Japanese companies, sending someone (usually a man) overseas means sending him with his wife (marriage is strongly encouraged) when he is young and his children not yet school age and bringing him home before they are. Or it means sending someone overseas whose children have graduated college already. Or, most painfully, it means sending a father far away without his wife and children, who must stay at home to move the kids up the education ladder, for however long the company requires.

Sending a manager out of the country for anything more than a year or two often means removing that person from contention for the top job, or any senior position for that matter. The expatriate suffers both loss of career and loss of family. I know executives who have spent several decades outside Japan without their families, and the miseries they described do not bear repeating. One I remember from about 1990 returned to Japan after thirty years overseas, mostly in Latin America, to find that his wife and children didn't know him and were not interested in learning to. Japanese women have a harsh and graphic expression for men like these. They are "wet leaves" that stick to your shoes and don't come off. Real nuisances. An American or European would quit rather than endure such a thing. But for many salarymen, the bonds of company loyalty are too great: the company orders and they obey.

Heedless of this tradition, MEI has for decades posted people abroad for prolonged periods, with and without their families as they chose, and promoted them when they returned. Kirk himself is a prime example. It is also common, as you can see in these pages, that many at MEI, like Kirk, adopt Western names that allow them to feel more at home abroad, especially in countries where the use of first names, a big no-no in Japan, is normal. Such a no-no that I remember my surprise when Kirk asked me to use his first name.

By 2000, MEI had a large management bench full of experienced leaders with a deep understanding of fast-changing global markets. Most spoke foreign languages excellently. Several were so deeply entrenched that their understanding was often as good or better than that of natives. I have an acute understanding of what it takes to do this. My Canadian grandfather was sent by his company to Paris in 1921, on to London in 1929, and never came home. I was born near London and my next thirty-three years were divided between England, France, and Canada. I have been in the United States only twenty-three years. I used to joke with Don Iwatani, formerly head of Panasonic North America, that he is more American than I am. While I was flattering Don for his cultural and linguistic fluency, I wasn't joking entirely: he came to the United States before I did and his children are as American as Old Glory. And I used to joke with Steve Ushimaru when he was head of Panasonic Canada that he is more Canadian than I am. Again flattering to Steve, but he lived there longer than I did and understands Canadians much better than a born binational like me ever will. So, who is the "foreigner"?

The first thing Kirk did when he became CEO was to recall a large number of managers with long experience in Europe, North America, and Asia, especially those with good records in sales. These are called Matsushita's *gaijin butai*, or foreign brigade. They were all people whose skills Kirk knew well from his time abroad. Some he had identified years previously as his lieutenants in waiting and groomed carefully for the day.

For many, returning home after so many years away was as disrupting to their personal lives as leaving Japan in the first place.

Steve Ushimaru planned to retire in the United Kingdom at the end of his posting there and had no intention of returning to Japan. Joe Shohtoku and his wife wanted to retire to Malaysia. Hiro Sakamoto returned from Taiwan. Their unheralded reappearance in Japan had a huge impact. Ushimaru was dubbed the "Sony Killer" in the Japanese press by no less than a senior Sony executive. But to show how far Sony itself has to go to restructure, Killer Ushimaru had been eviscerating Sony in Canada for years only Sony *didn't notice* until Kirk brought him home to do it all over again. There are many others, like Kurt Kitadai, who now runs Panasonic Electronic Devices, and Arthur Matsumoto, who started the first Unit Company.

Kirk saw the *gaijin butai* as vital to his reforms. "In undertaking major reforms," he told me, "the most needed executives were those capable of self-reform and rational, clear thinking. If I chose someone from inside [Japan] they might have failed. So I chose an outsider. That is why I called back Steve Ushimaru and he wonderfully met my expectations. When I chose him, I was already confident of what he could do."[16]

Kirk was able to combine the *gaijin butai* with like-minded players at home. Almost all of these domestic managers had pushed for reform and some had attempted it in areas under their control. But all ran up against limits to what they could do. One way or another, these managers coalesced over the years, forming a cadre with shared values. Without this cadre, and the *gaijin butai* to back it up, it is fair to say that Matsushita would not have reformed itself and market pressures would have destroyed the company.

Kirk told me that he looked for only two things in his new executive team: a rational way of thinking and the will to reform. If executives are like this, he told me, "all their staff will follow. Luckily enough, I had no trouble finding people because the sense of crisis was shared widely."[17]

One of the most important, if not the most important, of the new team was Atsushi Murayama, now president of Kansai Airport. Murayama, the pater familias of the foreign brigade, first met Kirk in 1987. He had just finished six years in the United Kingdom and was running personnel. "I was the person to ask him to go overseas when he had no experience," he recalled. But the two did not start working together on what needed to be done at Matsushita until 1997 when Kirk returned from his overseas positions, by which time Murayama was a senior board member managing personnel and industrial relations. "When I became president," Kirk recalled, "together Murayama and I made the plan for 'deconstruction and create.' He worked in the U.K. and the U.S. He has a broad perspective and he isn't afraid of friction. So he was the most suitable leader for restructuring."[18]

Murayama had a major impact on Kirk's ability to move the organization. Running the human resources operations of the company worldwide, Murayama told me, "I had something he needed to make his revolution work."[19] He knew where all the skeletons were, something that Kirk, who had spent practically his entire career in sales and who had been overseas for a decade, manifestly did not. Murayama began to reform his own area some years before Kirk became CEO. But, he told the Nomura Advanced School of Management, "My plan at the time didn't seem to go anywhere."[20] With Murayama an enthusiastic supporter of reform, Kirk had the one ally he could not be without. And, Murayama pointed out, they had two things in common: shared overseas experience—"We both learned the U.S. style of business ethics like corporate governance and the role of women"—and a lot of frustration with the way things were run.

"But," Murayama told me, for all those trying to alter the company, "it was very difficult to change such a long-lasting tradition" and it was hard to come up with visible results when anything you did was so limited in its impact. Then when Kirk became CEO, "this was when my experience worked. We didn't have a thorough talk about this, but we shared similar ideas. And his experience was mostly in sales and overseas, while mine was mostly at headquarters." When Kirk became president, "I took control of corporate planning as well as personnel, and set up a system so each would collaborate smoothly." Murayama had his hands on key levers of power.

"It was not only myself, but all the other managing directors and senior managing directors were frustrated," Murayama recalled. "Many had the same relationship with Kirk that I had and there was good chemistry." Several senior managing directors—Kazuo Toda, Joe Shohtoku, Motoi Matsuda, and Osamu Tanaka—met and they concluded that "we should carry out more drastic reforms." There was also a strong group of slightly younger executives, Murayama added, including Tetsuya Kawakami (now CFO, who led merger and acquisition initiatives), Fumio Ohtsubo (now CEO, who moved MEI into global dominance in flat-panel TVs), and Susumu Koike (now CTO, whose long semiconductor experience brought an understanding of the implications of Moore Time in crossing the V Sales Bridge). "We were fortunate to combine our experience with this younger group for a good team."

Kazuo Toda, who ran all domestic consumer sales until his 2006 retirement, told me, "I recognized the problem. We all did. But we could not change. Then Kirk Nakamura said, 'no taboos.' I was waiting for this for years." Toda would play two powerful roles: one, restructuring the domestic consumer electronics sales and distribution operation; and two, creating and managing the V Product process that reversed Matsushita's Niagara Falls product strategy, moves that were central to restored profitability. To Kirk, Toda's reforms of consumer electronics were of supreme importance. "This was really a must for us to review. We had to squeeze domestic distribution costs. In carrying out all the reforms of the company, the most difficult 'sanctuary,' in a sense, was the domestic distribution system because the founder himself established it. If I started with minor reforms and left the major ones for last, no one would have trusted me."[21]

Matsushita was also fortunate in that the managers of several of its subsidiaries, who had run very independent businesses, even though sharing common brands like National and Panasonic, were as determined to engineer an overall restructuring as were the senior managing directors of the parent.

I have already introduced Hajime Sakai, the head of what was then Kyushu Matsushita Electric, and his number two, Kazuyoshi Fujiyoshi, who now runs the Panasonic Communications Company. Both had well-known reputations as aggressive reformers at KME and as determined exporters of anything that moved. They were shy about nothing. Sakai had experimented with cell production, which became critical to Matsushita's ability to launch synchronized waves of V Products.

By the late 1990s, in what Murayama called timing "that might have been one chance in a million," MEI had assembled a combination of leaders from its overseas and domestic operations and its subsidiaries that was uniform in its desire for change, even if these leaders weren't all in agreement as to how change should be made.

For someone with tradition, both corporate and Japanese, running against him, Kirk had assembled a management bench that proved remarkably effective. He was able to meld his team into a rapid reaction force that drove his reforms quickly across the many dimensions he had to change and did it in the middle of the reversals the company suffered in 2001.

One of Kirk's more inspired moves was to make all top managers, including himself, bypass the system to sponsor reform initiatives personally. In digital still cameras, for example, Kirk sponsored the product himself just as he had sponsored the Brand Image Task Force I worked with at Panasonic North America in 1997, pulling together executives from different areas, like future CEO Fumio Ohstubo, to oversee the process. In the year before he retired, Kirk took personal responsibility for overseas sales, a major problem for the firm. His "skip level" system of task forces and assignments gave the reformers buy-in across several groups at once and bound large parts of the organization to the reforms. With Atsushi Murayama, he oversaw the Corporate Management Quality Innovation Division, which comprised four committees to oversee all aspects of reorganization:

- Corporate Culture
- V Products
- Supply Chain Management
- Quality Assurance

With Hiro Sakamoto, he pulled together the most complex job, the re-plumbing of the information technology insides of the mishmash of companies, divisions, and functions that he was trying to reform. Sakamoto ran the Corporate Planning Division, a power manager in a Japanese company quite unlike U.S. staff functions like Corporate Development. Sakamoto compares Corporate Planning to the *kuroko* (black person), attired head to toe in black, who assists the puppeteer in traditional Japanese Bunraku. You can see the *kuroko*, but you are supposed to ignore him. Similarly, Japanese corporate planning departments pull together all the threads of an organization. In a reform like MEI's, this function is outsized and influential, ensuring that all the parts work together during upheaval. In Kirk's system of task forces, he always has corporate planning operate as his secretariat. He did this with his PNA Task Forces in 1996–97. This put Hiro Sakamoto on all Kirk's task forces, making corporate planning the central coordinator of the entire restructuring process, regardless of function or division. In addition to his primary role in IT Innovation, Sakamoto also played a direct role in the Corporate Management Quality Innovation Division, in most strategic joint venture discussions, and in the merging of operations with MEW. From corporate planning, Sakamoto replaced Fumio Ohtsubo, now CEO, as head of the largest group by sales, AVC, which Kirk had run from 1997 to 2000.

Kirk's hands-on involvement so deep in a company is unusual for a CEO, but his time was limited and he wanted to make sure that everyone in the company saw he was serious. Too often in the past, MEI management had talked a good game and nothing had happened. He made it clear that things were going to happen whether everyone liked it or not. He put his personal stamp on what he expected from top managers: rapid and imaginative movement. For too long Matsushita was bogged down in processes and traditions that slowed everything to a crawl. The only way to shake things up was to get right in, make a commitment, and live or die by the consequences.

The results were immediate. I met managers who were shaken at first by the load that had been put on them. One begged me at dinner with Kirk in August 2003, "McInerney-san, please do not give Mr. Nakamura any more ideas. My job is too difficult already!" It got a lot harder very quickly. But Fumio Ohtsubo did well. Better than well. He is now the CEO.

Within twenty-four months of Kirk's accession, the firm was moving forward and the mood was upbeat.

It very nearly didn't happen though. Within months of taking office, the tech bubble burst, Matsushita's sales dropped 10 percent, profits suffered a $3.5 billion reversal, and the company went into the red for the first time since the postwar recovery. Kirk's tenure looked shortlived. A lot of the people who worked with him went through personal hell.

But Kirk rewards those who tough it out and take risks. In a reverse of the old Japanese maxim that the nail that sticks up gets hammered down, nails that don't stick up drive him nuts. In fact, he is more likely to run around with a punch and hammer the well-set nails right through the bottom of the floor so they will at least stick out somewhere.

For all that, he can be quite traditional about how he gets the nails to stick up. Cyril Wood told me of an occasion in 1992 when Kirk, who was then running Panasonic U.K., asked him to propose new conditions to Panasonic's U.K. dealers. Wood was reluctant to do this, telling Kirk that sales would drop. Kirk's response was that they would, initially, but would rebound with new growth soon after. Wood disagreed, strongly. Kirk asked him to think about it for a day or so and when they met again, Wood again expressed his reluctance. Kirk told him that, if, as expected, sales fell, he would support Wood, no matter what. Wood finally agreed. Sure enough, sales went down, and Wood was not a happy camper. But, when they rebounded just as Kirk had predicted, Wood had no more problem sticking his neck out. He now has Kirk's old job running U.K. operations. Many of Kirk's top executives have been tested this way: quietly but firmly. Some flunked the test because they mistook his quietness for lack of conviction. Big mistake.

Others tell a different story. As Murayama puts it bluntly, Kirk "sometimes goes off half cocked."[22] He has a powerful temper and can cut a presentation short by banging the table and shouting "Not good enough!" before storming out the door. He does not forget fools, nor does he forgive them. Everyone gets a chance, even two, but if you want to go for three, bring your letter of resignation because it will be accepted with alacrity.

There is no doubt that learning to motivate people without alienating so much of the operation that morale falls, and with it sales, has been a major element in Kirk's evolution. He is the type of person who, once he grasps what needs to be done, wants to move quickly and doesn't brook opposition. The problem, as in any organization, is that it cannot be run as a fiefdom. You have to get people on your side and doing this was, for Kirk, not a natural skill, but a learned one.

The Structure of Reforms: Value Creation 21 and Leap Ahead 21

In November 2000, just before the tech crash swept over Matsushita, the company had much of its new management team in place and announced its Value Creation 21 program. VC 21, which lasted from FY2001 to FY2003, was the first of two phases of reform and was itself broken into two parts, Schumpeterian "deconstruct" and "create" periods. In the deconstruct phase, the company was to be taken apart piece by piece. In the create phase, a new structure was to replace the old. Value-added systems, technologies, and branding were to be introduced. Leap Ahead 21, which ran from FY2004 through FY2006, was intended to take the VC 21 processes and turn them into increased profit and cash flow. These are the platforms on which MEI turned itself from being a product proliferator motivated by sales at all costs into a demand-driven generator of operating earnings.

At every point, reform was motivated by better understanding the touch points of cash in the system, higher cash velocities, and a clearer understanding of the sources of OFCF and how these have to be managed at every stage of the operation. The Soccer Ballization, if I can call it that, of MEI was not a simple wave of the wand, and it is far from complete. The reforms show the complexity of transforming a legacy company into an engine of negative working capital. Also, the level of IT sophistication needed to make a Soccer Ball work is not for the faint of heart. Ultimately, just as Wal-Mart is only a bunch of stores hung off a server, and exceptionally cash-efficient as a result, MEI is becoming a set of clients hung off a server. The key to MEI's flexibility, however, is managing what goes into those clients, a problem exacerbated by the fact that, unlike Wal-Mart, Dell, Apple, or Southwest Airlines, MEI exists in so many markets and product areas.

Value Creation 21 was a wholesale implementation of *The Digital Revolution* and *Future Wealth* to "deconstruct" MEI's old business model and "create" a new one for the twenty-first century, hence the "21."

Value Creation 21 laid out global reforms across a vast array of areas:

- Reform product packaging by:
  - ° Shifting from stand-alone products to systems.
  - ° Embedding service into products.
  - ° Reducing the environmental impact of the making and use of MEI products.
  - ° Introducing product-to-product networking so that everything from TVs to camcorders and PCs can communicate easily on a single platform.
- Reform operations by:
  - ° Restructuring manufacturing companywide.
  - ° Rebuilding sales operations and methods.
  - ° Restructuring the supply chain from end to end.
- Reform the company's asset structure by:
  - ° Reviewing all assets, closing unneeded operations.
  - ° Rethinking lease or buy decisions.
  - ° Redefining investment criteria and investment accountability.
- Reform all systems by:
  - ° Restructuring information systems to shorten the time it takes to turn customer information into value.
  - ° Restructuring management systems to eliminate duplications and inefficiency.
- Reform the organization by:
  - ° Putting in place a flat, weblike reporting structure.
  - ° Reducing headcount, especially staff.
  - ° Realigning the Division System to eliminate overlap and bring factories closer to customers.
  - ° Realigning overseas operations.

○ Restructuring human resources management.
○ Creating an in-house venture capital operation to spin off businesses.

Atsushi Murayama described the broad sweep of VC 21 this way. "Value Creation 21 packaged all the problems we had; everything was condensed into this plan. Every level of management was involved in the creation of the plan. Sooner or later everyone reached consensus on what we should do."[23] It was not just an organizational plan; it was also a tool for reenergizing individuals one-by-one throughout the organization globally.

The plan concluded with specific goals:

• Consolidated operating profit ≥5 percent
• Capital cost management (CCM is a rate of return on invested capital) ≥ 0
• Consolidated sales of ¥9 trillion

Kirk did not retire until his Value Creation 21 goals were well in hand. Reviewing the plan and its goals, you can see that the restructuring of the company was to be anything but cosmetic. What Kirk and his team envisaged was not a reassignment of responsibilities or a reshuffling of divisions; it was a root-and-branch overhauling of everything that moved and much that didn't. For the next five years Kirk repeated the themes of VC 21 in all his quarterly addresses to management. As things improved, certain VC 21 themes took on more importance than others, especially his focus on corporate IT as the tool for leveraging cross-company strengths and closing with customers as Dell and Wal-Mart had done. Another hallmark over the years was his constant driving at reduced inventories, especially after I introduced it as the core Soccer Ball Metric in measuring cash velocity and showed what driving down this one number could do to make operations faster, more responsive, and more

OFCF-efficient on a very large scale. As he said to me once, "people don't realize that the Soccer Ball structure is about so much more than cash flow." He did realize and, in the VC 21 implementation over the next few years, he would show how much more.

Kirk Nakamura moved the company from his VC 21 deconstruct to his grow and create phase in December 2002, but the annus horribilis of 2001, which we shall see next, forced the company to change at an accelerated place. Typical of Kirk, however, by shifting gears in the middle of the biggest crisis in the firm's history, he strove to boost morale and to focus the team increasingly on the future and less on the current nightmare of operating losses.

By July 2003, he was able to tell me at dinner in New York, "I think I have done everything I can to put the power to run the company in the hands of top executives. It is up to them now." He drove this point home with his team, telling them at the 2003 annual policy meeting that the company would redeclare its founding then and there. "Each of us acting with the spirit of a founder," he said.[24] Not THE founder. But each employee as a founder in his or her own right. Kind of like saying Konosuke is in the past now and, like it or not, you are the future. "At long last, all necessary frameworks and systems are ready, aiming at future growth. A new Matsushita now stands at the starting line."[25] With VC 21 in place, whatever was left of the old MEI was a memory.

Kirk kicked off Leap Ahead 21 in his March 2004 policy address. This was an altogether more sedate affair, largely because the biggest part of the 2001 crisis was behind the company and it could work on the more targeted operational challenges to making VC 21 effective. Sales and profits were up, market shares in essential V Products were on the move, and the new organization was in place. The company began to feel its strength return and see positive results.

LA 21 took the VC 21 emphasis in IT and redirected it to gain:

- Worldwide simultaneous launch of all Victory Products.
- Improved CRM.
- A network-based business model.
- IT-driven management systems.
- Stronger overseas units.

IT reform was a big area and full of problems. It doesn't take much to realize that at this point in its evolution, the company entered the twenty-first century with the worst jumble of systems and procedures imaginable. Even thinking about how to solve this would be a challenge of magnitude. Doing it would be harder still. But without coherent IT, managing cash touch points is impossible. This work is so complex that much of it is still incomplete.

In a way, VC 21 and LA 21 set the terms of Kirk's retirement. By mid-2003, he had decentralized decision making to top management, and the bulk of his reforms were in position. When the day came that they could perform to his Value Creation and Leap Ahead 21 fiscal goals and showed the ability to exceed these, as they did in fiscal 2005, there would be no purpose to his staying. In the last months of 2005, even in the middle of the kerosene heater crisis (perhaps because of it), the day arrived when he knew his team could work just fine. He e-mailed me, on my birthday in fact, in late February 2006, that he would leave at the end of June. A new era began.

Rationalizing the Organization: Domain Companies

One of Kirk's first "deconstruct" initiatives was to dissolve Konosuke's complex Division System and replace it with the Unit Company system he had developed in the United States. As he had done there several years earlier, he divided the company into

focused domains to ensure everyone got the message: one market, one domain. No more overlap, no more multiple branding,
no more mixed accountability. The goal of these changes, announced as part of the Value Creation 21 program in November
2000 that went into place on April 1 of the next year, was to be
efficient—use speed and simplicity—and regain the profitable
growth of fifteen years previously. The company was moved from
its old consumer products, industrial products, and components
divisions to four new lines of business:[26]

1. Audio, video, and computer networks
2. Home appliances
3. Industrial products
4. Components

For the first time in many decades, operations had clear lines of
responsibility and the people who worked in each chain of command could be held accountable for their actions. Onto these domains, Kirk mapped a series of acquisitions over the next several
years that brought into the fold all of Konosuke's affiliates, allowing further elimination of product, service, and brand overlap. It
also gave MEI a framework for subdividing the domains into more
responsive units. From this, MEI teams were able to identify what
assets and operations they actually needed, what they could dispose
of, and, for the first time, incredibly, who their customers were.

Sorting the operation into domains was only the beginning and
would, by itself, have done little for the company. Kirk went farther. He wanted each domain to follow a new set of business principles familiar to anyone who has studied Wal-Mart or Dell:

- Be flat, with the minimum layers of management supported
  by the Web rather than a dense hierarchy.
- Use the Web to put more employees in touch with more
  customers more often.

- Eliminate traditional distribution for Internet-based distribution.
- Put more products in the market with fewer inventories.
- Build service into products for greater value added and more customer retention, something Matsushita had never done.
- Replace vertical integration with an IBM-like strategy focusing on a moving window of core technologies, especially in ICs and system and service value added, supported by outsourcing and joint ventures where the company added little value or didn't yet have strategic technologies available.
- Drive for market share with top products and toss MEI's eight-decade-long obsession with product proliferation.
- Maximize cash flow.

Kirk shrewdly masked this departure from tradition by saying that Konosuke's series of radical changes, like the Division System of 1933 and Atami Conference of 1964, was an "excellent tradition" that he planned to uphold.

The ¥3 trillion AVC Networks (later Digital Networks) Area contained five domains, into which were bundled a set of products,

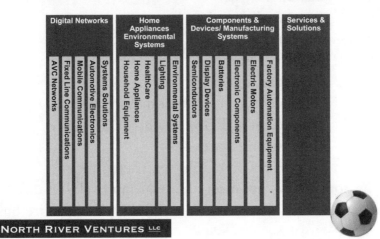

Matsushita Domains, 2002

Digital Networks	Home Appliances Environmental Systems	Components & Devices/ Manufacturing Systems	Services & Solutions
AVC Networks / Fixed Line Communications / Mobile Communications / Automotive Electronics / Systems Solutions	Household Equipment / Home Appliances / HealthCare / Lighting / Environmental Systems	Semiconductors / Display Devices / Batteries / Electronic Components / Electric Motors / Factory Automation Equipment	

NORTH RIVER VENTURES LLC

some of which were not yet in MEI's complete control. These I've marked with an asterisk.

- AVC
  ◦ Digital television
  ◦ Digital still cameras
  ◦ SD storage
  ◦ Plasma displays
  ◦ DVDs
- Fixed Line Communication*
  ◦ Telephones
  ◦ Fax
  ◦ Broadband equipment
  ◦ Digital imaging systems
  ◦ Printers
  ◦ PBX (telecommunications systems for companies)
- Mobile Communication*
  ◦ Mobile phone handsets
  ◦ Wireless base stations
- Automotive Electronics*
  ◦ Car navigation
  ◦ Car audio
  ◦ Car audiovisual
  ◦ Semiconductors and batteries
- Systems Solutions
  ◦ Security systems
  ◦ Broadcast and video systems
  ◦ Intelligent Transportation Systems (ITS)
  ◦ Point of Sale (POS) systems
  ◦ Government systems

The domains did not meet universal approval. It is difficult for anyone to change something he has done for his entire business career. And it is especially hard for the Japanese, for whom tradition is something you revere even when, as anyone who has visited the country knows, there is a lot of change going on. Fumio Ohtsubo, who succeeded Kirk as CEO, told me, for example, of his extra enthusiasm at reading a short text message Kirk sent him that asked for something in a form homonymous with one of Konosuke's core principles that every MEI employee learns by heart. We do not have this kind of regard for tradition nor the comparable subtleties in the English language. But in Japan, traditions cannot be simply swept aside because the CEO is on a deconstruct mission. This is why getting an aggressive team in place fast was so critical to Kirk's reorganization. It would be the only way of overriding opposition and getting the bulk of the company on side.

Within a short time, Kirk Nakamura eliminated some of the most confusing clutter I have ever seen. Domains allowed MEI to focus on market share and profit in each area, irrespective of the others, and save executives clear responsibilities and mandates. To counter the centrifugal pressures in such a structure, MEI embarked on a series of centripetal initiatives designed to leverage cross-domain strengths, including:

- Common technology, MIS, and manufacturing platforms
- The cross-domain V Product System
- Sales reform and the Global Vertical Launch System
- Common cash and capital efficiencies and investing criteria
- Common global brand architectures and brandline

But, before it could get to these, the entire process was interrupted by the tech crash of 2001 that devastated the company, yet that had an unexpected silver lining for its restructuring.

Annus Horribilis: 2001

In the closing days of 2000, just a few months after Kirk Nakamura became CEO and began the deconstruct phase of reform,
the tech market collapse swept over Matsushita. This crash combined into a perfect storm when the Japanese market, never
strong following the stock market crash of 1990, slipped into one
of its periodic recessions. Then, the felling of the World Trade
Center in September 2001 hit U.S. sales. In cellular telephones,
which had been the profit driver of the company for years, Matsushita's domestic market share dropped catastrophically from
34.5 percent in 1999 to 15.2 percent.[27] Matsushita lost its number
one position in the Japanese wireless market with all the earnings
support that went with it. Kirk was furious. "We destroyed ourselves," he said.[28]

In addition, the stock market, unaware of MEI's inner concerns during the late nineties, had bid up the price of the company's stock during the Internet craze of the previous few years,

Matsushita Share Performance

NORTH RIVER VENTURES LLC

driving it way out of alignment with the Nikkei. When the fall came for MEI, its shares were hit twice: once with the force of the bubble collapse of 2001; and then with the further plunge of the Nikkei, which didn't bottom out from its 1989 fall from grace for another two years.

MEI's widespread operations were no longer able to produce the countercyclical balance that had saved the company so often before, and in fiscal 2001, sales dropped in dollar terms to levels not seen since 1992. Domestic shares of home appliances, long a revenue staple, fell steadily from 25 to 20 percent since 1991 and could no longer be counted on for growth. Audiovisual products, another staple, went from 24 to 15 percent over the same period. There seemed to be no basement for Matsushita. Profits went from $1.8 billion in 2000 to a loss of $1.7 billion, a $3.5 billion U-turn. The sales reversal was the size of the company's wireless subsidiary, Matsushita Communications Industrial.[29]

Caught out of position, with everyone on the move, and with no countercyclical lifesaver in its products or geographies, the company was stunned.

2001 was truly Matsushita's annus horribilis.

When I started this book, I took the 2001 reversal as a reversal: serious, but in the event, overcome. After all, Matsushita that year was the twenty-sixth-largest company in the world by sales and the tenth-largest industrial that was not in the oil or the automotive business and it holds almost the same ranking today.[30]

I missed the point entirely. One of my first interviews for this book was with Takami Sano, a senior managing director, and I blithely asked him, as one of the current generation of top executives and lead reformers, when he first saw the need to restructure. I assumed, of course, that like Atsushi Murayama and Kazuo Toda, he would say something like, "1992" and then describe the events since then that had formed his thinking as a top-ranked officer today. When he said, "Five years ago" (2000), I thought he must be kidding. What I took as a given, that major problems were evident to all the top people for a decade before that, he did not. And he was not alone. When I asked Shinichi Fukushima, the managing director in charge of human resources worldwide, the same question, I got the same answer, "the 2001 loss."[31]

These responses illustrate the role of Matsushita's annus horribilis in energizing reform. Sano spent the years before 1999 in batteries, a market Matsushita dominates worldwide with shares ranging from 25 to 50 percent in some categories and where he was used to a long tradition of double-digit profits. "When I worked in batteries, I always said, 'Forget what HQ says because we are faster and smaller.'"[32] Not only did Sano's group rule its markets and make money, it didn't see itself chained to anyone else's idea of how to do business. If there were problems, batteries didn't have them. But once he moved to headquarters, "I noticed a lot of problems" and, used to getting things done, he became an important architect of restructuring.

While Matsushita was being hit hard, therefore, it wasn't being hit everywhere, and for many, absent some dramatic event, radical restructuring would have been seen as an unnecessary disruption. When the numbers turned south in a big way, however, it was easier to galvanize the firm across all divisions. Joe Shohtoku, whom we met as a leading member of the *gaijin butai* who led the restructuring of Matsushita's overseas business, said that 2001 "created a strong sense of crisis and rethinking."[33] Fukushima recalled that, like himself, "people were so shocked that the arrogance of the past was dragged out of them. 2001 woke people up."[34]

Sano's comment revealed further weaknesses on MEI's management bench going into 2001. Sano himself had a résumé of success, something very few of the younger managers in the company, who would have to come up with the finer details of the restructuring and execute them, actually had. The average age of a manager at MEI is forty-seven, and by 2001 it had been seventeen years since the company had experienced profitable growth. The last time the company boomed, these managers averaged thirty years of age, much too young to learn how to manage a growing, profitable operation the size of Matsushita. Among those with such experience, how many were officer material like Sano? Precious few, undoubtedly. In other circumstances, the reforming group of senior managing directors would have time to bring forward younger managers as they showed their promise. The 2001 crisis eliminated that option.

No less than the early reform advocate Atsushi Murayama did not at first see how serious the crisis was. "Even in October 2000, four months after Kirk came in, results still looked good. At the time, I didn't understand the position of the company."[35]

Kazuo Toda, who took control of all domestic sales and managed the V Product "hammer" as I call it, diagnosed MEI's weaknesses going into the crisis: "Ever lower prices and fewer larger retailers made it difficult to serve a major channel of small retailers like MEI's National Shops. Ever more Japanese were driving to big stores, where we didn't sell and we didn't provide any kind of countermeasures for our smaller retailers. Our production costs were much too high to make our products competitive. And, with all this, we couldn't change our mind-set."[36]

As the crisis unfolded, Kirk's management addresses took on a tone of desperation. He started 2001 pushing for reform and setting his Value Creation 21 goals. In March, however, he told managers, "We are now being questioned about whether or not we know how to run Matsushita."[37] In July: "We are in a critical state, having nowhere to fall back to. If we cannot achieve a quick rebound, Matsushita will become history."[38] By December, he was using language that was, for any CEO, extreme: "We are truly in a situation where one more step back will take us over the precipice."[39]

For many, the pressure during this time took them to the breaking point. The incoming CFO, Tetsuya Kawakami, in particular went through a very difficult time. He was not Kirk's choice, and it seems that he was forced on Kirk as the price of becoming CEO. "My initial relationship with Kirk Nakamura was rocky because he wanted *me* to change." In other words, don't just change your department; change yourself. Kawakami told me that he realized immediately how poorly he had been trained for the job, revealing the weaknesses of Matsushita's homegrown management bench when faced with a major crisis. "I think my experience was not good enough for this job, given my long experience in MEI divisions and without any outside expertise."[40] By many accounts, Kirk made his life especially miserable and he sickened alarmingly.

The situation became quite ticklish, when, coincident with his and Kirk's appointment, and right before the tech collapse, MEI revised its first half fiscal 2000 forecast (ending, Japanese style, in March 2001) upward. Then Kawakami said, "I was forced to make a downward revision. But the real closing was even worse. From April 2001, we had a loss every month. Kirk wanted to cut total assets by more than ¥1 trillion. When I was first told to do this, I thought it was impossible."[41]

Most companies would have retreated under such pressure. Reform would have stopped dead while all resources were turned to cost cutting and boosting sales. Kawakami recalled that "one of the most important characteristics of Kirk Nakamura's reform is that although we were mostly operating in the red, we were still undertaking drastic restructuring."[42] Instead, as desperate as Kirk's tone became, he used the unarguably awful numbers to give himself permission to push ahead faster than anyone could have imagined. He told his team, "We have to recognize that this sudden and enormous operating loss is an indication that many problems exist within our internal organization and in the nature of our business operations," and he used the crisis to "break the spell of successful experiences we enjoyed in the past."[43]

To break the spell, Kirk pushed hard over the next few months on several fronts at the same time, stressing the company to its limit:

- Restructured at an accelerated pace, getting domain companies in place and planning for their further reform beginning in March 2002.
- Planned the acquisition of five of Konosuke's affiliates, the timetable for which was announced in January 2002.
- Set aggressive operational goals:
  - ° Cut COGS by ¥300 billion ($2.5 billion).
  - ° Cut inventory days 20 percent.
- Accelerated the replacement of assembly lines with cell production systems.
- Introduced a supply chain management system.
- Launched the V Product program that is still the lifeblood of the company, demanding that the company get 25 percent of its domestic market as well as top share for all product lines worldwide.[44]
- Forced all executives to be accountable for consolidated group sales worldwide rather than domestic operations alone.

To accelerate the process, Kirk put all MEI's top executives in charge of one or two of these initiatives as well as their own responsibilities in his task force system. This way he decentralized accountability in order to drive more change more quickly while preventing a complete sales and profit collapse. This got everyone to buy into his program much faster than a Japanese CEO would, or could, normally do. To focus everyone on the task at hand, he used IBM as his example. That company had forced through most of its recovery in a single year, 1994, and, he told his team, that is what they must do also.[45] Murayama, one of those chosen to double up, told me, "From September to

March we realized that we had to do a huge amount to improve the situation."[46]

Kirk used this year to slam managers for underperformance in every conceivable area. In March 2001, just as the scale of the crisis was unfolding, he ripped into them for their failure to bring inventory levels—central to the Soccer Ball System—into line, telling them, "Groupwide activities to halve both lead time and stock have not shown any results."[47] By January 2002, he was quoting a book published in Japanese by Seiichi Takarabe titled *Does Matsushita Have a Future?* and telling his top people that Takarabe had told him that "Matsushita's management philosophy is dead."[48]

In February 2002, Kirk convoked an extraordinary management conference in which he lambasted managers for coming up with rosy forecasts for the fiscal year starting in April that were all weighted to the latter half of the year. He had already warned them against doing this in March 2001 and told them bluntly "to resubmit more responsible business plans" that didn't let them wriggle free of commitments to boost sales immediately.[49]

All the while, Matsushita's cash position deteriorated from the ¥1.16 trillion of 1990 to ¥352 billion in March 2002, a frightening slide that gave management less and less room to maneuver. The company's credit rating, AAA until 1992, fell regularly through the 1990s, falling to A in March 2002, raising the company's borrowing costs and further tightening the squeeze.

During dark periods like these, companies are forced to strip away everything they do until they get to the bare essentials of their ability to add value. Those that survive usually do so by rediscovering their core DNA. Gerstner, as we have seen, led just such a process at IBM, which is why Kirk chose IBM as an example of what to do. In April 2002, he told his management team that IBM's "spectacular losses" of the early 1990s came because "the company's previous success caused it to be slow in responding to the changing times," which was, he said, "precisely analogous to the situation in which Matsushita now finds itself."[50]

The risk, of course, is that you peel back the layers of the onion to find that your DNA has degenerated beyond recovery. Murayama told me of this phase,

> *One thing I can say is that we had an established sales network and competitive products to sustain ourselves, and we thought we could develop system LSI and put this into new products. We were very strong in image creation and visual products, and that we were already strong in white goods. Throughout the 1990s, when we tried restructuring, what I was careful about as head of personnel was that we keep and increase the number of our engineers to reinforce the future. It is not that we had such a clear technological view, but although the number of employees went down in 2001, the number of engineers actually increased.*[51]

When you think of it, this is not much on which to base the recovery of the world's twenty-sixth-largest industrial company. But it had to do.

I asked Murayama the question that bothered me most because it was the one trait of the company that I felt could kill off any reform effort: morale. How, I asked, did the company keep morale up during this time? "There were some divisions that had no future," he said,

> *and these had to be discontinued. There was nothing we could do about them. What sustained the entire group was the effort of each business unit head. They clarified the direction, and these managers' efforts convinced employees that we were heading in the right direction. I think that what also supported morale were Japanese-style industrial relations. Each division has its own union and the restructuring was discussed with each union and they could express their opinion. The divisions cannot make decisions without the union's support. So, although the head of the division makes the real decisions, union support is critical. I was the*

go-between in the company with the unions. Kirk has never worked in manufacturing, so he had no experience in this kind of union relations.[52]

Matsushita let over 10,000 people go, something that, like IBM nearly a decade earlier, it had never done, the postwar years aside. Kawakami told me that Kirk agonized over the decision and asked himself three times in front of his senior managers if he should go ahead with this. As he often does, however, he took this problem with him on vacation, using the time off as a retreat to get to grips with a hard decision that could potentially end his career and the company. He returned to his desk clear in his mind what had to be done.[53] "This was," Kirk recalled, "the most difficult thing for me to do. A huge number of people left the company, which was virtually unprecedented in the history of the Japanese business community. In retrospect, many people say that my actions changed the employment traditions of Japan."[54]

So, how did the company win the support of the unions for such deep changes? "When faced with the biggest crisis since the founding of the company," Murayama recalled, "they knew they had to do something or the entire company was in danger. Of course, they demanded benefits for retirees. But, after this was done, they took it back to their union board, which was essential to persuading the employees of the company's position."[55] In addition, in his July 5, 2001, management conference speech, Kirk announced the Panasonic Start-up Fund to offer MBO financing to operations it had to unload.

To leverage this dreadful year and get V Products moving fast, Kirk pushed his entire top team into the line. Kazuo Toda pulled together the basic system: a coordinated launch of high-value, premium-price products designed to disrupt all MEI's major markets at once, from white goods to electronics, and to keep disrupting them in wave after wave across the company. Senior managing directors were assigned to sponsor each, just as Kirk assigned his top team to sponsor task forces. He sponsored digital still cameras himself—a new product for the company, and therefore high risk—to make sure everyone got the message: no retreat; only advance.

He used more or less the same system to drive through all his other reforms simultaneously, putting immense strain on his team. Some, like CFO Kawakami, became ill with the stress as Kirk drove his managers, not to the wall, but right through it. Like Fumio Ohtsubo, however, Kawakami did more than survive. He thrived, cutting total assets by ¥1.5 trillion, rebuilding net cash to ¥1.12 trillion, and becoming the deal-maker at the center of the reorganization and one of the go-to managers in the company.

While all this was going on, senior management was increasingly conscious of the risk of a hostile takeover and breakup of the company. Kawakami told me that with the company's market cap down by a third, even in the weakening M&A environment immediately following the tech crash, MEI knew it was a sitting duck.[56] He listed several factors in addition to falling share prices that came into play at the same time, making management very nervous:

- MEI's strong cash flows.
- The unraveling throughout Japanese industry of cross shareholdings that had made hostile takeovers difficult.
- Increased institutional holdings and more foreign shareholders, which increased the risk of shareholder activism.
- Panasonic's high brand potential.
- The strong captive sales channels of the National/Panasonic shops in Japan.
- World-beating video technology.

These characteristics, especially during a downturn, attract the salvage crews of world markets: MEI was worth more in pieces than it was whole, and this had to be obvious to anyone who thought about it for more than five minutes. By this time, Kirk had management thinking about it for a lot longer than five minutes.

Unless return to shareholders was increased quickly and by a lot, the takeover threat would not go away. It is the force behind MEI's share buyback program, one of the most aggressive in Japan, and behind the constant emphasis on shareholder value. Kawakami pointed out that management believed that once it accomplished its Value Creation 21 goals, the risk of takeover would be reduced. The acceleration of the Leap Ahead 21 program that followed Value Creation 21 might eliminate the threat altogether.[57]

By the end of the annus horribilis, not only were operating earnings positive, a trend that has increased annually since, but the company became hardened, decisive, knew its own strength, and knew how to make tough and far-reaching decisions. Not everything was working properly—that would not happen for several more years—but enough had been done that management's character had changed. Perhaps also for the first time, it began to understand as a team what it takes to get to the top, what it takes to stay there, and what its competitors lacked in product, service, and management ability.

When you look at Matsushita's peers in the Fortune Global 500—those manufacturing firms not in the oil or automotive business—the list is short but telling:

- IBM
- GE
- Hitachi
- Siemens
- Hewlett-Packard
- Samsung

Only one of MEI's peers is Japanese and all but Hitachi have bigger market caps. The rest are from the United States, Germany, and South Korea. Of these, by 2000, only two, IBM and GE, had undergone root-and-branch makeovers, both when they were much smaller than MEI and during periods of market growth, which made their circumstances more forgiving. Management could make changes in the knowledge that, on balance, the markets for their products were in their favor. Matsushita had to change in a stalled domestic economy where real recovery was still years off and during a tech bubble collapse. No one outside GE and IBM had any experience in how to rebuild a company as large as MEI and no one at all on how to do it in the middle of a downturn.

During the twenty years Jack Welch ran GE, he created a Trotskyist system of permanent revolution. When he became CEO, GE had sales of $26.8 billion. He dismantled most of the old management system during his first year, as Kirk did at MEI. After four years, Welch cut 112,000 employees, or 27 percent of the labor force. Eighty-one thousand were dismissals. The balance of these employees were sold off with their divisions. Over the next decade, Welch constantly pruned the company's people and operations. Welch was forty-six when he became CEO and had time. Kirk came to the top of MEI just days after his sixty-first birthday. Time was not his long suit.

Lou Gerstner came to IBM from RJR Nabisco, where he was CEO, by way of American Express and management consultants McKinsey, and knew what the job required. Corporate makeovers are McKinsey's specialty. Gerstner, like Welch, reversed most of previous management's decisions, but, before he arrived, 100,000 employees (many were neighbors of mine working in nearby Armonk, Somers, and Yorktown, New York) had lost their jobs. Gerstner was fifty-one, ten years younger than Kirk, and after fourteen years as a CEO, first of RJR, then of IBM, he had moved on by the age Kirk was when he became CEO.

Both Gerstner and Welch were at the ends of their long tenures when Kirk Nakamura took the helm of MEI. When Kirk retired in 2006, he had a total of just six years in the top job; Gerstner had more than twice and Welch more than three times as much experience. It is fair to say that without an annus horribilis to hit everyone over the head hard with the need for radical change, there is no way Kirk Nakamura had time to turn MEI into a modern company, even though he had the support of many players. Murayama laid out this silver lining: "I think that without the shock of 2001 we could not have consolidated our reforms."[58]

Both Gerstner and Welch had a free hand as to whom they hired. Both could bring in whatever expertise they felt they needed. And they could dismiss underperforming executives and tens of thousands of workers as they saw fit. Welch was so famous for unloading people he gained the nickname "neutron Jack." He annually dismissed the bottom 10 percent of management.

Matsushita was in no such position. The company managed to get 10,000 of its people to take early retirement,[59] less than 10 percent of the number of people sacked by IBM or GE. As for senior management, except for the usual retirements for those reaching the mandatory retirement age and those it could politely usher out the door, the company had to move ahead with those it had. This meant that the team was tested together and learned under pressure about its strengths and weaknesses, which in turn accounts for much of its resilience.

Kirk, as we saw, used IBM as his example, telling management that if Gerstner could turn that company around in what Kirk called a V-shaped recovery—down and up fast—then Matsushita could too. In four simple points, he outlined what IBM had done, telling the company that it had to do the same thing:[60]

1. Optimize the business to scale properly.
2. Clarify business priorities and concentration.

3.   Reform organizations.
4.   Expand service business.

These simple points became the envelope in which Kirk would carry the full range of what MEI must do.

In July 2002, he was able to signal to his team that the first glimmer of turnaround had begun in the quarter just ended, saying, "this was truly an auspicious start."[61] Not only had the annus horribilis come to an end, but also, from that moment Kirk's tone changed. After December 2002, he stopped using phrases like "the precipice" and referring to Matsushita as "history," which littered his talks through his first eighteen months as CEO. And he never again used these occasions to hector management for irresponsible business plans. While he hit managers hard for bad numbers, especially Soccer Ball Metrics of cash and capital efficiency, he was no longer as condemnatory as he had been and was increasingly able to refer to successful examples of restructuring and new products and to isolate the one or two areas of failure, like cell phones, or specific strategic concerns, like inventories. For the duration of his presidency it was clear to him that a new team had weathered the storm, that they were capable, and that they could meet the continuing challenges. This is not to say that all MEI's problems were behind it or that no further work lay ahead. Just that the new team, which was largely untested in late 2000, and composed of Murayama's "one chance in a million" grouping, had proven itself. Thereafter, Kirk's focus shifted from the defensive—pull back from the brink, reorganize, and get V Products into the breach—to the offensive. By March 2005, when events finally caught up with Sony and Howard Stringer was brought in to rebuild that company, Matsushita had been on the offensive for nearly three years, locking in what, in the event, proved a major advantage.

To understand how big three years is, look at Volkswagen. Bernd Pischetsrieder was brought in as CEO in 2000, the same year Kirk became CEO of Matsushita. But he waited until 2004 to hire McKinsey turnaround artist Wolfgang Bernhard, who got moving on reorganization only in 2006.[62] *Panasonic* shows that Bernhard would need five years to do this, at least. That's over a decade to do what Kirk did in twenty-four months and the work hasn't begun yet. Both are now gone.

Reintegrating the Affiliates

Among the many anomalies in the Matsushita system were the partially owned affiliates designed to do things that Matsushita itself could have done. Konosuke created most of these in the 1950s and '60s as part of his strategy of broadening the capital base of the postwar company as he expanded its market coverage. But the biggest, Matsushita Electric Works, a ¥1.2 trillion ($10.4 billion) unit, was founded in 1935 during a different era, long before the modern Matsushita emerged. MEW was thought of not as an affiliate or even a subsidiary (it was minority-, not majority-, owned by MEI) but as a sister company with its own long, proud traditions. MEW was pried from Matsushita's control by the Americans after the Second World War in the belief that Konosuke was running a *zaibatsu*, a Japanese combine which the Americans broke up just as they had Standard Oil at home a half-century earlier and the Bell System more than three decades later.

Whatever Konosuke's reasons for creating so many affiliates with some overlapping and some unique products, these had ceased to be important long before 2000. What mattered by then was that many independently managed companies were using Matsushita brands. These companies did not share identical interests, even though they often used common sales channels, especially overseas. Panasonic North America or Panasonic Europe, for example, sold all Panasonic-brand products, regardless of source, meaning that fax machines might come from different companies in a variety of packaging that would make them impossible to brand effectively. No amount of reorganization of MEI, no matter how detailed, or successful, would have any impact on MEI's brand if all these operations remained independent. This was clear to the senior managing directors at their first top seminar meeting to discuss reform.

All the affiliates were publicly listed. To bring them into the fold, Matsushita would have to buy them at market prices. Tetsuya Kawakami, CFO and architect of these mergers, told me, "When I was general manager for group subsidiaries (managing the accounting relationships between MEI and its affiliates) I proposed buying our affiliates but no one thought it could be realized. No one believed it was possible to delist MCI and KME. Also, the price of MCI stock was high, at ¥15,000 per share, making it financially impossible. Kirk felt that if we couldn't bring in MCI, the whole effort made no sense. But, when we brought goodwill accounting up to SEC standards and the price of MCI stock fell to ¥5,000, the deals made sense."[63]

In January 2001, only a couple of months after putting the domain structure in place, MEI first bought Matsushita Electronic Corporation, a joint venture with Philips that Konosuke founded in 1952. This deal brought in-house a lighting, CRT, and semiconductor business that MEI integrated with internal groups to build new semiconductor, display devices, and lighting companies. MEC became the core of a black box technology strategy that allowed MEI to focus on proprietary technology and drop its reliance on vertical integration, a big step away from its deepest traditions.

A year later, in his January 14, 2002, address to the company, Kirk pointedly identified six major areas of product overlap, including sensitive areas with huge growth opportunities like car navigation, and said these were draining resources and slowing growth. He announced a realignment of his domain company system to make overlap elimination easier and then the $5.3 billion acquisition, approved that morning, of Matsushita Communication Industrial, Kyushu Matsushita Electric, Matsushita Graphic Communications Systems, and Matsushita Kotobuki Electronics Industries. At a stroke, eight decades of Konosuke's clutter were over and coherent branding could begin. Done in the middle of MEI's annus horribilis, these deals signaled to everyone that there was no going back, that there was a new MEI with a structure and coherence unlike any version of the company that had gone before.

Once these deals were done, Matsushita reassigned products between groups and rationalized the organization. Kyushu, which called itself the mini Matsushita because it duplicated so much of what was done at the parent, had had serious problems before this rationalization. Its product line was all over the place from water purifiers to telecommunications. In some markets it was big. In others it was small. But, like MEI, its efforts were diffused over too wide an area to be manageable. Kazuyoshi Fujiyoshi told me in 2005 that while it was still public, KME could not explain to analysts what its business was. "They always asked, 'What is your business?' and we always confused them. And whenever we talked about our future plans, they would always say we talked as an intragroup competitor. This was a real challenge for us."[64] Differentiation under these circumstances was impossible.

Remember that Fujiyoshi, and his predecessor, Hajime Sakai, had started reforms of their own at KME right after my visit in early 1997, when Kirk asked me to tour Japan with my *Digital Revolution* recommendations, and that Fujiyoshi showed me much of what he had done in November 1998 when I returned. But there were limits, he told me in late 2005. "We were a listed company, as were all the many parts of the company that we integrated with. We were aware of the need for change but we couldn't move so quickly."

Under the new name Panasonic Communications Company, KME took all the wireline, fax, and Internet Protocol communications products of Matsushita Communications and Matsushita Graphics Communications, consolidating these with its own. It offloaded its car navigation systems, as did MCI and MEI's AVC, onto the Panasonic Automotive Systems Company. KME's old TV parts and lead frame businesses were closed. Its refrigerator motor business went to the Panasonic Motor Company and its ceramic parts business to Panasonic Electronic Devices. In April 2005, KME's water and environmental products went to Matsushita Electric Works. The company emerged as a single purpose entity with the world's number one market share in cordless telephones (of which it sold 200 million units a year) and small PBXs, number two position in personal fax machines, and number three position in multipurpose business fax machines. A power in all its markets today, PCC is a model for the rest of the company.

With the diffusion of missions gone, PCC focused on a common platform, the Internet Protocol, and putting common designs, handsets, and parts in all its products. Japanese factories went from sixteen to twelve and overseas operations from eight to six. The benefit to MEI of the fax reorganization alone was ¥7 billion. PCC today is one of the few in the world to have a complete line of in-home communications and security products for which, with its digital imaging products, it has a full range of audio and visual capabilities. With the elimination of MEI's confining web of geographic mandates, PCC can now sell its full portfolio anywhere in the world it wants to. In an irony not lost on management, while the rest of the company is focused on building sales and profitability overseas, PCC's big weakness, after decades of forced exclusion from domestic markets, is growth in Japan.

As always in Japan, however, the people side of streamlining on such a scale is a sensitive issue. For Fujiyoshi, "We knew inside the company that consolidation was necessary. But we were not just in the business of firing people. We had to ask ourselves what to do with all the people who couldn't move and do something for these people, like helping them find jobs and adding to their pensions. Also, it is in the nature of business that skills need upgrading, and there are always people who cannot upgrade with us because they want the status quo. So for them we boosted their pensions to help them retire without a grudge."[65]

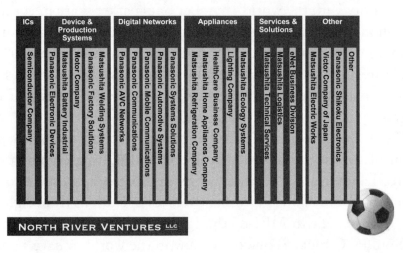

Matsushita Domains, 2006

ICs	Device & Production Systems				Digital Networks							Appliances					Services & Solutions				Other			
Semiconductor Company	Panasonic Electronic Devices	Matsushita Battery Industrial	Motor Company	Panasonic Factory Solutions	Matsushita Welding Systems	Panasonic AVC Networks	Panasonic Communications	Panasonic Mobile Communications	Panasonic Automotive Systems	Panasonic Systems Solutions	Matsushita Refrigeration Company	Matsushita Home Appliances Company	HealthCare Business Company	Lighting Company	Matsushita Ecology Systems	Matsushita Technical Services	Matsushita Logistics	eNet Business Division	Matsushita Electric Works	Victor Company of Japan	Panasonic Shikoku Electronics	Other		

NORTH RIVER VENTURES LLC

Once Kawakami had rolled up the affiliates, he could finally be certain of his own abilities, so much in doubt during the crisis of 2001. In December 2003, MEI announced that it would spend $1.4 billion to increase its share of sister company Matsushita Electric Works from 31.8 to 51 percent. MEW has a separate management culture though there is some product crossover. Both MEI and MEW sell under the National and Panasonic names, depending on market. MEW's main expertise is in the efficient management of home and office environments. Probably no other company in the world knows as much about how to make homes and offices energy efficient. Bringing MEW into the fold was a big undertaking—it was a ¥1.2 trillion enterprise—and it added an entirely new expertise to Matsushita. In spite of the similarity in names, therefore, pulling this deal together was much more like a classic takeover than anything MEI had done in the 2000–2002 realignment. But in other ways it was contentious in a familial sense. "This was a bold decision," Kawakami told me, "that other generations could not countenance because we are sister companies so our rivalry was intense, more than between unrelated companies. For example, Mr. Nishida, a former president of MEW, said that the biggest driving force of MEW growth was news that they were falling behind MEI in performance."[66]

Few companies in the world make serial acquisitions successfully. Most that do, like Cisco, acquire small companies for their technology. Others, like McGraw-Hill, which bought my first company, are constructed on a careful plan to grow by expanding into so-called adjacencies. But most mergers end in failure, like Compaq's purchase of DEC. Only one or two large companies—Chemical Bank, which now goes by the name J. P. Morgan Chase—ever get into the merger big leagues. Almost all mergers are between cash- and capital-inefficient Lead Balls that, no matter what the parties tell the press about synergies and market share, are trying to manage decline. Most deals are just money in the pockets of investment bankers and consulting firms.

Matsushita has a somewhat unhappy history with acquisitions outside its area of expertise, having acquired MCA in 1989 in an overreaction to Sony's twin moves to acquire CBS Records and Columbia Pictures. The deal was a fundamental misapprehension of how software, content, and media work together in the information age. Matsushita sold MCA on to Edgar Bronfman in 1994.

I also believe that the MCA deal soured because MEI's organization was so poor that it did not understand its markets or how they were evolving. Had the Nakamura reforms been in place at the time, the company's judgment might have been better; *imitatio Sony* might not have been seen as the path to enlightenment. In the event, MEI unloaded MCA fairly quickly, where Sony stuck with its game plan more than a decade longer, eventually being forced into a painful restructuring of its own.

Today, however, if you map Matsushita's M&A capability and its V sales bridge onto its domains, add in the V Products system and the streamlined board, compensation system, and sales organizations that I will describe later, and then look at MEI's balance sheet, MEI can make acquisitions. Not only can the company acquire and integrate entire V sectors, but the coherence of its internal operations make the likelihood of an accretive deal strong. The suggestion would have been laughable in 2000.

The impact of the roll-up of its affiliates midstream in its annus horribilis was salutary. It signaled that the firm was going forward, not backward, come hell or high water. Atsushi Murayama told me, "When we pulled all the listed companies together and signed with them, that's when I knew it was going to work."[67]

Sales Restructuring

Matsushita's number one sales problem both in Japan and abroad was the lack of demand creation. To change this, the company had to transform itself from a product-push operation to a demand-pull operation centered on the point of sale. This may look like a straightforward reversal of polarity. Indeed, the Soccer Ball System says that companies that manage the sales process make all the profit in their markets. But Matsushita suffered for years from a chronic failure to manage the sales process for its products. This meant that no matter how high sales were or how great MEI's products, force-feeding customers made profits elusive.

Domestic and international sales operations were complex and hard to manage before 2000, and they proved tough to reform afterward. Three top executives stepped in. Senior Managing Director Kazuo Toda took charge of domestic consumer sales reform and Senior Managing Director Joe Shohtoku took charge of overseas sales reform. Takami Sano took control of global industrial sales. Toda would also oversee the V Product system and Shohtoku the restructuring of MEI's global capital outlays and internal financial reporting.

Toda's group moved to change domestic consumer products sales in 2000, reasoning, as Toda said, that "the system was already too old. Because people thought MEI was big in consumer products, a change there will *encourager les autres*. I was asked to take on AVC and start a revolution in sales."[68] He did this in two stages. In July 2000 he laid out internal changes that were implemented during the annus horribilis of 2001. In July 2002 he planned reform of the distribution chain that was implemented in April 2003. The biggest challenge, he told me, was the legacy of National Shops left by Konosuke that, I knew, many considered untouchable. But, as Toda pointed out, Kirk had insisted that there be "no taboos" in the reform, so the National Shops were open season.

As we saw earlier, Konosuke built the National Shop system for the best of reasons: to put the company closer to its customers than any of its competitors. One of the complexities of the National Shop system is that Konosuke used other people's equity whenever possible. He believed that ownership made people more responsive to customers and more likely to ensure strong profits, the alpha and omega of business. The problem, as Kirk discovered in Nagoya and later with the affiliates, both of which were partly owned by MEI and partly owned by others, is that competing agendas are hard to manage, especially when cash flow is at stake. Matsushita's 19,000 National Shops[69] (now the Panasonic/National shops) presented a somewhat different challenge because they were wholly owned by the merchants who ran them.

In Konosuke's time, the power of his personality and his assiduous grooming of his captive retailers held the system together.

By the 1990s, he was gone and the face of Japanese retailing had changed. Toda estimated that by 2000, small shops accounted for only 14 percent of the market but 45 percent of Matsushita's domestic consumer electronics sales. In effect, MEI's reliance on small shops mirrored a Japan of thirty-five years previously when small retailers accounted for over 75 percent of the market.

Toda's team quickly found that sales were an end-of-pipe consideration in a product-driven operation. This would have to be reversed and sales staff built into all product decisions early. They identified thirty-two sales companies inside Matsushita's domestic operations that had no sales function at all, resulting in a lack of accountability all round and a selling organization that was itself "caught in a spiral of organizations that are not liable for sales."[70] Moreover, the cost reductions of 2001 had forced out a large number of MEI's best salespeople even as pressure to grow sales increased, pushing down morale. These findings were indicators of further problems requiring a complete overhaul of:

- Receivables management
- Budget management
- Inventory management
- Schedule management
- Sales mind-set

As for the National/Panasonic stores, Toda's team found that most had experienced double-digit sales declines but, because they were captive franchisees and could not source products elsewhere, they were not happy campers. Moreover, their fixed costs were too high and their labor efficiencies low. Matsushita's complex structure was hard for them to manage. These companies had been left to their own devices for decades. Yet, as Toda recognized, they were invaluable assets if treated properly.

I asked Toda why MEI bothered to support these stores at all under such changed market conditions. He told me, "In June

2002, I surveyed all our specialty stores and found that half were good operations and half were poor. But we had always looked at average numbers for all our stores as a group. With the severe competition, it would have been a big mistake to rely on average sales data." In addition, "the way we supported the National Stores was decided by the policies of the company," which meant a common policy for everyone regardless of results.

Once Toda had a better picture of which stores were doing well and which were not, he changed direction. "We made a big decision. Before we went for egalitarianism. Now we decided to reward performance, which is, in fact, more fair than what we were doing." Matsushita started by differentiating its retailers by sales results. "We renamed the top shops 'Super Professional Shops' and concentrated our support there. We brought in the same contract terms that we used for mass retailers. We gave them more technical and consultation support through special call centers. We also helped provide successors for owners when their children were no longer interested in following owners into the store business."[71]

Toda calculated that MEI's small retailers would grow if they were encouraged, had the right products, and most important, took advantage of Japan's aging society, which, he felt, didn't want to drive to distant stores and needed a quick local response to problems. The last two points, he reckons, "are more important to the elderly than price." In other words, the aging infrastructure of National/Panasonic Shops, if rejuvenated carefully, could become a channel for premium products rather than cannon fodder for big box outlets.

The team put in place a comprehensive policy of visits by senior MEI executives to get a handle on Panasonic/National store issues before they became problems. It restructured the functions of the sales companies that supported these stores, streamlined their number, and made them accountable for sales to the National/Panasonic stores.

In addition to Matsushita's captive channel in Japan, the company rebuilt its sales operations for major retailers. To do this, Kirk brought back to Japan one of the most redoubtable of the *gaijin butai*, Steve Ushimaru. I met Steve in Toronto in 1997, where he ran Panasonic Canada, when Kirk had asked me to help sell Panasonic cell phones to my longtime client Bell Canada, an experience I will describe in a later chapter. In a foreshadowing of MEI's later V Product strategy, when I met Steve, he was in the middle of beating Sony in the commodity TV business with a more expensive product. I remember being amazed by this: who else on the planet was gaining market share in TVs by selling on anything other than price? Also, he seemed to be enjoying himself thoroughly. Kirk told me before the meeting that Steve was the best executive in MEI's sales organization worldwide and I could see why. He was marked for greater things.

When Steve was sent to the United Kingdom in the late 1990s, I assumed that he would soon be asked to run the U.S. operation in Secaucus because of his North American experience. In the event, he returned from the United Kingdom to Japan when Kirk's reform began in earnest. Steve's modus operandi, learned in Canada, is to flatten organizations, eliminate formality, and form strong teams. "When I got here, no one was accountable. You couldn't tell who made decisions. My philosophy is that the person you are talking to is your customer. This makes your colleagues your customers. If you can take care of your colleagues, you can take care of your customers. Your boss and your subordinates are your most important customers. We train ourselves at off sites and I work all these meetings. VPs from other divisions visit often, make short presentations, and learn from what we do."[72]

Ushimaru has a Jack Welch approach to his team. "My mission is to get 'champion employees' and if I have a lot of them, I get the best results. My top priority is to get more champions on my team. If I have more of them, sales will take care of themselves." In effect, Ushimaru wants to remake the corporate culture.

*We got rid of all Japanese formality. I don't like people stand-
ing up when I come into the room; no one wears a tie; my office
door is always open, and I don't like people bowing. I told Kirk
that we have to put the sales operation in Tokyo and get it out of
"old" Osaka. There is no smoking here, we are casual, and we use
flextime. When you have finished your job, I want you out of here.
Too many Japanese hang around the office till late at night doing
nothing. Everyone—dealers, media people—say the "air is light"
in your office, totally different from Sony.*

Steve exhibits boundless energy, showing his office by running
up and down the stairs between floors (no elevators, please), rushing into rooms, rapidly showing what each team does, and giving
no one time to even think about formality. In a country where top
management is expected to show the proper amount of gravitas
and assiduously cultivates correct protocol, Steve's leaping up and
down stairwells in a golf shirt and slacks is quite a sight.

The hallmark of his system is to move his teams into the field
to launch new V Products with massive displays in all major Japanese retailers at once. This overnight "vertical launch" capability
hits the market hard and is coupled with big media campaigns.
"We try to meet our customers before they come to us. We don't
respond to their requests; we try to exceed their expectations be-
forehand."

Integral to his strategy is to build demand through a top-rated
website, which, he says, is especially popular among college students. On the other side of his marketing and human resource
management, Steve, like all good Soccer Ball managers, is an inventory hawk, seeking every possible way to eliminate it from the
sales pipe.

Internally, he puts every aspect of his operation on his group's
intranet so that "everyone knows what is selling by model, and
where, daily." He insists that as much as possible about as many
programs as possible be posted, so that no one can claim to

be in the dark. In another, very North American change, he insists on 360-degree performance reviews so that superiors,
colleagues, and subordinates, with no exceptions, review team
members.

His lightning quick responses had a huge impact on Sony,
whose executives as we saw dubbed him the Sony Killer because
of the rapid increases in market share his system generated
at their expense. Sony probably expected MEI to stick to its
Japanese traditions as it had always done, ceding Sony room
for action. Indeed, a Sony executive told me a few years ago
that MEI's decision-making process was "very old fashioned."
Steve's return after decades abroad was the last thing Sony (or
Matsushita, for that matter) was prepared to deal with. The
diminution of Sony's core electronics business that resulted did
more than anything to force its own painful restructuring under
Sir Howard Stringer. By then, Ushimaru had given MEI a vital
five-year lead. MEI now gets top market share in Japan for most
of its V Products.

Matsushita's sales and operating profit goals is a 60/40 over-
seas/domestic shares split. Kazuyoshi Fujiyoshi, head of Panasonic Communications, has a lot of experience in foreign markets
and remarked to me that getting to this ratio will bring home
hard to many domains just how deep the overseas challenges
are.[73] Moreover, sales in overseas markets present a host of problems MEI does not face in Japan where it has its captive Pana-
sonic/National stores and a powerfully resurgent brand team.

In most major markets, as in Japan, small retailers have been
replaced in recent decades by bigger ones. But as it did in Japan,
MEI ignored the shift for years. When I started working with
MEI in the United States a decade ago, there was no system to
track this shift and so no sense that sales support should be taken
away from the declining number of smaller accounts and shifted
to bigger ones. The result, of course, was lost sales as the market
moved to big box stores and category killers and MEI's marketing

and sales resources did not respond. Also, restructuring overseas tended to lag behind events in Japan and did not really get moving until progress in Japan was well established.

In 2004 and 2005, Panasonic Europe went through a major change, weeding out nearly 60 percent of its accounts, all unprofitable, and rationalizing both fixed and operating costs in a deconstruct phase. In the create phase, Panasonic EU focused on several major accounts like Dixons in the United Kingdom and Media-Markt in Germany. The challenge, as Hitoshi Otsuki, the head of Panasonic Europe, explained to me, is that "we still do not have any real pan-European dealers and we must also work separately with dealers within major groups, like Dixons."[74] Added to this, some countries have independent agents that sell only one product, like batteries. Buying patterns across Europe do not synch up well, making the V Sales Bridge harder to manage than it is elsewhere. Income levels vary widely and tastes vary as well. Italy and Spain, for example, kept buying analog TVs well after others had switched to digital flat panels, forcing Matsushita to support older products long after it wanted to. Yet Spain was long the company's most profitable market in Europe. The solution is to cease analog production and to OEM these products for as long as consumers still want them. But Otsuki asks, "How do we differentiate ourselves under these circumstances?" Luckily some products, like SD memory and digital still cameras, are new categories in which buying patterns are more common across Europe and where, he says, "we have a more advanced situation."

For its major accounts, Panasonic Europe put in place a rolling inventory management system that it calls Automatic Availability, which gives these accounts better control of their own cash flow and reduces the risk of discontinued lines—much higher in the price-performance-vulnerable digital than in the analog world—and stock overages. Panasonic Europe does what Soccer Ball major account management says: to get real lock-on, sell your customers increases in their velocity of cash.

Impact of Sales Process Reform

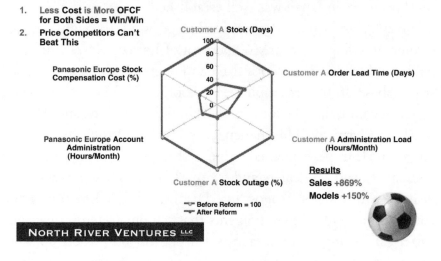

1. Less **Cost** is More **OFCF** for Both Sides = Win/Win
2. Price **Competitors Can't Beat This**

Panasonic Europe Stock Compensation Cost (%)

Panasonic Europe Account Administration (Hours/Month)

Customer A **Stock (Days)**

Customer A **Order Lead Time (Days)**

Customer A **Administration Load** (Hours/Month)

Customer A **Stock Outage (%)**

Before Reform = 100
After Reform

Results
Sales +869%
Models +150%

NORTH RIVER VENTURES LLC

Panasonic Europe's system is point-of-sale driven and for one major account, orders placed on Thursday are shipped on Tuesday. There are more wait states that Panasonic Europe would like to eliminate to speed this up, but local law apparently forbids some levels of simplification. Nonetheless, the system took sixty days out of the account's inventory and 50 percent from its order lead time, and virtually eliminated stockouts for Panasonic products, something others are a long way from achieving. You can see on the chart how these contribute to sources of free cash for both the major account and Panasonic Europe, the essence of Soccer Ball Management. But the piece that is most interesting is that the administrative load on the customer of managing its Panasonic Europe relationship dropped almost 80 percent. To a major account manager, these data are pure gold because they reveal deep insights into the customer's operating hot spots that can be leveraged to great advantage over the competition. For Panasonic Europe, the rewards were not long in coming. Sales to this account grew by nearly nine times, the cost of administering the account dropped by almost three-quarters, and the cost of returned stock fell by 97 percent. This combination is the road to operating free cash flow heaven.

Otsuki says that the weakness in the system is that the European economies vary so much in their sophistication. In the more advanced countries you can make advanced cash velocity programs work. By advanced he doesn't mean GDP per cap but degree of market regulation. The deregulation that President Carter pushed through in the United States thirty years ago that gave us FedEx, Wal-Mart, Southwest Airlines, and Dell has occurred only sporadically in Europe. In the United Kingdom, for example, customers accounting for 45 percent of Panasonic sales use the Automatic Availability system. In France and Germany, which are more heavily regulated, only 9 and 5 percent respectively use the system. It is very hard to change regulations in Europe, and this makes it difficult for a company like Matsushita to use advanced delivery and cash management systems to differentiate itself. These barriers hold everyone back equally, of course, but they make the core of the Soccer Ball System difficult to implement: if no one is buying cash velocity because it is, basically, against the law, super efficient major account management is, to all intents, off the table.

In the United States, the story is different. Mike Aguilar, the senior VP of Supply Chain Strategic Initiatives, has an easier time because he can manage the process on a national scale. Nevertheless, he told a conference in May 2006, "We had to change virtually all of our processes."[75] For example, the company shifted sales bonuses from channel sales to point of sale: salespeople don't get paid until the product clears the retailer's cash register. This had the effect on everybody of moving the "supply chain from the back office to the front office," where "it would be the single most important thing that will ensure our profitability drive increased sales."

The big selling feature, of course, was that Panasonic North America stopped selling product and began selling cash flow: "We went to our channel and told them," Aguilar said, "if we can do this, there will be a huge increase in free cash flow that we've never experienced, and you've never experienced, and a tremendous decrease in markdowns." This kind of operational integration, as I call it, produced fast results:

- High-end TV sales shot up 500 percent when the market as a whole rose 200 percent.
- On-hand inventory went from seventeen weeks to four and shrank to two weeks during the 2005 Christmas selling season with no stockouts.
- PNA moved from a tier two or three supplier at many of its top retailers to a tier one supplier in all of them.

Takami Sano, executive vice president for industrial sales, made the interesting point when I talked to him about sales reform that industrial sales are the only global organization in the company. But "We competed with many 'excellent' companies like Nokia and IBM and I could compare ourselves to them. We had many people coming from many divisions to sell to one customer. All had different policies. Some were helpful to customers and some were not. We had 130 divisions, and before I came to this position we had, as you might say, brand destruction."[76]

The challenge is complicated by the nature of the industrial market. "Take Toyota. They have many partly or wholly owned companies that make components of various types. We compete with them, collaborate with them, and sell to Toyota's tier three suppliers who are our competitors, like Pioneer. In the case of navigation systems, a Toyota-owned company may have strong points in some parts but we make better components."[77]

Sano's puzzle had to be solved in three dimensions. Industrial accounts were being mismanaged, the competitive structure of the business was complex, and both dimensions crossed the full range of global markets. "We are in sixty countries and have 8,000 customers of which 5,800 are located overseas."

He came to run industrial sales from batteries in 1999, a year before Kirk became CEO, and did an immediate *tour d'horizons* of his customer base. What he got was an earful. He was told that MEI's business practices were out of date, that the company was slow and unresponsive and did not know how to share in a timely way the technologies its customers valued most, that the company demonstrated no vision or strategy, that customers were getting sales calls from all over MEI and they couldn't tell who was in charge of what, and that the company was incapable of making decisions on anything that overlapped divisions.

To make sense of this he had his team map out what he calls a "technostory," a marketing methodology for ensuring that MEI sells high value-added, in a coordinated way, and at the right level in the customer organization across all industrial domain companies. Technostory starts with the assumption that MEI should be selling systematic, and therefore profitable, solutions to identifiable customer problems rather than shoehorning cheap bits and pieces into any market opening possible. Done right, MEI adds maximum value and its customers get maximum value, which should be a win-win. The term "technostory" derives from the assumption that both parties are working at the leading edge of technology in their markets and have to push that edge to compete successfully. So they have a common technology story. MEI can leverage this commonality to bring to bear profitably the full line of its products and processes. By sharing their respective technology stories, as it were, customer and supplier move ahead faster than otherwise and reduce risks for each other.

What technostory advocates, in effect, is modern account management, which says that value is generated by the maximum level of operational interoperability between customer and supplier. The priority of the executive team is to identify exactly what level of interoperability gives customers maximum leverage from their own value added, and more important, gives them the maximum operating free cash flow from the arrangement.

Technostory concluded with a series of customer case studies showing how this should be done.

The technostory model is one that I have advocated for decades, that you have to turn your company sideways, as it were, pushing the people normally the farthest away from customers in your upstream operations, like R&D, into direct and formal customer relationships. Only when customer contact is consistent across all aspects of the organization—when *all* operations are on the surface of the Soccer Ball—does the company become a functioning antenna for customer value opportunities. The farther any one sector of operations is from the company's customer, the more pronounced the Hubble Effect—which, to recall, says that the farther you are removed from your customers by your organization, the faster they move away from you—and the larger the lost opportunity.

To make this work, Sano broke the barrier between the divisions, developed common platforms, drove tighter net-based communication between divisions and with customers, and forged tighter C-level and operational links. When I went to see him for this book, Sano had just been told by Toyota, perhaps Matsushita's biggest customer worldwide, that Toyota was awarding MEI its excellent company award for its GPS. But, he told me, GPS was a collaborative product that integrated elements across domains, and this could not have been done without the technostory system in place.

Sano is the first to point out that technostory is the beginning, not the end of the story. Marketing can be a big problem when selling outside Japan. "In Germany we had problems. We translated back and forth and we thought we had understood what the customer wanted but we didn't and we lost." Even though technostory is a language, in a sense, for communicating between MEI and its customers, it still has to be inflected properly to be sure the meaning is clear. "In the case of software, it is difficult for us even in Japan to communicate." There are also problems with what to sell. As an industrial operation, Sano's mission is to sell to all comers. This is not easy because, as he says, "the basis of competition is always changing and we have to hunt, literally." And it is compounded by another problem. "How much of our black box technology should we sell to Sony when Sony competes with our other divisions (like AVC). But we have to show them the latest."

All of these sales restructurings have the effect of pushing aside poor products and poor sales prospects, focusing the company on profitable opportunities where operating free cash flow is most likely to be generated. For a company that had always placed sales volumes ahead of profit, these changes, when added to the restructuring of the firm's lines of business, were invigorating.

Board Restructuring

In 2003, the company restructured its board. Until that time, MEI ran with a typical Japanese board that is unusually large by U.S. standards that consisted exclusively of senior executives. In Japan, these executives are often titled "director," signifying their role in the top policy-making forum of the company. Directors are promoted along with their increased responsibilities to managing director and senior managing director. These officers usually supervise junior directors somewhat like group presidents in the United States.

Japanese boards tend to be unwieldy and are often inbred. Where U.S. and European boards are full of outsiders who are supposed to oversee management on behalf of shareholders, and where U.S. companies, in particular, use boards to bring in influences and customers that may help the company in new directions (though this is by no means the rule and plenty of boards are captives of the CEO), Japanese boards and management are usually one and the same.

Like everything in Japan, this is beginning to change, and Matsushita made board restructuring a priority. Board terms were cut from two years to one, and in 2003, the MEI board was split in two. Many of board rank were retitled executive officers; the size of the board was cut by about half. The new role of the executive officers is to run the lines of business while the role of the board is to oversee strategy. In another major change, perhaps more far-reaching in view of the global reach of Sarbanes-Oxley legislation on U.S.-listed companies like MEI, outsiders have been invited to join.

MEI today has something more like a German supervisory and management board structure. As with the German setup, the lines between the two can be somewhat porous with supervisory board members having responsibility for specific line operations and reporting to the chairman on those operations.

The company's most senior board members in 2005 were salesmen. This itself was a sizeable change, pushing the company away from its product-push past into a demand-pull future.

Driving Core Efficiencies

Matsushita's central strategic problem at the outset of Value Creation 21 was, as we saw, that several competitors and its customers had achieved superior Soccer Ball efficiencies of cash and capital and Matsushita had not. This meant that the company was being torn not just in two directions at once—by competitors and by customers—but also by the same set of underlying forces. As I explained in earlier sections on the Soccer Ball System, companies like Dell and Wal-Mart, with their high velocities of cash and capital, have more in common operationally than either of them does with Matsushita. This in turn meant that the shift in structure would have the effect of leaving Matsushita stranded with an ineffective way of doing business. Value creation would be impossible.

A top priority of the Value Creation 21 Plan was to rebuild the firm on two Soccer Ball metrics:

- Cash velocity, which included reform of supply chain management, inventory management, cell manufacturing, and corporate cost accounting.
- Capital velocity, which included reform of capital allocation, introduction of domain companies, integration of the affiliates, and new capital expenditure guidelines.

Very little fell outside these two metrics, which are mutually supportive. Change in one area, like the creation of capital-efficient domain companies, would also improve cash efficiency and vice versa.

In essence, these two thrusts reversed the polarity of decision making in the company from factory-to-customer to customer-to-Matsushita, forcing executives to account for their actions in ways they never had to before. Kirk told his managers in early 2001 that if they didn't make these changes quickly, "we alone will have to carry the risk of sudden market change instead of sharing it with our customers."[78] Core out the company, put all its resources on the surface, and respond to the market faster than anyone else.

Kirk explained that driving for cash and capital efficiencies made a company profitable by its nature. Slashing costs far and wide and shifting divisions do not, in and of themselves, make the business system enduringly profitable. And to survive, Matsushita had to be profitable. "We have," he said in March 2001, "achieved no growth in the last four years. We are not even producing the minimum return required."[79]

By failing to meet operating goals, line groups set themselves up for a harsh choice: fix yourselves, quickly, or prepare to be divested. Never before had such responsibility been put on the head of individual MEI managers.

In his March 2001 management conference, just as the scope

of the tech implosion was hitting MEI, Kirk made a move that, for my money, is the most important move he took during his tenure as CEO. He decided to evaluate managers on consolidated worldwide sales. This may seem like a small change of emphasis and he announced it in only three sentences, the third of which was "This is an epoch-making change."[80] "In the past," Joe Shohtoku told me, "we discussed our business on the basis of the Japanese parent alone. For example, AVC would talk about itself. Now we talk about the whole company first. You have to show your global position. All operations worldwide are assigned to the domains. Management is autonomous."[81]

But this change did not come easily. Atsushi Murayama recalled that "consolidation was really important and we didn't know which way to go. Parent alone? Consolidation? To get overseas sales into executive evaluation we had to overcome resistance from those who thought the overseas operations were separate ones" for which they were not responsible. Worse, "although people talked a lot about cash flow, they were really obsessed with sales." One of Kirk's biggest moves was "having MEI focus on cash flow."[82]

After reversing the polarity of the company, on December 5, 2002, Kirk announced that, beginning in the new fiscal year on April 1, 2003, all managers and all domains would be judged on two indices only: CCM, a rate of return on invested capital that must be positive; and cash flow rather than on their sales and profit numbers as in the past.[83] Until this time, performance evaluation was based on a complex cocktail of ingredients laid out on a point scale: so many points for CCM, so many for profitability, and so many for inventory, environmental management, growth potential, and quality. The convolution of this mix naturally encouraged managers to play the numbers game rather than to drive cash and capital efficiencies essential for top performance.

To get the company focused on cash velocity, Kirk chose a single working-capital metric, inventory, because it could be measured with relative accuracy, and its impact ranged from the furthest reaches of the supply chain all the way to customers. Track this number, and all the firm's cash touch points could be better managed. In addition, good inventory management allows a company to change its sales approach. Instead of talking to customers about products, as I said before, you can sell them improved working-capital management. This allows higher levels of operational integration with customers, richer C-level conversations, and more opportunities to sell the company at a premium rather than its products at a discount. Yoshi Yamada, the head of Panasonic North America, told me that using the Soccer Ball System this way had "completely changed my thinking about how to talk to customers."

In 2001 as losses mounted, Kirk repeatedly told his top managers that the failure to cut inventories from the system left the company open to large profit reverses whenever markets softened. He hit hard on this point, observing that Matsushita Seiko president Teruo Nakano had, by 2001, already focused on inventory reduction for three years, cutting inventory days from forty-six to twenty-six, with the result that the company saved $58 million and posted a profit even as sales dropped.[84] But for many managers this was hard to accept. They were used to a world where inventory buffers were central to their operations. When this was taken away, they had to live with a very real fear that they were doing the wrong thing and would pay for it.

Yoshi Yamada drew my attention to the propaganda effect of this spotlight on inventory days, explaining that in the Matsushita system so concentrated on manufacturing, these numbers were ones that everybody understood unambiguously. "Kirk is very clever to focus on this," he told me at one of our first meetings. By getting people to come together on something they had already thought about and knew a great deal about how to manage, he could get results more rapidly than if he used a wider set of metrics. The problem, however, would be complacency: not in the sense that no one cared about inventory levels, but in the sense that managements often accept certain levels in their sectors as givens. They cannot see how they can get below these numbers simply because no one else does. To get beyond this, Kirk was strident, slamming Matsushita's inventory levels and making these a benchmark in his cash-efficiency goals. "I will not allow internal inventory transfers" to jury-rig the numbers of Matsushita's domestic units, he told his team in 2002.[85] He came back to this theme time and again over the years, telling the Top Seminar in 2004 that he was disappointed that the company had not made more out of its cell manufacturing system.

Combined, these moves had the effect of forcing managers to change where they were looking, and what they were looking at. Once managers began to look at cash and capital efficiencies on a global scale—these numbers are meaningless on an unconsolidated basis because they allow managers to bury problems in overseas units—they began to make decisions unlike those made in the past. Many of management's new strategies, like vertical launch, which I will look at later, were put on decision trees that looked nothing like their predecessors.

These decision trees globalized the thinking processes of large numbers of MEI staff who had never had to think much beyond their hometowns.

As in everything else in this book, this is a shift from sales first to operating sources of cash first. In this case, however, the shift was designed into the core of the firm's accounting. One can see this as harmonizing management accounting with shifts in manufacturing, inventory management, and account management. I see it as more than that. Until a firm structures its internal accounting to drive toward operating sources of cash, all the rest is peripheral and can be changed back relatively easily. But once the line is crossed in the accounting guts of a firm, pushback is much harder.

What made this accounting move significant was that the company had never held any of its top team accountable for worldwide performance of their operations let alone for the cash and capital efficiencies of these operations. Until this change, managers drained overseas units of cash to boost the performance of their domestic operations. This had two negatives. First, it distorted the system's information about itself. There was no incentive to understand where money was being made, or lost, and therefore no reason to determine what actions to take. Second, it patriated money that increased MEI's tax base to levels much higher than those of its competition, making MEI stock inherently less attractive.

When the Value Creation 21 plan began, overhead fees were charged to overseas sales groups as a percentage of sales. This was replaced by a fixed fee based on the business plan of the group, forcing it to live with its commitments, not its results. When a division wanted to invest in a factory overseas, it split the cost with headquarters, effectively minimizing its own risk. MEI replaced this with a capital-efficient system in which the domain company deposited 100 percent of its investment cost with headquarters and headquarters in turn invested that 100 percent in the new operation, forcing domains to take on all the risk of their actions. Dividends back to the company that were based on the results of domestic operations are now payable on a fixed rate of consolidated shareholders' equity. Once looked at in this way, it was clear that some overseas operations had been heat sinks for money for years.

There is always resistance. Early on, as the annus horribilis unfolded, CFO Tetsuya Kawakami, who was on the outs with Kirk at the time, was asked to put a new system in place. He pulled together a team of younger managers. "They did it fast, in four months. I didn't like their interim report, but said nothing. After they completed their final proposal, I understood that the biggest anti-reformist was myself, which was why I couldn't meet Kirk Nakamura's expectations."[86] Atsushi Murayama recalled, "The accounting department resisted to the very last moment."[87] The problem, once the new accounting platform had been designed, was, given Kawakami's questionable standing, who would present it to the boss? Kawakami was, Shohtoku told me, convinced at this point that if he presented the plan himself, it would be shot down, irrespective of merit. It fell to Shohtoku, whose team had been involved in the plan's evolution and who had a much better and long-standing relationship with Kirk, to walk the plan into Kirk's office. Typical of Kirk, when he sees something he likes, he understands immediately how it will work, asks a question or two, nods, and it is done. Which is exactly what happened. Shohtoku returned to meet with Kawakami and his finance team where he was met with jubilation. When Kirk later met with the team that did the work, he clapped, which must have been a relief and a shock. But it sent a strong signal: one, do it yourself; and two, incrementalism is unacceptable.

Setting Investment Goals

Once all the foregoing pieces were in place, MEI had a basis for setting investment goals and making decisions for the first time since Konosuke Matsushita left the scene. In his time, he appropriated these decisions to himself and his reasoning was his own. There was logic to it, as I described in Chapter One. But that logic was lost on his successors. The 2000–2005 reform of MEI established a systematic basis for investing that did not depend on the whims of one individual.

Domains were in place with clear lines of responsibility. The V Sales Bridge showed the company its sales and profit strengths and weaknesses. Sales operations were reorganized and the V Products system was established. Lines of authority were clarified, compensation and capital allocation metrics established, and the company realigned to focus on cash flow rather than sales at any cost.

In addition, the company had begun to think of market exit as part of market entry planning so that it had a much better handle on managing product cycles and it had the Panasonic Start-up Fund in place to finance MBOs for offloaded operations.

Combined, these changes give executives a logic for making investments of significant size. The MEW deal showed management what could be done. In addition, MEI's $15 billion in cash and low debt-equity ratio gives it more than enough power to hit hard in any of its chosen markets. Matsushita's own Soccer Ball Metrics allow it to determine valuation, assess breakeven, identify risk factors, determine accretive potential, and measure management. Few firms anywhere know how to do this.

Within a few short years, MEI emerged from a cocoon. What was once a lame company with little control—really no control—over its destiny is now an investment vehicle to be reckoned with. In addition, it can invest outside Japan as easily as in it, making the company a large factor in the decision making of other companies worldwide for the first time.

Reducing Downside Risks

A problem with the old MEI structure was its built-in exposure to downside risk. The company had few controls over how products were sold, how its brands were managed, and how products were designed and made, and no adequate measures for cash flow or investment management. Market exit was not well understood, and the company often found itself making products after demand had evaporated. The timing mechanism of the company didn't work. Maybe it didn't have one.

Having replaced its make-everything mission with one to make profitable products for which customers will pay a premium, and having shifted away from sales maximization to cash-flow maximization, MEI needed a system for deciding which businesses to stay in, which to nurture, which to fix, and which to exit.

The lesson of the CRT business was, as it had been for the dot matrix printer business a decade before, that the company had no exit strategy for failed operations or declining markets. Takami Sano looks at downside risk management from an organizational perspective. What matters to him is that each domain company has to be "an excellent company in its own field. At the same time, the domains should not be too independent. Five years from now we must be able to leverage across domains by networking. To do this we must be number one in each market."[88] Getting to top position means that many product areas must be filtered out. Already a quarter of the firm's products are V Products, and this percent will rise quickly as more legacy products cease production, are sold off, or get replaced by advanced versions the way CRTs were replaced by plasma displays.

Kirk laid the firm out on a matrix like the chart below and made the growth/profit quadrant the criterion for survival. With the new management system in place, line executives who failed to meet global operating goals set themselves up for a harsh choice: fix yourselves, sell yourselves, or close shop.

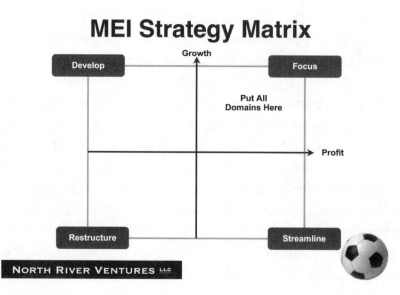

MEI Strategy Matrix

This new matrix put Japan's famous jobs-for-life social contract squarely in the hands of line executives, removing it from the CEO. Common in America, perhaps, but not in Japan.

In 2000 you could not have made such a chart and mapped on it something as simple as a fax machine because it was not clear whose responsibility fax was or even which company was being mapped. Today, MEI can look at itself as any rational operation would and make a clear assessment of its downside risks. Repeatedly during the preparation of this book, managers told me that one of the biggest changes in their thinking was when to exit. They say they would do it sooner than they had in the past. Why? Because for the first time they know they have to and can see when they will have to. Exit is now central to the V Product planning process. Matsushita no longer enters a market or launches a product without a realistic plan for exit when that product can no longer drive profit at the company's targeted levels.

IT Restructuring

In his March 2001 management conference speech, Kirk hit hard at MEI's $8.2 billion inventory, identifying days in inventory as his primary Soccer Ball Metric, and promising to cut days of sales from inventory, reducing inventory by $3.2 billion.[89] The big problem, he said, was that "an incomplete SCM system" was exacerbating the financial impact of sales declines. Once sales dropped, poorly planned production runs built up inventory, hitting working capital at the very moment when the firm needed strong working capital. Conversely, the same process meant that when products sold well, the company ran out of goods to sell. Lose, you lose; win, you lose. For good measure, Kirk added that in rapidly deflating markets, any failure in the supply chain would hit immediately, as customers switched to cheaper and better-performing products while Matsushita still had its own lower-performing products stuck somewhere in inventory. These inventories would have to be flamed off at deep discounts in a never-ending downward spiral: rising inventory→rising working capital→fire sale→profit collapse→sales implosion→rising inventory→.

Because, he said, MEI was becoming "insensitive to market transformations," the company found itself selling against companies that "are much quicker in responding to market changes than Matsushita, such as promptly introducing supply chain management." In a comment designed to frost plenty of cookies, he then described how Nokia, Matsushita's arch competitor in cell phones, sent orders to suppliers over the Internet based on instant information being fed to Nokia from the market. Matsushita, he said, was still going to retailers several times a year, collecting their order forecasts, which were inaccurate and out of date by months already, rolling these data into its own forecasts which were then doubly inaccurate and now out of date by half a year or more, and then manufacturing to these numbers. In Moore Time—and nothing changes in Moore Time faster than a cell phone—what Kirk described is terminal.

For the next five years, Kirk did not let up on his push for better SCM systems and lower inventories. He framed his initiative as "Super Manufacturing," a slightly disingenuous phrase designed to get MEI people to think about returning to their manufacturing roots while in fact redefining the whole concept of manufacturing.

In Leap Ahead 21, the company turned to IT restructuring. In truth, though, the work began the moment Kirk took office.

Stan Makita,[90] the MEI executive officer in charge of information systems, recalled that the big challenge at MEI was that very few in Japan understood the systems that had built FedEx and Amazon. This meant that they didn't grasp that the company would have to improve its business processes and the speed of its IT utilization at the same time.[91] As I said in Chapter Two, the Iron Laws of Information operate in parallel, not in serial, and if your management isn't ready for this, you have a problem. Matsushita had this problem.

Within days of his appointment as CEO (twenty-seven to be exact), Kirk created the Corporate IT Innovations Division under Makita with a mandate to pull SCM, Merchandising, and CRM into a coherent global system. This was Kirk's first attempt to leverage corporate capabilities across domains. While Makita was in charge of execution, Kirk sponsored the program personally and asked reformer and member of the *gaijin butai* Hiro Sakamoto to be the managing director responsible to the board. As corporate planning *kuroko*, Sakamoto had insight into so many parts of the company that he was the natural choice if IT reforms were to be effective.

Makita's team faced several challenges:

- A lack of companywide system optimization. Everything had historically been run by individual factories and sales companies with no attempt at integration.
- Management was information system–indifferent. Senior management didn't know much about IT.
- Information systems took a passive attitude. No one took the initiative to do anything new and few IT people saw themselves as agents of business process transformation.

Makita recalled that at the time, "it was too complicated. Nobody understood it or how long it took to make a product or which route it took to market."[92] The team basically had to start from scratch, reviewing all processes globally. It broke the task into three areas of immediate concern, which, like everything else during the reform, had to be dealt with simultaneously:

- SCM and inventory days
- Merchandising
- CRM

To show how seriously Kirk took these three areas, he doubled up on his "skip level" reporting, by having Sakamoto take personal responsibility for a part of the SCM restructuring, Kazuo Toda oversee two CRM areas, and Susumu Koike manage the entire merchandising piece. Practically speaking, he was putting his entire top management line into IT and making them, along with himself, personally accountable for an incredible level of detail. Remember that *Panasonic* opened with Sean White and me visiting a Panasonic showroom in New York where nothing worked. Even in the late nineties, it was common in Japan for executives of major corporations to stay far away from IT, letting underlings handle the details. We reasoned that the problem with the Panasonic showroom was that no one in senior management actually knew how to use a PC, so they were satisfied to be shown a Potemkin village on their New York visits. Seeing nothing, they changed nothing. As soon as Kirk became CEO, however, he bought cell phones for all his managers and started text messaging them all day long for results. Putting IT into the hands of his managers was vital to making his skip level system work: he refused to wait for formal meetings or reports through the hierarchy to be kept up to date and see who was really on the ball, and he made changes fast when he saw the need. If you weren't firing on all eight cylinders, he knew about it as each cylinder misfired. And why.

The team soon found that MEI met its promised lead times about a third as often as its competitors and that MEI often took six times longer to get a product to its customers. The group made significant progress in the early years, especially in SCM. It reorganized over thirty core systems and over one thousand databases. Over 34,000 products were modified and 10,000 employees moved between areas. Even so, progress was hard. The group had to deal with a lack of common certification processes, differing data definitions, domain-specific and redundant applications, little (or no) hardware and software integration, and widely dispersed data centers.

Makita's team broke processes down into key areas, improved each, and tied the results to the company's operating profit and CCM goals. This way, everyone involved could see that IT improvements were not just pie in the sky, but had real earnings impacts. MEI cut inventories by thirteen days.

In 2004, LA 21 shifted the bulk of MEI's attention to IT. Over the five years of reform, the team spent just about as much as it returned, but after losses in the early years, the company is now close to returning twice its costs on an annual basis. IT is becoming a significant source of OFCF. Sales per employee are up 1.4 times while the number of salespeople is down. In flat-panel TVs, for example, procurement time is down 70 percent, time to launch has been cut by 42 percent, and factory processing time is down 75 percent, delivering MEI inventory-yield and capacity-yield advantages that the competition is finding hard to beat. IT, Makita points out, has moved from an incomprehensible mess to "a strategic weapon."

Even a casual look at MEI's working-capital data, however, shows that the company will need another IT revolution, probably in outbound logistics, to drive its cash velocity to top grade standards.

In his March 2005 management conference, Kirk was finally able to show his team what they could do with the SCM advantages they had won. Pointing out that the rest of Japan was at the time moving from slowdown to recession, he noted that MEI was entering a recovery "ahead of the industry as a whole. This advantageous position is the result of our groupwide commitment to inventory-squeezing initiatives. In other words, now is our chance to take a significant lead over our rivals."[93] Go in for the kill.

The End of Vertical Integration

Vertical integration is out of fashion today. The reason is not hard to identify: Henry Ford's belief in making everything that goes into a product—he even bred the sheep for the wool in his car seats—depends on stable markets with long production runs. Once a market starts to move in Moore Time, there are too many parts to change at once. Because each of these parts has someone's political agenda attached, responding at speed becomes impossible. The Soccer Ball System says that it is much easier for a company to focus on what it needs to do to add value for customers *directly* and to outsource everything else.

I've seen this evolve over thirty years. When Sean White and I started our first business we made it a point to visit every major telecommunications manufacturing operation in the world, making detailed notes on systems, yields, returns, and so on. At the time, it was not uncommon to see large factories built on the old Bell System model. Bell was the world's largest nonmilitary employer and it had a stranglehold on the bulk of the U.S. communications business. Its manufacturing arm, Western Electric, now Alcatel-Lucent Technologies, had a guaranteed market for its automated telephone exchanges. Western routinely made these from the ground up: the company even pressed its own sheet metal. As recently as 1984, you could still see such operations. With Bell's long-term plans in place, its supplier could pump out product with little risk. Bell's assured cash flows in turn assured those of Western Electric.

Things changed fast in the 1980s when deregulation and digitization swept the world. Phone companies demanded more, more quickly, and they all had different needs. Suppliers like Western were divested and their cash flows were no longer guaranteed. Vertical integration went out the door as response time became critical.

In 1990, Sean and I visited one manufacturer that didn't get it. The company still pressed its own metal and had locked in place contracts with its internal divisions to supply everything it needed, including, critically, semiconductors. When its sales people reported a shift in demand to products that needed different silicon, the semiconductor division responded that the ICs to support this were not on its agenda for the foreseeable future but that the telecommunications division could not go elsewhere for its chips. The salespeople were told to get on with the job, meet their quotas, and stop complaining. No surprise, this company was forced to leave the market and was unable to reenter successor markets for the high-bandwidth systems that now predominate. A century-old business simply vanished, all because vertical integration prevented response as the cost of information dropped and markets accelerated.

Matsushita's problem in the 1990s was that markets overseas had begun to move faster than those at home, where the bulk of the company's resources were. And home wasn't getting the news. For overseas salespeople, this meant that the tail—themselves—had to wag the dog, which never works.

Having spent a decade as the tail, Kirk Nakamura saw the risks of not moving and also the difficulty of getting a company with strong manufacturing DNA to change. He chose a deceptively simple way to deal with this problem. Within days of becoming president, under the moniker of making MEI a "super manufacturer," he called for three things:

1. A focus on only those products that could grow fast, make money, and dominate their markets, the V Products.
2. Proprietary black box technologies.
3. Drastically reduced inventories.

Managers could put this formula together any way they wanted—though he pushed hard for flexible cell-based production methods to replace MEI's traditional production line system—as long as they got results. He took his usual skip level responsibility for two areas, plasma displays and digital still cameras. Matsushita made the program work through a system of alliances, outsourcing where needed, black box technologies to assure profit and intellectual property rights, and a combination of renewed supply chain management systems and cell-based production to cut inventories. Sales increases were instant.

The result looks nothing like vertical integration. But it has the merit of emphasizing in-house resources, and you routinely hear Matsushita people claim that they have chosen "vertical integration" when they have chosen no such thing. Fumio Ohtsubo, the new CEO, accurately says that "unified management is more the way we see it."[94]

Sometimes, however, appearances can be deceiving. When I asked Susumu Koike, now chief technology officer and then head of semiconductors, how many of his ICs were in my FX9 camera, his face broke into a big smile, and he replied emphatically and with great pride, "*Hyaku pacento!*" (100 percent). But if you look at Panasonic DSCs, there is plenty of other company's work in the product. When I visited the Household Appliance Division's refrigerator factory and expressed surprise that they were still pressing their own metal, the plant manager assured that this "would be going very soon."

What makes the three-part formula for ending vertical integration work is the third point, reduced inventories, a centerpiece of the Soccer Ball System. Once you focus on the core point—that businesses live on cash, not profits—cutting inventories becomes the priority for every manufacturer. Low inventories mean a tight supply chain upstream and a powerful outbound logistics system designed to pull proprietary technologies through to the market. Kirk successfully got his managers to focus on inventories—real numbers that are quantifiable and against which management performance can be measured quickly—and this way broke the old MEI vertical integration culture. Manufacturers got their pride of place by making value. SCM drove down inventories, resulting in an OFCF and cash velocity win-win. In the next section we will see how MEI manufacturing changed.

Cell Manufacturing

In the Soccer Ball System, cash efficiency depends on low inventories and these depend on the successful integration of SCM upstream, cell production in-house, and powerful outbound logistics downstream. We have already looked at the first of these. Now it's time to look at the second.

In his first policy speech, in July 2000, days after becoming CEO, Kirk pushed for a shift away from traditional production lines to cell production in an effort to cut inventories through the supply chain and make the company more responsive to customers. He assigned one of his top reform colleagues, Atsushi Murayama, to spearhead this process through the Corporate Manufacturing Innovation Division. By the end of October 2001, half of MEI's worldwide operations and 82 percent of the plants in Japan had been converted, up from only 35 percent the previous March, reflecting a furious pace of change. Kirk expected this system to enable the company to leverage its new supply chain system into superior working-capital numbers. For the next five years this took much of his attention.

Typical of his MO, Kirk chose specific operations to showcase the others. In this example, he used the rapid rollout of plasma display panels, first from the Ibaraki plant, where they were initially produced, and then at the new Amagasaki factory. These operations regularly double output ahead of schedule without seeing a drop-off in yield, and are now the largest PDP facilities in the world, something the company attributes to the multicellular production, which it believes is far more responsive to changing demand patterns than its old production lines.

Using cells, the new CEO, Fumio Ohtsubo, while still head of AVC, astonished the company as much as the competition with the speed with which PDP production came on-stream. By the end of March 2002, average production per person had risen by 1.4 times and in some cases as high as 1.8. Production lead time fell to 70 percent of previous levels, and partially finished inventory was cut by an average of 40 percent.[95]

It soon became apparent, however, once the first wave of cell production cut inventory days sharply, that further reductions would not come easily and the company had to rethink its processes much further. From 2002 to 2004, inventory reduction stalled.

In 2004, MEI pushed its cell manufacturing initiatives a step farther, launching a Next Cell Production Innovation Project. As usual, Kirk took personal ownership of the project. He brought in Kyushu veteran Hajime Sakai, the most senior executive officer in the company, who provided the linkage to the domain companies it was intended to serve. Sakai had serious street cred in manufacturing and was an early implementer of IT reform. Masashi Makino, another officer-level executive, runs the operation.

The purpose of the Next Cell Production Innovation Project was to crossfertilize domains with each other's strengths. Part of the problem, Sakai told me in late 2005, was that "we had managers; but we needed innovators," people who could rethink entire supply chains from the ground up.[96] Makino went further, telling me that the IT system was not good enough to let managers "see" inventory. But, if V Products could be made with V processes, as it were, the company could continue to hit the market hard with rapid rollouts as it has in PDP and with high-yield processes in automotive systems. Putting quality and speed together were central to profitable growth, but Matsushita had too little of either.

To fix this, the company made two assumptions:

- Inventory pools indicate a process that is not adding value and must be changed.
- Inventory pools indicate costly waste.

Inventory, therefore, should be invisible in the manufacturing process. This may sound extreme, but in all responsive, high-speed operations, the less visible the inventory, the more visible OFCF and cash velocity. But moving in this direction meant re-thinking large parts of the operation:

- Product development process
- Human resources management
- Factory systems
- Black box technologies

In some cases, like automotive products, large customers like Toyota long ago installed a cell-based pull system from their side, but MEI had push-based lines on its side. The asymmetry became increasingly problematic. When Matsushita replaced its old push lines with push cells, the push/pull mismatch continued, and after initial improvements not much more happened. For a company steeped for decades in the subtleties of production line management, it was easier to keep tinkering with the existing system than to throw it out. No surprise though, when pull was eventually matched with pull, deliveries per day quadrupled, and finished goods inventories dropped 67 percent.

One of MEI's biggest challenges in this changeover was measuring cost. On its traditional production lines, the company looked at average cost. But making inventory-invisible pull processes work meant identifying every component of cost—not just the cost of every component—in order to determine where value was being added or subtracted. The risk is that eliminating value-destroying processes in one place simply creates them elsewhere. Sakai put it this way: "If a company cannot come up with a product that is not full of 'nonvalue' processes, the company is obsolete."[97]

By February 2002, most of MEI's factories were converted to cell systems. But having cut factory inventory days by 28 percent in the first two years of cell production reform, stagnation set in, and inventory days fell only 14 percent over the next three years combined. Even though some operations, like Sakai's own Panasonic Communications Company, cut work in progress by 98 percent, corporate goals are becoming harder to reach. This prompted a new initiative now under way to cut factory inventories (about 58 percent of the total) by 30 percent in 2005 and another 50 percent in 2006. The next challenge is to reduce inventory in the shipping pipeline.

I regularly warn CEOs and CFOs that cutting the first 30 percent of inventory is the easy part. After that, you must rethink the company's structure, probably three times: once at twenty days, again at ten days, and hardest of all, at five days. Each of these "day barriers" is like a sound barrier; you can't go through it with the structure you used at lower speeds. Matsushita is at the threshold of the first of these barriers. This barrier, and the ones that follow, cannot be crossed without further reform of IT, creating network-based operations like those of a Cisco, where the CFO can track all operations in real time and close the books at the push of a button. MEI is immeasurably more complex than Cisco, however, and a lot larger.

Getting to where Cisco is remains Matsushita's biggest challenge and will occupy Fumio Ohtsubo more than anything else during his tenure.

Building Service into Products

In *The Digital Revolution*, Sean White and I pointed out that Dell posed a unique threat to Matsushita because through its distribution system it had seamlessly integrated service into product. It was hard to say where Dell's product ended and its service started. Moreover, we pointed out, it would be far easier for Dell to turn its distribution guns on Matsushita than it would be for

Matsushita to counterattack Dell in PCs. In fact the asymmetries ran deeper than that. For Dell to eviscerate MEI it had only to take a small, profitable piece of MEI's markets: Michael Dell's classic "pool of cash" attack where you find a competitor with a low velocity of cash and suck the operating free cash flows out of its markets until it withers like a desiccated bug. But for Matsushita to attack Dell in PCs with MEI's antiquated distribution system would be suicide.

What is at work here is subtle and one of the worst-understood phenomena in industry today. Remember my earlier chart on the Rule of Inverse Service Cycles. The rule says that the only way to counteract ever-compressed Moore Time product cycles is to extend customer relationships, or service cycles, to infinity. Otherwise, you get a customer for a single short generation and then have to spend SG&A like crazy to replace that customer when he or she goes elsewhere. If service is baked into the product, you avoid this. For a decade, Dell's integrated distribution did that, and the company grew and profited. Now Apple does it, melding hardware, service, and content into a single fabric for managing entertainment. IT effectively wraps products in a service envelope. Once a customer is embedded in your fabric, you can go back to that customer time and again with proprietary and highly profitable offerings.

The simplest way to understand this is to think of how Einstein showed that space and time (product and service) are not single dimensions but are part of a combined fabric called space-time. Space and time cannot be divorced. Neither can product and service. Or content. As the cost of information falls, these relationships become readily apparent to companies fast enough to see them. But for those on the other side of the McLuhan Frontier, they are not and never will be.

Kirk grasped this in a second and in his November 2000 management conference, he told his team that they would have to figure out ways of differentiating products with services, and that these services would have to be baked into MEI's offerings Dell-style, going so far as to say that "businesses that do not create elements of service must . . . be eliminated."[98] By March 2001, he had divided his attack in services into two streams, virtual services that built the Internet into company offerings and a new front of service businesses.

Value Curve Challenge, 2003

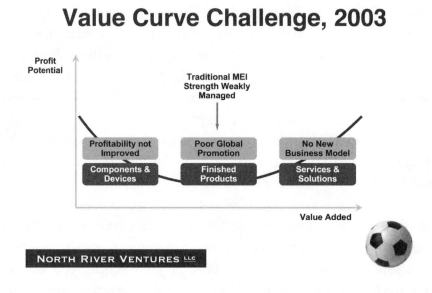

For the rest of Matsushita, however, grasping the implications of this is really hard. For a company used to loading containers with VCRs in Osaka Bay and bidding them goodbye, service meant after-sales warranty fulfillment, which meant cost, and cost is not good. What Kirk understood was that for Dell, by contrast, baking service into the system meant customer lock-on and better margins. Integrating service and product is central to OFCF generation in all modern markets. Indeed, it is safe to say that all the best companies do it. Whether an IBM or a GE, nobody today gets top rates of return without product-service integration.

The company has made considerable progress in call centers and is pushing an extreme customer satisfaction program in the United States. But actually selling product-service across all of its domains is still a ways off.

In mid-2003, using this updated version of his Smile Curve to show Matsushita's product-service weaknesses, Kirk recognized this work was incomplete. Saying "We must evolve into a company that always suggests new lifestyles,"[99] he created a Customer Value Enhancement Committee to meet on the same day as the group presidents meeting. But this, like IT, is unfinished business, and even though it has been on the group presidents' agenda for three years, it will take much of the new team's attention for some time to come.

Rebalancing Global Sales

The prolonged imbalance of domestic and overseas sales was a big problem. In its simplest sense, a global company like Matsushita should have sales around the world proportionate to GDP. For example, MEI sales in the United States, a country 2.4 times the size of Japan in GDP, should be 2.4 times those in Japan. Instead they are about 20 percent of those of the home country. Japan, not overseas markets, is the company's profit engine.

In July 2003, once most of Matsushita's major reforms were either in place or launched, Kirk turned his attention to this challenge and asked Executive Vice President Joe Shohtoku to right the imbalance.[100] Shohtoku (whose English is so good that I once told him, and his wife, that they could easily get retirement jobs prepping American Ph.D. students for their orals) had long experience in the United States, Malaysia, and China. His team was a major force behind the implementation of the shift to reporting on consolidated sales and the new investment and dividend policies, and Shohtoku had led the restructuring of many of the overseas manufacturing operations since 2000, so he knew global markets and how the MEI system worked.

The problem Shohtoku faced was sales stagnation in Europe and North America combined with a China market that was growing fast, but that was still immature. The weakness he saw in this mix was that MEI had not participated in the burgeoning cellular market where it had so many advantages.[101] At the same time, Shohtoku knew full well that the company could not count on growth in Japan because that market was still in stasis.

In addition, manufacturing demand for MEI's industrial products had begun to fall in North America and Europe as manufacturing shifted to China, especially, and MEI did not have a global account management system strong enough to sell to those American companies that had begun outsourcing to China, or to harness their shift to more value added at home. In March 2004, Kirk set his goal for 2005 sales to China at ¥1.5 trillion ($14.3 billion), significantly more than fiscal 2004 sales in the U.S. of ¥1.1 trillion ($10.5 billion).[102]

In many markets, global consolidation and vertical disintegration meant that MEI would have to sell to outsourcers and not to primary customers, losing control of its major accounts. Sean White and I had warned of this problem in 1996 in *The Digital Revolution*, observing that to cut costs as their market shares shrank, large U.S. automakers were consolidating their suppliers around a small number of top-tier companies, like Lear, who delivered entire car interiors. Matsushita, we said, faced a decision: was it going to move up the value chain in automotive systems, or become a supplier's supplier well down the pecking order and with little influence on its customer?[103] At this time, industrial products were MEI's biggest seller in the United States. Today they are a much smaller part. This meant that Shohtoku's team had to not only increase sales overseas, but do it in a way that didn't just shift the numbers from the States to China, but boosted U.S. and European sales. And they would have to do it without having cell phones, which the company had counted on as a growth driver, for those markets.

Shohtoku's team pushed through a series of moves to unify the global brand, which I will discuss in a later section, and made MEI's vertical launch capabilities global so that products did not have to prove themselves in Japan before being sold overseas and the company could improve OFCF from a simultaneous, and fast, sales lift. The team also led the shift from push-style marketing—closer to merchandising really—to a demand-pull system to synch up with its shift in manufacturing. In combination, these have the effect of increasing operating sources of cash and diminishing the cash conversion cycle. The big challenge is that even if economies are sluggish, as they are in Europe, the replacement cycle for V Products, which can grow much faster than the market, may still be too slow to be an engine of sales. In certain countries like Spain, as we saw, the shift to digital products is slower than elsewhere in Europe. This makes close-in account management essential. Without it, markets have insufficient reasons to move.

Most reforms to date have been in the Japanese core, and many processes have yet to be introduced overseas. Outbound logistics, critical to cash velocity and OFCF, need a lot of work. Until MEI can bring its attention to this, overseas sales will not be the salve the company is looking for.

In addition, there are strong centripetal pressures from customers. Honda buys more from Panasonic in the United States than in Japan, and will have an increasing amount to say about MEI's American operations, irrespective of what happens in Japan. Honda has its own ideas about cell manufacturing, pushed hard for changes in Matsushita's U.S. automotive supply operations, and got them. While this looks like a manufacturing issue, it's a sales issue. In the Soccer Ball System, operational integration with customers is necessary for optimal profitability, making manufacturing and sales hard to distinguish. Either both work hand in glove with customers or neither does. For Matsushita to rebalance its overseas sales, there are more painful adjustments to make.

China is a priority for any operation as big as Matsushita, as Konosuke recognized three decades ago. Hiro Sakamoto, head of corporate planning and member of the *gaijin butai*, coordinated Matsushita's initial goal of getting cross-domain sales in China up to ¥1 trillion. Matsushita is now much better positioned in this growth market, and the firm is expanding its white goods sales there on the back of the exploding consumer population, its first attempt to move home appliances into a new major market in many decades.

Building a Common Corporate Culture

A two-decade-long culture of slow growth and declining profitability stood in the way of reform. In his January 2001 policy speech, Kirk Nakamura addressed the issue directly: "I believe it is the responsibility of management to overcome a stagnated corporate culture and prepare a stage on which the next generation of employees can perform to their fullest."[104]

The impact of a stagnating culture can be devastating. An excellent example was Matsushita's understanding of the impact of the Wal-Mart business model. Yoshi Yamada, the head of Panasonic North America, shook his head as he told me how, because Wal-Mart itself appeared only recently in Japan and because it has not done well there, its vacuum-cleaner impact on markets was not known, let alone understood. In the United States, fully one-third of the population shops in Wal-Mart stores every year, which is like the entire population of Japan shopping in one store every year.[105] There was nothing in the MEI culture or organization designed to loosen the flow of information about Wal-Mart and get people to react to it, let alone with any vigor.

Right from the get-go, Kirk decided that all this had to change.

By cross-fertilizing groups with new management, introducing cell manufacturing, eliminating excessive reliance on vertical integration, pushing customer service into products, and making everyone accountable for their actions, he enabled the transformation of the corporate culture. But as always, people have to make it work.

One of Kirk's main tools was his constant storm of initiatives. He presented to his people quarterly, and each presentation in the early years of his presidency was packed with new ideas, new goals more extravagant than the last, and large chunks of new business models. No Japanese company had seen a Jack Welch–style blitzkrieg of corporate innovation, and many employees struggled to keep up. Kirk's problem was that he had little time and had stored up some of his ideas for decades, and to get them in place he unleashed them in a torrent.

Among other things, as we saw, he pushed through a system of instant messaging on his top managers. Japan may be a country where the young are text messaging crazy. But there is a protocol for management discussions. Reports are detailed and presented formally at regular intervals and only after a lot of group discussion to make sure no one objects. Kirk accepted this but ordered cell phones for all his top managers and hectored them day and night on their progress. Managers got Kirk's message: to hell with the meeting, report now.

Kirk's downpour of initiatives would have stalled in obfuscation, however, if it had not been for the tech crash of 2001. When the crash occurred just six months after Kirk took office, he was blindsided. His personal anguish was barely disguised. In the face of large losses and sales declines, he had to lay off 10,000 people and close operations, actions that were unthinkable to a man who had told *The Wall Street Journal* that maintaining jobs was the company's "highest mission."[106] In the United States, a CEO would be fired for not doing this. In Japan, by contrast, a CEO would be fired *because* he did it. But a company in Matsushita's state did not have this luxury. Kirk was new to the job, markets were sinking, management was in turmoil, and the company had to hold on to the leadership it had.

In the Japanese press MEI faced an onslaught railing against its highly inflated claims of reform. This was mortifying and drove a wedge into the company through which Kirk was able to reshape its culture and get the job done. The collective shock to the system of a large sales collapse and its associated losses and dismissals brought MEI as a whole around to Kirk's way of thinking. Kirk was able to pull his top team together, slash costs, increase sales, and get positive results quickly enough that the company coalesced behind a new culture.

Shinichi Fukushima, managing director in charge of human resources, told me, "Our reliance on Japan for sales growth and a legacy of jobs that had to be kept drove huge inefficiencies and lack of productivity. This had to change." One of the biggest obstacles to doing this was re-creating a culture of growth and profitability. "I joined in 1971 when the top companies in Japan were the Bank of Japan and MEI. This is no longer the case. So trying to bring people in who have experienced profitable growth is difficult. When I joined, no one could have imagined red ink. The year 2001 woke people up. I never want to go back to those days. But, today we need the same, but positive, sense of crisis."[107]

"In 1990, our company was still excellent," Fukushima said. "With the collapse of the bubble economy that year we had a rehabilitation plan but many parts of this earlier plan didn't work." This was why, when Kirk became CEO a decade later, he insisted that "there are no taboos." What had to be changed would be changed. The biggest problem Fukushima had with Kirk's root-and-branch restructuring was that "we had to be very careful about communicating this with top management, the domain companies, human resources, and the labor unions. We had to sell the process." He stressed to Kirk that for the process to work, management must explain what it was doing clearly to stakeholders, it must be transparent, and it must be modest. Lacking these, it would lose credibility.

Not all went well. "When we started equal opportunity for women in 2000 both men and women asked 'why?' Our first slogan was 'Women Brighten the Workplace' and this did not go over well." (I can understand why.) Also, "promoting young people created problems with Japan's traditional hierarchical approach. But the biggest challenge was getting a flat, weblike organization. Before, we had a fixed system. Many people thought that we were just changing names and titles, until they saw it work."

Fukushima explained that to get the right level of collaboration to make things work, "many of the things being done are done by task forces. These can be put up and taken down very quickly to solve specific problems." Skip level task forces have the additional effect of circumventing the traditional, tightly bound Japanese hierarchy and moving the approval levels needed for decision making far down in the organization, where it is more effective.

During the 2000–2006 period Matsushita created a role, albeit small, for non-Japanese in management. Joachim Reinhart is the COO of Panasonic Europe and is an executive officer, the first foreigner to achieve that rank. Cyril Wood is the head of Panasonic U.K. In the United States, Panasonic Automotive Systems brought in outside experts like Tony Faulkner to reshape production systems. These changes show a company that is trying to feel its way into a global shape. Does it "localize" by having more people native to the country it is in run operations there? Does it promote more non-Japanese to officer, even board, rank? What does this imply for the firm's common language? Will foreigners disrupt basic communications between Japanese, which are part of the firm's (and Japan's) social fabric, if all high-level meetings are conducted, as they are in many EU firms, in English? Could the firm survive this? Or should the company be decentralized by moving several domains overseas? The avionics operation is based in Seattle now. Is that a model for the future? And what does this imply for the Japanese nature of the company? You can see daily that Toyota and Honda, for example, are working their way through this as their sales in foreign markets surpass those at home, and management structure has to adapt. Matsushita is in the early stages of the same process.

The culture of low expectations was hard to eradicate. Once the pressure of 2001 was off, backsliding set in. For fiscal 2003, Kirk told all the domains to set their own sales targets without the usual "guidance" from headquarters. When he got these, he hit the roof. Left to their own devices, domain management set sales targets below levels for the year before. At the March 28, 2003, management conference he slammed managers for this. "From your business plans, I can see that all of you have become accustomed to lower profitability and tend to take low figures for granted." Tough talk. He went on to criticize managers for back loading even these anemic sales projections onto the second half of the year and in doing so, "procrastinating on our business challenges." Just in case anyone was sleeping through this (doubtful), he pointed out that planned CCM and cash flow were projected downward and "that your business plans do not show strong determination to put into practice management that focuses on CCM and cash flow under the new management systems."[108] He then put up a series of slides showing investment bank analysts' findings that were equally gloomy, making it clear to everyone that he was not the only one who was not fooled.

Role of Women

In Japan the role of women in business is complex. As a rule, there is no such thing as a successful middle-class economy without a powerful role for women. Where women's roles are artificially limited, the economy is too, and everybody suffers. Since Japan is a middle-class economy, women have a stronger role than is obvious to foreigners, who rarely encounter women at any level of management. Partly because Japan does not have many MBA schools, there is not much of a platform from which women can move into management. But this is changing and Matsushita's case is intriguing.

By studying business, law, and medicine, U.S. women gained professional profiles over the last half-century that makes hiring them a no-brainer. That is not to say that 50 percent of all CEOs are women, because they are not. But they are unquestionably on the move at every level in corporate America and their value in decision making is indisputable. More like essential. I tell my Japanese clients, "If you don't have a woman in the room, something will go wrong, only you won't know what it is, even after you've failed." I usually get polite smiles.

For many years I saw few women at meetings in Japan. Today, they are an increasing and noticeable presence. Their rank is not often high, but their roles are often decisive. There are several reasons for this. First, Japanese women are educated, Japan's population of male managers is aging, and the combination is opening opportunities for women. Second, women are delaying marriage and children to further their careers and secure their own earning capability. Third, Japanese managers are learning from their foreign experiences. Reform leader Atsushi Murayama talked about how he and Kirk learned a lot about bringing women into management during their time overseas. "At the very beginning of reform, we talked about equal opportunity. Kirk and I had been in the U.S. and we had experienced a lot of problems and we had to encourage the position of female workers. We had some experience with this after working in the U.S. That's why we both started to work on the position of female workers and we had long discussions on this."[109] Finally, a Soccer Ball–structured company is deeply integrated with its customers, whether consumer, commercial, or industrial. The closer a company comes to understanding enough about its own cash and capital efficiencies to manage its customers' experience of its products and services, the more women it needs to make decisions and work with customers. Getting this right means having women in all parts of the value chain and at all levels of authority. Getting it wrong means building in unacceptably high levels of risk.

Kirk moved early. In May 1995, he hired leading New York City education authority Dr. Ellyn Berk to run the highly successful Panasonic Learning Lab on Park Avenue, which replaced the old showroom there. The Learning Lab became the prototype for the Panasonic Centers he later opened in Japan. Then, in 1997, he brought in Connie Pohl from AT&T to run cell phone sales. His legacy still holds here a decade after his departure. The most senior woman in MEI outside Japan is Megan Lee, vice president of human resources at Panasonic North America.

From the moment he became CEO, he pushed for more female decision makers, telling *The Wall Street Journal* less than a month after he took office that the most important lesson he learned running Panasonic North America was to give young people and women more responsibility. He told the *Journal* bluntly, "At Matsushita, we have only one female section chief. There's something wrong with a company like that." For good measure he added that women were high in his plans for cutting time-wasting bureaucracy because they "immediately sympathize with that. But when you do that with the middle management, they just don't get it."[110]

In my travels through the company, women in all parts of the firm are unquestioning in their commitment to Kirk because they understand the depth of his commitment to them. They also know how few Japanese companies have CEOs that share his view that women build value for customers. Many speak, for example, of his unfailing courtesy and of his legendary anger at men who are not so courteous. One manager told me how, when her boss publicly snubbed her at a company retirement party, Kirk looked over at her and stormed out in fury. He tore a strip off the man and the next day she received an abject letter of apology. In a telling reply, when I asked him for this book about what he would tell a young person coming into the company for the first time, he said, "I want him or her. . . ."[111] Also, women's perception of Kirk is quite a bit different from that of the men who work for him. "People say he is tough, harsh, and demanding," Megan Lee told me, "but the person I know is very compassionate."[112]

Satoko Matsuda, head of Matsushita's Corporate Diversity Promotion Division, told me that when Kirk became CEO, he immediately "took the initiative to take diversity management out of human resources and make it a function of corporate management policy," and that the reason for this was his U.S. experience. "In Japan," she said, "companies are dominated by men. Mr. Nakamura believed that this kind of monoculture wouldn't work for a global company. Monoculture was fine for an age of mass production but not in an age of more diverse products."[113]

To end the monoculture, Kirk wanted the commitment of top management and formed an advisory committee. Top executives, Matsuda said, "recognized that the accelerated participation of women *is* a management issue. As a result, more employees are conscious of this matter." But, she pointed out, as everywhere else, when women first move up in the ranks, they have no role models "of good female management for them to understand." When the company surveyed managers on this, it discovered that not only women made this point, but so did male managers. To fix this, each year twelve women are singled out to become mentors for others. Then she turned to Megumi Kitagawa, one of the most valuable members of the support team MEI provided in the researching of this book, and reintroduced her as one of them. I should not have been surprised; Kitagawa is frighteningly efficient.

Matsuda listed several positive outcomes:

- More female managers
- More women playing an active role in the company
- More women with higher goals
- More men with changed views

That being said, moving women forward in Japan is no bed of roses. Men and women speak different languages, and, unlike males, females use verb conjugations that imply subservience. Matsuda referred to this problem repeatedly and stated how hard it is to run a meeting that way. Men have a way of speaking that denotes complex levels of camaraderie and mutual obligation, bonds that women cannot share linguistically. Men frequently go out drinking late after work where they establish and manage the lifelong relationships essential to navigating their careers. Women, Matsuda told me, are excluded from this and have no way around it. Moreover, many, if not most, she said, have commitments to family that preclude this sort of late-night camaraderie. This in turn means that they often have to build careers pursuing solitary activities outside the team framework so deeply embedded in Japanese male culture. Partly for this reason, in the spring of 2006, MEI announced a plan to let a thousand employees telecommute, a commonplace in the United States, but seen by Japanese women as a significant benefit. The more telecommuting there is, however, the harder it will be to maintain a monoculture. Individuals will have to act on their own with an impact on male-female relations at work that will be far-reaching. Regardless, "We are still more of a monoculture," Matsuda emphasized and, "out of the 80,000 women working for us in Japan, only 89 are managers. There are 11,000 male managers." In addition, female managers are dangerously concentrated. Only one division, Household Appliances, has a large number of female general managers (eight), and they are all in design. None hold officer rank.

Matsushita has experimented with bringing in ranking women experts from other companies just as it has begun to bring in men. But these women report that the culture of the company itself, irrespective of the male monoculture, is often hostile and hard to manage. As a result, they often get pushback from male and female staff alike on even simple procedures for which they have more than enough expertise.

Some women are playing roles that are powerful, if unseen. Before I wrote *Panasonic* I asked Yoko Nakamizu, in sports marketing, to read several Japanese books on Kirk Nakamura and give me her conclusions. She advised me to build the book on Kirk's work in the United States and the United Kingdom, which Japanese texts had all ignored. She observed that my work with Kirk in the States gave me insights into Matsushita's restructuring that no one else had and that these were essential to understanding what was done and why. I had planned to give this period a light gloss and to focus mainly on 2000–2006 when Kirk was CEO. At her suggestion, I restructured *Panasonic*, reviewing all my decade-old notes to Kirk and rereading *The Digital Revolution* reform template, seeking out retired executives who worked with Kirk in Secaucus, and revisiting the results of his task forces, especially the *Panasonic Ideas For Life* team, and spending much more time with Yoshi Yamada on the ToughBook than I originally intended. In effect, *one woman* determined much of how the world will come to see Matsushita.

In addition, Matsushita is bringing up a generation of trilingual women with multinational experience—Megan Lee is an excellent example—without which the company cannot fulfill its global ambitions. As Kirk said in 2000, women get it. Matsuda put the point bluntly: "It's really a question of whether or not MEI wants a global future."

Megan Lee's case is illustrative. Born in Korea, she spent three years in Osaka as a teenager and came to the States at twenty-four. Amazingly, in spite of arriving here ten years older than

Henry Kissinger was, her American English, unlike his, is accent-less. She joined Panasonic North America in 1987 because PNA needed bilingual staff. In 1993, while Kirk was posted in the United States, she moved to human resources. There she partici-pated in a PNA management development program that Kirk asked me to review because he felt there was a problem with it. (There was.) Kirk returned to Japan shortly afterward, and a year later, in July 2001, Megan was sent to Japan for a year. "At the time, Fukushima was under a lot of pressure to get the women and international issues resolved. I worked for him in the Pana-sonic Global Executive System. He wanted to create a structure at a high level to manage global human resources. At the time there was no common system."[114] Lee planned for one year in Japan and stayed for three. Once the system was in place she returned to PNA as head of human resources in October 2004, making her the first non-Japanese, let alone woman, in MEI history to go to headquarters, take on a global mission, and return as a ranking ex-ecutive. It is easy to see how the company's future is in the hands of women like Lee even if the men don't recognize this yet. Fukushima himself told me that he saw a limited future for unilingual men like himself in his job.[115]

REFORMING BRAND: PANASONIC IDEAS FOR LIFE

The hardest lesson in branding is that brand has little to do with products or advertising, the two things to which most companies gravitate when they start brand initiatives. Brand is managing how your customers *experience* your products. That is, brand is every-thing you do and how your customers live with what you sell them, day in and day out. This makes it the primary mechanism by which high-profit opportunities are identified and exploited. If anything you do does not directly manage your customers' expe-rience of your products and services, it is someone else's job.

In the Soccer Ball System, managers constantly filter out activities that do not manage their customers' experience, activities that are not on the surface of the Soccer Ball. This was Kirk Nakamura's reform message from the moment he became CEO: everyone in the company, irrespective of role, has to work with customers. In MEI's shot-put structure, this was far from the case. Manufacturing/product-centered MEI had very little brand capability. When Sean and I returned from Japan in early 1997, this was one of our main observations to Kirk and it became a priority once he became CEO.

For any manufacturing- or engineering-driven company, successful branding means a wrenching change. All the products and manufacturing in the world are no substitute for ethnographic information fed deep into the corporate structure in real time, twenty-four hours a day. For companies that operate globally, this means incorporating ethnography across cultures and geographies, forcing the company to recompose itself with a shallow, flat topology that can respond quickly across multiple markets.

By 1996, Matsushita's many different divisions, affiliates, and sales companies worldwide, with their own ideas of what customers were experiencing and how to manage these experiences, had unbranded the company. Unlike Procter and Gamble or Unilever, which are single entities with multiple well-managed brands, MEI and its affiliates with their National/Panasonic dyad were a multicompany/multibrand entity. Matsushita had a set of sales messages that were so complex—some were mutually exclusive—that they were incoherent. The only thing in common across this multicompany/multibrand structure was the Panasonic and National logotypes. All that held together the company's brand image, such as it was, was a style manual.

A Gallup and Robinson tracking study done for Panasonic North America in the mid-1990s showed that Panasonic's overall "excellent/very good" rating was 54 percent, while Sony's was close to 80 percent.[116] Moreover, Sony's image led Panasonic's by an order of magnitude across a broad range of categories from "product leadership" to "reliability" to "latest technology." This study forced us to conclude that Matsushita had no strategy for managing its brand in what should have been its primary market. It had no clear idea of how its customers should "experience" Panasonic or what they should expect from Matsushita as a "customer-for-life" partner.

Matsushita and its customers were moving away from each other. Add in the impact of Moore Time, and the speed with which the company and its customers were divorcing was increasing by the day. I remember being struck by just how unfunny this was.

Over the years, its centrifugal nature moved Matsushita away from Konosuke's endless injunctions to create demand. The firm increasingly substituted merchandising for marketing and demand creation. Konosuke's art of getting customers to preselect Panasonic well before they buy was lost.

There had been one or two sales slogans in the 1970s—like the vaguely defensive "Panasonic: Just Slightly Ahead of Our Time"—but nothing new in years. By the mid-1990s, many inside the company asked if there was anything even slightly ahead of our time about Panasonic. The company led in few markets and, as we have seen, was more inclined to enter markets established by others than to create markets by itself.

The Brand Image Task Force was one of the six Kirk assigned me to work with in 1996–97, and he asked me to recommend a brand expert. I e-mailed my friend Gerry Butters, head of a management team I advised for years at Nortel Networks. Gerry had gone to AT&T Network Systems, where he managed its rebranding as Lucent Technologies. Within an hour I got his answer: Landor. He said they were the unquestioned best and suggested I call Hayes Roth.

Landor rebranded GE, Federal Express, British Airways, and Procter and Gamble (one of its largest account worldwide), to name a few, and Hayes, now chief marketing officer, brought in a team to present to Panasonic in Secaucus. Their findings were illuminating. Landor's database of brand recognition showed that the Panasonic name still had high value though there were serious weaknesses. This gave us something to work on, though for how long was anybody's guess: In Moore Time a great brand can be dust in the blink of an eye.

The Landor team concluded that at Matsushita, marketing—and branding—had no consistency across the company's geographies, products, customer segments, divisions, or consumer groups. It found:

- Multiple product lines with multiple messages
- Multiple brandlines
- Individual marketing teams with no coordination
- Multiple expressions of the brand across Panasonic and Matsushita groups
- Limited marketing budgets in a primarily manufacturing- and sales-driven culture

In addition, Landor could identify only one strong leader in MEI's markets, Sony, and found that MEI people were constantly, and negatively, comparing themselves to Sony. Landor called this "Sony envy."

Even though Dell, for example, was already selling as much as Panasonic was in the United States, and had a distribution structure and customer experience management expertise that it could turn on Matsushita, and Sony, or anyone else for that matter, it was clear to me from my work on *The Digital Revolution*, and my subsequent visit to Matsushita operations in Japan, that MEI people were only vaguely aware of the danger to MEI's already weakened brands. One or two were, however, like Kazuyoshi Fujiyoshi, whose Kyushu operation traditionally sold overseas. "When it was up to individual groups, brand was a problem," he recalled in late 2005. "Today, we need an integrated approach and we are at the beginning of this."[117]

In November 1997 and March 1998, Landor conducted a series of focus groups and surveys of consumers and businesses across the United States. This study confirmed much of what was already in its databases, finding that Panasonic was well regarded in several areas like value and reliability, but had limited recognition outside its customer base, was seen by consumers as little more than a TV and VCR company, and was suffering from a poor customer service image among business customers. The firm had little value at all in areas like innovation, style, market leadership, or prestige. Landor recommended a complete overhaul.

At about that time, Tom Murano came to PNA from Unilever, where branding is well understood, to get a handle on what had to be done following the Brand Task Force and Landor reports. The first hurdle was integrating twelve uncoordinated marketing efforts and pulling disparate groups together, a painstaking process that took Tom hundreds of interviews. Late in 1998 Tom met with Landor and at about the same time Bob Greenberg moved from the Panasonic Consumer Electronics Company to oversee the U.S.-wide brand effort. The three central players in Matsushita's global rebranding effort for the next eight years were in place.

In 1998 and 1999 Greenberg had Landor conduct a full qualitative and quantitative program across the United States to get a better idea of customer and employee views of the Panasonic brand, and this only served to confirm its initial findings. In 2001, he commissioned Grey Global to undertake additional studies. The summaries of this learning make painful reading.

BrandAsset® Valuator[118]	"A brand with little (and declining) differentiation, especially among younger audience"

ImagePower®	"A strong brand, losing distinctiveness, trailing Sony on critical measures"
Landor	"A good, quality brand with no clear image beyond category cost of entry; behind the times/outdated, no emotional tie with consumer or business to business customer"
Grey	"No clear image beyond category cost of entry; behind the times/outdated"

In 2001, Greenberg asked Landor to develop a new message for the market. Greenberg brought the top twenty PNA managers together for a Landor exercise designed to get through long-established silos and identify a BrandDriver™ that is differentiable and ownable. The BrandDriver is the central statement of a company's ability to generate value; it is what the company does for customers. The FedEx BrandDriver supports the brandline you see on everything FedEx does, "The world on time." Nothing could be more succinct. Anything FedEx does to improve how it delivers the world on time, irrespective of technology, reinforces the brandline, giving FedEx clear avenues for growth at minimal risk to its brand. British Petroleum (BP) used the same process that Greenberg initiated to come up with the brandline "Beyond Petroleum," genius for an oil company.

Brandlines are a world apart from the marketing slogans Matsushita had used since its inception. They are more enduring, reflect deeper value sets, and are designed to maximize market shares and minimize risk.

From his background in consumer products sales, Greenberg

Brandlines	Marketing Slogans
Shorthand communication of brand message	Typically capture a core theme associated with a given campaign or product
Target multiple audiences: • internal unifying/rallying/motivating • external expression of promise/ expectations	Focus on generating sales
Intended to endure over time	Target primarily at consumers/customers rather than broader audiences
Closely associated with the brand identity/signature	Generally short-lived May be trendy or faddish
Used in multiple applications to maximize effectiveness of permanent media	Limited to advertising only

could see that the main obstacles to getting an effective brandline at MEI were the many companies sharing the Panasonic name and their diverse brand strategies. On top of this, his rebranding initiative would have to cover a stupefying range of products and services from shavers to pencil sharpeners, from batteries to automotive audio, and from white goods to entire TV studios. Any rebranding would have to cover all of these—MEI had started buying up affiliates early in the process—and had to bridge the unknowns of future products, services, and possible acquisitions. Brand reform would also have to capture something of Konosuke's original ideas if there was to be any buy-in from Japan. What emerged was a set of attributes laid out in a keep, lose, add matrix.

From this matrix came the BrandDriver that now supports the Panasonic brand worldwide: "Pragmatic Visionary."

Keep	Lose	Add
Reliable	Slow	Modern
Relationship-builders	Apologetic	Expert
Good value	Cautious	Authority
Life-enhancing	Outdated	Improving
High-quality	Boring	Energetic
Customer-focused	Not a leader	Smart
Global	Poor service	Solutions
Friendly	Ease of repair	Innovative

The Pragmatic Visionary BrandDriver says: "For over 75 years, Panasonic has set the standards for excellence in electronics. It is our passion for perfection—our tenacity in applying our unparalleled expertise to creating innovative products and services that surprise and delight our customers—that sets us apart. We are pragmatic visionaries, driven to always exceed expectations and add relevant value to our customers at work and play."

Pragmatic Visionary was as useful inside the company as outside. It was a positioning Konosuke espoused all his life. It covered everything MEI made, and, critical to the reforms then under way, it gave permission to everyone to do whatever they had to do to make their visions really useful to customers, regardless of market. This message also enabled MEI to explore every possible means of managing customer experiences of its products, without being bound to manufacturing. Pragmatic Visionary tells stakeholders what the company will do for customers: keep them ahead of the curve in the most useful way possible. And that is the key to brand: a mechanism that bonds a company and its customers to the same goals, just as Sano does with his technostory.

With the Pragmatic Visionary strategy in hand, Landor and Grey Global distilled the core message into the brand vehicle *Panasonic Ideas For Life* with Christian Slater as the voice of Panasonic.

In December 2002, Bob Greenberg and his team briefed me on the new brandline. For the first time in its history, Matsushita was being asked to commit to a brandline intended to endure for years, even decades, and one that would apply to all aspects of the company's operations and relations with its customers, regardless of division, product, or geography. *Panasonic Ideas For Life* is a declarative statement: Panasonic will have a direct, beneficial impact on your life, wherever you are, whether at home or at work. *Panasonic Ideas For Life* is a lifelong commitment to customers: we will stay at the leading edge of your lifestyle and workstyle, whether you are a consumer or a business, irrespective of technology or location, forever.

Such a brandline would be as inescapable for MEI itself as it would be for its customers. If it weren't a *Panasonic Idea For Life*, why would a customer be interested? Why would we offer it?

Also, the brandline fit so tightly with Konosuke's core vision, as Greenberg had intended it to, that it would become viral. Yes, it was an American idea in a Japan-centric company, but who could resist what it promised? This, I felt at the time, actually increased the risk of pushback from *honsha*.

Nonetheless, it was immediately clear that *Panasonic Ideas For Life* worked across domain companies and in Japan as well as overseas. It had the potential to leverage quickly and effectively all the other changes coursing their way through the company, like V Products and universal design, and do so globally. I e-mailed Kirk the next day with my recommendation that he make *Panasonic Ideas For Life* the company's global go-to-market statement.

In January 2003, Kirk ended his management conference in Osaka with a PNA *Panasonic Ideas For Life* video and in his March 28, 2003, annual policy meeting, he made *Panasonic Ideas For Life* the brand envelope for all Panasonic products. The *Panasonic Ideas For Life* brandline is now central to MEI's "One Brand Strategy" to end the National name, "unifying the global brand to Panasonic."[119] This transformation began in overseas markets as Matsushita launched Panasonic white goods and home appliances traditionally sold in Japan under the National name. In July 2003, Matsushita began selling HFC refrigerators in China under the Panasonic name. Moving all MEI products into the fast-growing China market under the Panasonic brand effectively limits the use of National to Japan and forecloses it from growth markets. This presages the end of the National name, Konosuke's first brand, and will give the company a single global identity for the first time in its history.

Panasonic Ideas For Life will pay big dividends in MEI's purchase of a majority position in MEW. I will devote more space to this in my section on the greening of Panasonic, but MEW's expertise on managing space—at home or at the office—is probably unparalleled in the world. No one knows more than MEW about how to make living and work spaces more energy-efficient and easier to use. Nothing fits better under the *Panasonic Ideas For Life* rubric even though MEW today uses the National name. To integrate the brands, MEI began by dividing the empire, as it were, into two realms: MEI manages time for its customers and MEW manages space. Both are *Panasonic Ideas For Life.*

MEI began reforming the Panasonic brand in New York, not Tokyo or Osaka—a first for Matsushita—making *Panasonic Ideas For Life* another part of the reform program, like domain companies and V Products, that Kirk Nakamura initiated in the United States a half decade before he became CEO. It encapsulates his thinking more clearly than perhaps anything else he did during his period as CEO: a seamless transition between Konosuke's core values and the realities of modern markets. Improving people's lives at home and at work had been Konosuke's goal right from his double-pronged socket in 1917.

But starting in New York had its challenges. "We couldn't touch the Panasonic logo," Roth told me, even though Landor's research showed repeatedly that something new was needed.[120] One way of dealing with this was with the bold band that runs above and below the brandline and sometimes right through it so that the brandline is immediately recognizable at a distance. IBM does something similar; you can tell an IBM TV ad at sight, well before the name hits, because of the Big Blue bands across the top and bottom of the screen. Luckily with ToughBook already up and running, the team had an ideal product—"Life Proof"—to take to market right away.

The Christian Slater voice-over has been effective in unplanned ways: both Jay Leno and Conan O'Brien have introduced him on their top-rated interview shows as the voice of Panasonic.

The program also "raised the bar" in Bob Greenberg's words, driving a different quality of employee: "If you can't add value to someone's life, you shouldn't be working here."[121] For the future, Greenberg told me, "We have to rethink how we are interacting with the users of our products." This will, he believes, require ever-deeper ethnographic studies to keep *Panasonic Ideas For Life* vigorous and fresh and to give up control to the customer. For example, he says, "we have to shift the public's perception of Panasonic away from hardware, like camcorders, to 'Panasonic enables me to capture my creativity and share it.'" In other words, Matsushita's new brandline must move the company away from the old commodity competition, like Sony and Samsung, and toward the new, like Apple.

After three years, the *Panasonic Ideas For Life* brandline has had a big impact. PDP, a critical V Product in MEI's sales bridge, took on a life of its own and now dominates the global and North American markets for flat-panel TVs. Today, Greenberg is using the brandline to build a new lifestyle, called "Living in High Definition," that embraces a wide range of Panasonic products from PDPs to SD memory cards, and from DSCs and Blue Ray DVDs to camcorders and security systems, under a single *Panasonic Idea For Life*. In the past, each of these products was sold individually and was not marketable collectively. Demand creation wasn't even thinkable. "We call it 'enabling the personal expression of creativity,'" he says. A big change from selling camcorders at a discount.

THE PANASONIC CENTER

I opened the book with the story of Sean White and I visiting the Panasonic showroom on Park Avenue in New York and how Kirk Nakamura shut it down after reading our 1993 comments in *Beating Japan*. In the mid-nineties, he replaced the showroom with the Panasonic Learning Lab, a space for schoolchildren to use Panasonic products to teach themselves school lessons, managed by New York educator Ellyn Berk, who had built the $25 million Panasonic Foundation in 1984. The Panasonic Learning Lab was a sensational place. Children from all over the New York area came there in busloads to use Panasonic technologies to help them learn in new ways. The idea, she recalled, "was to show how kids could learn through technology and that Panasonic alone understood this."[122] In this way, it brought into the information age something that Konosuke thought about all his life because of his own lack of education, which was how to educate others, especially the young. Berk's discussions with Disney revealed that no less than the master entertainment company on the planet thought that education could not get children into a branded IT environment. Only entertainment could do this. Sony was evidently on two tracks, moving into game consoles and movies, both of which took it further away from education. The field was open for Panasonic and Kirk took it.

"The underpinning of the Lab was that it didn't matter who came to the Lab or where they came from. When they got into the Lab, it was magic. The Panasonic Learning Lab became a good resource for schools in the area. When we started [1995], teachers didn't even know how to go on the Internet." They would learn this at the Lab. I remember that during my many visits to the Lab, the most interesting thing was not the schoolchildren—they were jumping right into whatever Panasonic offered them as fast as kids' hands shoot into a candy jar—but the teachers for whom Ellyn set up a special computer station. Here teachers could learn to log on and prepare lessons from web-based resources. Ellyn initially built the station just to keep the teachers out of the way while her highly trained staff worked with the children. But it soon became apparent that the Panasonic Learning Lab had as much value for the teachers as for the kids and she began to create special programs for them.

The Panasonic Learning Lab attracted attention from around the country and Sean and I recommended in *The Digital Revolution* that Kirk make it a centerpiece of Panasonic's North American branding. Education, we said, was a natural for Matsushita and the field was wide open. We also recommended making El-lyn's teacher resources, which she had turned into an attractive home page, into a web-based homework resource for American children. We imagined parents all over America replacing "Have you done your homework?" with "Have you done your Panasonic Learning Lab?" And teachers doing real-time projects in class with Lab resources. Not even Microsoft could get buy-in like this, we said.

One of America's largest mall developers approached Ellyn and asked to put Panasonic Learning Labs in all its malls. This thing had legs.

But it wasn't going to run. Kirk was recalled to Japan in mid-1997. For unclear reasons MEI funded the Lab through a subcontractor and so did not see its real budgets nor have the day-to-day operating control Ellyn felt MEI needed to have. In March 2000, three months before Kirk became CEO, Kirk's successor at PNA closed the Lab. To say Kirk was unimpressed is putting it politely.

When Kirk became CEO he revisited the Panasonic Learning Lab on a grand scale. The company built two Panasonic Centers, one in Osaka and one in Tokyo. The first of these, the Tokyo Panasonic Center, opened in September 2002. These centers are large, interactive spaces where customers can work with Matsushita products and think up new uses for them. Education is a big part of the picture but in the larger sense that education is a brand builder of the first order, an axis of communication between MEI and its customers along which the two educate each other about needs, ethnography, and lifestyle. The Panasonic Center in Tokyo is part TV studio where productions use equipment fresh from the labs. Feedback into MEI's broadcast systems operations is instantaneous. What started as the education of children and their teachers in New York now educates everyone.

Matsushita integrated the Panasonic Centers into its *Panasonic*

Ideas For Life brandline. They embody all the "add" traits of the 2001 BrandDriver exercise: modern, expert, authority, improving, energetic, smart, solutions, innovative. Putting all these into one space to show how Panasonic's Pragmatic Visionary BrandDriver works in the real world is a significant departure from the company's practice. Panasonic Centers don't entertain; they teach and let Matsushita be taught in turn. They therefore carve out a space in the world of advanced technology that, for some reason, has been left untouched by all the other major brand powerhouses on the world stage. While entertainment and its delivery vehicles change all the time, the need for a Pragmatic Visionary working with people at the leading edge of their life and workstyles will never go away. It can be used to identify and exploit profitable opportunities virtually forever.

PRODUCT REALIGNMENT: VICTORY PRODUCTS AND UNIVERSAL DESIGN

Until 2000, Matsushita's emphasis was on making the broadest possible range of electric and electronic products with one or two exceptions that Konosuke made, like mainframe computers. Konosuke believed that the electric world revolutionized human behavior and that the future of MEI was in providing for every aspect of that change that anyone at the company could think of. As the twentieth-century wave of electricity covered more human activities and spread over more of the planet, Matsushita's mission was to be there. Konosuke used to say that MEI products should flow with the ease and cheapness of water. And that, more or less, is what he offered.

As we saw, this emphasis pushed the company in an innately conservative direction: wait for large markets to establish themselves, then enter them with better-made, easier-to-manufacture, and cheaper products. The extent to which the company had proprietary control of technology, though important, was secondary. What counted to Konosuke were sales volume, reliability, and cost. He was convinced that putting those three together was the core to adding value and was, therefore, the sum total of brand. In Konosuke's day, he was right and he had the sales and profits to show for it.

The problem with his marketing theory was that in the electronic world, more specifically the computerized world, cyberspace expands more quickly than any company can keep up with it. Even if you could offer enough products to expand as fast as cyberspace, you could not possibly do so profitably, as no less an information powerhouse than Microsoft is finding out. Indeed, the conquest of cyberspace, Konosuke-style, was a formula for the destruction of the company. Only no one at Matsushita seemed to have figured this out. Or, if they had, they had no solution.

Critically, there was nothing in the Konosuke system that inherently drove it toward maximum velocity of cash or to identify and optimize all the drivers of OFCF. The company was putting more shot all the time.

Further problems with the Konosuke model emerged as the decades moved on. Even without the rapid inflation of cyberspace, Matsushita was competing across a huge front from white goods through batteries and factory automation to air conditioners and professional TV production and consumer electronics as well as many, many other markets. In each of these, product and marketing cycles were different; there was no attempt to coordinate new launches across the company—to create a Matsushita buzz—even if the domains were rationalized and all the affiliates consolidated. There was also no system for pruning the company-wide portfolio and, as we saw, no criteria for understanding exit and exit timing.

With an array of products that was broad rather than deep, MEI was vulnerable to more focused competition. Its profit structure was held up for long stretches by single products. The company was increasingly strung out across product lines in one dimension, and through time in another. "Matsushita produced hit products, one after the other," Kirk recalled. Rather than simultaneous hot products in several sectors, the entire edifice was supported by one product in one sector for a while, and then another in a different sector until, "after a certain point, we did not produce hits."[123]

VHS, for example, had supported the company for many years. Later cellular took the lead. When telecommunications led the tech crash in 2001, cellular went down fast, exposing the rest of the company's weaknesses. Management was rightly terrified by what it suddenly understood as a huge flaw in its business model. Any new strategy would have to solve both the space and time problems to ensure that Matsushita always had several market dominators in harness.

To stop its front from imploding during 2001 and early 2002, the company rushed V (for market victory) Products into market as quickly as possible. Every domain had to produce immediately a list of products that would sell fast, and then get behind each of these with an almighty push. The domains got eighty-eight of these in place during this period and then struggled into 2002 to get the market to recognize their value and buy them. Everyone who was involved remembers it as the hardest time in the company's history, as the crisis filtered out managers, products, and processes.

To complete MEI's maneuver, in October 2001, Kirk announced a sweeping review of R&D[124] to:

- Select and concentrate on key markets
  - ○ Reduce the number of products
  - ○ Reduce the selection within product groups
- Select and concentrate development themes

     ° Reduce the number of areas in R&D
     ° Prioritize these
     ° Reinforce top areas
- Integrate all development resources to create a uniform strategy

Then, in early 2002, he called an extraordinary management conference where he pushed for a new, long-term approach to V Products, one where domains would turn their focus from emergency sales recovery to an institutionalized system for identifying top-selling products, hitting the market hard, gaining profitable share, and exiting in a timely way rather than hanging on for decades. "The business model which was so effective for Matsushita in the twentieth century—releasing a stream of new products with more diverse functions—has lost its effectiveness."[125] Getting the first generation of V Products out the door was not enough. More were needed. Lots more. And each one had to be strategic.

To get something like this done, Kirk as always turned to one of his tried-and-true executives. He asked Kazuo Toda to create and manage a formal discipline for introducing V Products. Toda's background in everything from audiovisual consumer products to home appliances gave him a considerable range of expertise. There is very little that the company does that he has not worked with since he joined in 1964. What Toda created, and drove across the whole company, was a system whereby all Matsushita acted like a jackhammer, hitting all its markets with a repeated series of hard blows.

The V Products process accomplished several things:

- Moved the company away from diffused, commoditized, low-value products, onto a smaller number of differentiable, high-value products with long-term profit potential.

- Coordinated the launch of these products across domains so the market, and the company itself, could see a steady pulsation of high-value products from all Matsushita.
- Ensured that the pace of introduction was computer-like with orders of magnitude improvements over a short time, regardless of product sector.
- Empowered management to think far enough outside the box to make the necessary innovations happen.
- Brought promising managers to the attention of the executive quickly.
- Bypassed the hierarchy and traditional decision making.
- Got sales and marketing into the product design phase.

Added to this, in a statement found rarely in the mouths of CEOs in 2002, though more common today, Kirk insisted that all products be designed to improve the environment by reducing the energy required to make them and the energy required to use them. More on this later. For the moment, however, you can imagine thousands of executives and managers having been clobbered by the tech crash, being told, first, to pull fast-selling products into the line and sell them in unprecedented volumes; second, to redesign operations to launch a strategic new series of market dominators; third, to absorb five subsidiaries, and oh, by the way, make all your products and processes green. And have it done by Wednesday at three.

Kirk cautioned his team in September 2002, "Matsushita used to be known for its strong production engineering which brought us various 'process' innovations. Today the advantages of manufacturing are not enough to survive the global competition. We need to be a company with strong 'product' innovation."[126] The company had always led from behind, assuring itself that someone else had established a market for a product before entering. Microsoft had done this in computer software as recently as twenty years previously. But the market had changed. The first to market with high-velocity operations became the key to market domination, as Apple was about to show with its iPod/iLife combo. Matsushita was not cut from this mold, and a great deal had to change if the company was to succeed. Atsushi Murayama recalled, "We had similar initiatives before, but our previous efforts were purely ceremonial. Kirk Nakamura had a much clearer definition, that these products should be core products of the whole company."[127]

Kazuyoshi Fujiyoshi told me that one of Kirk's additional messages early on was that the company's DNA is manufacturing, and that it is the leveraging of this DNA that will move MEI in a very different direction from Sony.[128] The V Product strategy encapsulated that approach, wrapping potent new offerings with a powerful new manufacturing strategy that rolled out new V Products, upgraded existing ones, and rapidly exited, leaving resources available for the next V Product.

Each V Product had to have a core Matsushita black box technology that could not easily be duplicated and that gave the company overwhelming market advantage for decades. Everything else should be outsourced or managed through joint ventures. This way MEI could gain enduring profitability quickly without being slowed down by the tail of vertical integration downstream trying to wag the dog upstream.

Kirk was deliberately vague about the nature of black box technologies. They needed to have three elements, but how these were put together he left to line managers:[129]

- Protected by MEI intellectual property rights.
- Materials or manufacturing expertise for black box technologies.
- Contain not just technology but manufacturing knowledge.

He wanted line groups to get close enough to the market to figure this out for themselves, make their case, and go for it. Fast.

Otherwise, he worried out loud, contract manufacturers anywhere in the world, especially in China, could undercut Matsushita. Perhaps his biggest barrier to doing this was the natural
reluctance of tens of thousands of people deeply ingrained with
the old Matsushita philosophy that MEI should wait for a market
to establish itself—which could take years—and then carefully
prepare a mass assault, a process that could also take years. Few
were ready for the change in direction and many, I know from experience, still have trouble with it.

In TVs, white goods, and the like with their long replacement
cycles, slow pace of technology change, and minimal shifts in
price-performance, MEI's "slower is better and don't ever inno-
vate" approach worked well. The company never did anything in
a market that didn't have proven unit potentials, often in the millions. Moreover, the idea of creating a market, the way Apple did
with PCs and then with the iPod, was anathema. And with good
reason. Apple created the PC business and then got clobbered by
underpowered and underfeatured IBM-compatibles. This drove
home the point: never stick your neck out. But that was a quarter
century ago, things had changed, and so had Apple. The iPod
would soon show that you could create, and dominate, a digital
market overnight. From his overseas experience, Kirk knew that
MEI had to be ready for this, or disappear.

Toda's program had several parameters:

- Features that rivals do not have
- Products with differences customers can see at a glance
- Unprecedented products that can open new markets
- Launch all these simultaneously on a global basis (vertical
  launch)

Once the V Product/black box process was under way, Kirk
turned to reversing another of Konosuke's long-held dicta, that
growth was its own reward. He saw clearly that the logical corollary

of rapid cyberspace expansion was specialization and profit rather than growth for its own sake. To a great extent the V Product program solved that problem by forcing everyone in the firm to focus on what worked. Once he had them doing this, and gaining the market share rewards for doing so, Kirk added a Jack Welch twist: Matsushita must be in the top two of every market, or out.

The V Product program delivered breakthrough sales, yields, and profits at unprecedented speed. Shanghai Matsushita Microwave Oven, for example, introduced a single-function grill oven in April 2002 that it expected to reach sales of 4.5 million units over the next three years. It hit 6.9 million. By the end of June 2002, Matsushita products were beginning to outgrow several markets, giving the company increased, even dominant share. In home appliances, Matsushita outgrew the market by over 30 percent that quarter alone. Panasonic had never led Sony in camcorders in Japan. In mid-2001, Sony had a 40-point market share lead, which most people would call insurmountable. Yet within only a year and a half, the two were running neck and neck.

In some areas of the company, black box processes, like how to push up yields and push down inventories at the same time, proved more valuable than black box technologies themselves.

To get to the top two, and stay there, MEI uses a philosophy of universal design. What the company means by "universal design" is not quite what we mean in English. We take it to mean a common platform for use across multiple products, as car and computer manufacturers do. What MEI means is that each product should be designed for use by the most people possible. It should be universally accessible, by design.

Thus, MEI's digital still cameras are simple to use with extra-large LCDs and huge lettering in the menus, making it easy for people like me with PC vision—if it's 24 inches away it's in focus, otherwise it's not—to use them without bifocals. At the same time, these products, for those of us used to setting film cameras manually, are quite sophisticated. The 30-degree tilted-drum washer/dryer is a single unit that washes and dries clothes at the push of one button and is easy to use, even for someone in a wheel-chair. Kind of like making your TV remote simple: great idea, but who does it?

Universal design will have plenty of challenges in a global market of diverse needs, but it shows a deeper understanding of human behavior across multiple markets than MEI evinced be-fore. This is proving critical in sales. Universal design is the be-ginning of a new brand architecture that will revolutionize the company's *Panasonic Ideas For Life* positioning.

Toda's V Product management system runs deep in the com-pany. Over a nine-month period each year, a function/line matrix in every group proposes products that must meet the V Product criteria for universal design value added, profitability, and market impact. Along parallel tracks during the first two months, sales, marketing, technology, and universal design teams work on the product, which then goes to a two-phase process of review that re-ports directly to Toda. Once completed, the V Product is approved

V Product System

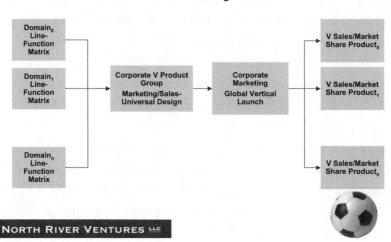

Domain$_0$ Line-Function Matrix			V Sales/Market Share Product$_0$
Domain$_1$ Line-Function Matrix	Corporate V Product Group Marketing/Sales-Universal Design	Corporate Marketing Global Vertical Launch	V Sales/Market Share Product$_1$
Domain$_n$ Line-Function Matrix			V Sales/Market Share Product$_n$

NORTH RIVER VENTURES LLC

and added to the lineup. Like the task forces, the V Product system ignores the Japanese hierarchy.

All groups move V Products in synch across the firm. The result is a companywide series of waves of new products flowing into the market and rejuvenating the brand.

The list of V Products is as wide as the company itself. The idea was to ensure that the responsibility first for recovery and then for growth was shared across divisions and not seen purely as the load to be shouldered by one group in a hot market. Matsushita was too big to be supported by one group as it had been in the past. Besides, everyone's attitude needed changing, no matter where they were in the company.

In this part of *Panasonic*, we are going to look at a few of these V Products. The first, ToughBook, shows how long it took Matsushita to internalize the possibilities for change in the early years of Kirk's reforms. But when it did, how deep the lesson was. The second, plasma display panels, where incoming CEO Fumio Ohtsubo won his spurs, shows how the company managed a fast changeover in a mature market, TVs, that was undergoing change so rapidly that it threatened to pass MEI by completely if the company stuck to its old way of doing business. The third, digital still cameras, shows how the accelerated pace of decision making allowed Matsushita to enter a market in which it had no experience and to crush the competition there within only a few years. The fourth, 30-degree tilted-drum washer/dryers, shows how a traditional market like white goods can be rethought from one end to the other just as the market for mass storage can be rethought. The fifth, automotive systems, shows the interaction of inventory and yield. And the sixth, semiconductors, shows MEI's focus on system LSI.

You will see how MEI drives OFCF through its V Product design and manufacturing processes and the mechanics of taking the shot out of the shot put and making a Soccer Ball.

Combining V Products, vertical launch, and universal design shortened time to market. In DVD recorders, for example, the company was able to introduce its DMR–50 generation worldwide in two months, starting in March 2003, compared to seven months for its predecessor, and to sell three times as many year over year. MEI gained the ability to hit the market hard in selected areas, something it had never done in its history and that, therefore, no one expected it to do. Moreover, as Ken Morita, who runs MEI's plasma display unit, pointed out, "You have to prepare substitutes for your product in advance and know how to exit at the right time."[130] The V Product system became more than the engine of product creation; it became the tree-pruning machine for the company, setting up de facto criteria for getting out of shrinking and unprofitable markets.

ToughBook

In 1994, Kirk Nakamura started the Panasonic Personal Computer Company in Secaucus, New Jersey, with only seven employees and got Martin Kono Consumer Electronics Company, now head of Panasonic, to run it. PPCC was one of Kirk's first experiments with the domain company structure he eventually used to transform Matsushita, and was the only U.S.-based unit company to morph into a full domain company.

The idea was to attack a profitable niche in the highly commoditized PC market with a line of hardened, milspec (military specification) PCs called ToughBooks. Successfully done, such a unit could tap profit pools in an otherwise margin-challenged business, secure sticky customers, and do a lot for the then suffering Panasonic brand. ToughBook became the prototypical universal design/V Product. Making it work took time and taught MEI a lot about what it would take for V Products to succeed in fast-changing IT-driven markets.

Matsushita had some experience in the personal computing business, but it had not been auspicious. Yoshi Yamada, now head of Panasonic North America, explained to me that in 1982, the company launched a hand-held product for the insurance business but sold only 120,000 units. In 1985, it attempted a transportable IBM-compatible with a built-in printer. But, as with many compatibles at the time, BIOS was a problem and production stopped in 1987. When the Phoenix BIOS came in, the compatible market finally started to move, and at the end of the 1980s, Matsushita began supplying products for Tandy (Radio Shack) but that did not go well and the company began selling laptops under the Panasonic name in 1990.[131]

Yamada had been in the United States during much of this time, returning to Japan in early 1990 to manage PC exports. In the early 1990s he revived the Tandy relationship, selling laptops to Grid Computer Systems, which Tandy had acquired in 1989 (and sold to AST in 1993), and which specialized in U.S. government business. Grid asked Yamada for a laptop with a magnesium cabinet, something he thought unusual, and it got him thinking. Grid, though Yamada didn't know it, was getting squeezed out of the PC market by the same forces of commoditization that were upending the PC business for everyone and was in the middle of a transition to niche milspec products that required hardened cases. Indeed, of the first generation of PC suppliers, only Apple remains, and only just. Yamada eventually sold magnesium-encased PCs to Grid, Tandy, Siemens-Nixdorf, and AT&T for marketing under their own names.

By 1994 Yamada was head of overseas marketing when a Panasonic dealer in Atlanta showed him an Itronix hardened PC and suggested that there was a great opportunity for these products among utilities and telephone companies for whom the need for automation was great—unionized labor was, and is, killing them—and for whom the average flimsy laptop was useless in tough, outdoor conditions. So he checked out Itronix. He looked at the number of employees, the price of their products ($8,000 to $10,000 each, a lot for a $2,000 PC) and realized they were selling into a profitable market with a good opportunity for growth. But the two companies did not compare. MEI had more PC engineers, more cash, and way more manufacturing expertise. None of this would have made any difference against then market leaders IBM, Compaq, and Dell. But, Yamada reasoned, it would be everything against a small guy like Itronix. Panasonic could hit the market in a much bigger way and sell the same product for $5,000, a great margin for Matsushita, but a huge hit for Itronix.

He returned to Japan and asked for a laptop that could be dropped a meter and that you could pour coffee and tea all over. To Japanese engineers, used to beating each other's brains out for the lightest and slimmest product on the market, Yamada was mad. The idea of making a great big ugly clunker to go up a cherry picker in a Kansas winter was off the wall. Besides, he wasn't sure he knew how big the market was.

Undaunted, in 1994, Yamada proposed that Kirk, who was then running the U.S. operation, start a sales company to sell hardened computers under the Panasonic name in the States. In 1995, Kono's Panasonic Personal Computer Company launched the ToughBook marque. But things weren't easy sailing. Itronix had a wireless component to its offering based on ARDIS (Advanced National Radio Data Service, originally a joint venture between IBM and Motorola and now the backbone of the BlackBerry system) and Matsushita had nothing. It took two years to catch up. Until it did, sales went nowhere.

Today, ToughBook sales are growing about 30 percent per annum and revenues per unit, growing at over 10 percent, are well over three times the industry's average selling price for a PC, which is shrinking. Hewlett-Packard, for example, is growing PC sales by only 8 percent and its margins in the business are less than half Matsushita's. Dell is growing one-third as fast and its margins are a third lower.

Matsushita derived a major lesson from ToughBook, even though it took close to two decades to learn. First, you *can* enter a highly commoditized business that regularly crushes everyone in it, and you can do very well, if you know where to point. It is possible to grow, take market share, and make money. But you have to be focused and move with determination. In the PC business, Matsushita stumbled around for years with all sorts of misfires before it got a global PC product that clicked. Today, Matsushita sells ToughBooks to British Gas, British Telecom, Deutsche Telekom, and Verizon, among others. In 2005, SBC ordered 22,000 ToughBooks packaged with the EDGE service of its Cingular wireless subsidiary. ToughBooks accompany U.S. forces in Iraq. A global business, started outside Japan like *Panasonic Ideas For Life*, and now a domain company in its own right, ToughBook became the prototype V Product.

For Matsushita, most of the change wrought by ToughBook was not in the product but in the global business operations it applies to its products. Get this right, MEI learned, and the company can focus quickly, something it had never really known about itself. Moreover, to be increasing unit prices and margins in a rapidly deflating business in which names like DEC, Wang, and Compaq have vanished is a singular achievement.

For Yamada himself, the success of ToughBook put him in a position to run Panasonic North America, and gave him officer rank in the company. The V Product system was beginning to breed the next generation of leadership.

Plasma Displays

Remembering that Matsushita, for all its manufacturing expertise in traditional electronics, had never been in a business remotely like plasma display panels, the fact that it now dominates the business worldwide is staggering. In a recent issue of *Consumer Reports*, Panasonic swept all plasma display panel (PDP) categories and all Quick Picks.[132] Matsushita finished 2005 with 46 percent of the U.S. plasma market and outsold the top LCD by nearly two to one.[133]

The way it did so is a lesson to everyone.

Plasma display panels are not for the fainthearted. Making them takes an investment of many billions, the type of risk Matsushita had never taken it its past. To make it in this business you have to have two things absolutely right: yield management and global mass marketing. Miss either one and you kiss off billions—in a month or two. This is a market where all the problems of collapsing price-performance, mass marketing, quality, and volume hit at once and in the same spot. To make it here you have to have a tolerance for pain. You can see why the executive at the head of PAVC, who was ultimately in charge of this drive, Fumio Ohtsubo, became CEO on Kirk's retirement.

A PDP is today's television, but it has nothing in common with the TV we grew up with. The analog TV we remember was based on cathode ray tubes invented by Karl Ferdinand Braun in 1897. These products and the techniques for manufacturing them are well understood and the industry is open to just about anyone. Prices came down over the decades, and features improved. But this industry had none of the violent price-performance downdrafts of the computer industry.

The main challenge of PDPs is that they go computers one better. For most of the last quarter century, PCs, for example, have been fairly even in price. You paid $2,000 for a new machine and every eighteen months or so you could expect the performance to double on the Moore Curve. In recent years, prices have fallen to under $1,000 as companies like Dell have made inroads in logistics and inventory management, stripping costs and functions out of the system, and manufacturing techniques have improved. Still, performance was the main variable; price was not.

In PDPs, however, price and performance both shift fast. A few years ago PDPs, which are very hard to make, cost tens of thousands. They will soon cost small fractions of that. The consumer capital to consumer disposable line is about to be crossed in plasma displays as it has been in cell phones. This is the first major market for big-ticket items to perform in such a way. Getting into it is tough, but staying in it is even tougher: one bad mention in Walt Mossberg's *Wall Street Journal* column, and you're toast.

To understand the risk in PDPs, think of a computer chip. It's small, often smaller than a stamp or a fingernail, and it is produced on a sheet of many chips at a time that is then cut as if by a cookie cutter into individual chips. If one is a dud, you throw it out. It's small and the loss is not so great, unless your yield rates are abysmal.

But a PDP, rapidly pushing north of 65 inches—some couches are smaller—is one gigantic computer chip. The entire single chip panel has to be made in a clean room—actually, a clean factory— and even small deficiencies in yield mean incredible wastage of immensely expensive items at the factory and large volumes of returns from customers. Poor yield hurts you twice: waste in the front end and collapsing customer service on the back end. PDPs are, therefore, a brand nightmare: tiny mistakes magnify quickly into a collapsed public image. Because PDPs are so large—they have already turned the movie industry into a first-run-in-the-home rather than a first-run-in-the-theatre business—a mess-up in PDPs will quickly infect you in other markets. If your PDP is lousy, why would I buy your camcorder, especially if you are trying to package them as a system, which is what Matsushita wants to do.

The line executive who had to make this work, Ken Morita, was put in charge of the PDP initiative in April 2000. Matsushita's share of the legacy TV business, he told me, was only 6 percent, typical of its shares of many markets at the time.[134] Masaaki Fujita, the head of the PDP Business Unit, added that MEI made 450 different models of TVs that took too many engineers and were too inefficient to be profitable.[135]

Morita recalled that while the company wanted parallel V Product successes, when he came to the PDP job, "the top priority of the firm was how to make a success of PDP." But, "we had no factory" for this kind of product.

Morita's last point is a big one. You can't just turn a CRT factory, or CRT employees, into a PDP operation. There is absolutely nothing in the CRT business that is helpful in its successor PDP business. This was not obvious to MEI at first and it came as something of a shock, Fujita recalled, "when we realized that the CRT business model simply wouldn't work."

Most companies faced with a discontinuity that requires such huge investments to cross leave the business or go under. The history of the last two hundred years is littered with such failures. In the late 1790s, my family owned the largest private shipbuilding yard in Europe. Their ships helped dispose of Napoleon, carry the China trade, and cement the British hold on India. In the 1850s and '60s, one of my forebears committed two mistakes at once: he declined to recapitalize the company by taking it public and he failed to move into the new technology of steam. By the end of the nineteenth century the company was an undercapitalized rump. By the mid-twentieth it had ceased to exist. In the computer age this process accelerated to the point where the CEO of DEC, Ken Olsen, could found his company in 1957, create the second-largest computer company in the world employing 100,000 people, be feted on the cover of *Fortune* magazine as America's leading industrialist, and just over a decade later see his company vanish. Forty years from start to finish. All because Olsen miscalculated discontinuities on two fronts: on one, the impact of PC price-performance on computer usage, and on the other, the cost advantages of Unix-based operating systems.

You would be excused, therefore, for saying that MEI was making a big mistake by rushing into PDPs. I certainly had my doubts. In the late 1990s, Sean and I were ushered into a meeting room in Osaka to discuss our thoughts on when high-definition TV would take off in the United States so MEI could properly time its PDP introductions there. We politely told the group—who we knew would find our answer hard to take—that HD was an over-the-air medium and that traditional over-the-air was dead. Only the poor got their TV signals that way. The middle classes got their TV signals from satellite, already digital if not yet HD, and cable, the owners of which had no desire to clog up their bandwidth with HD signals. Moreover, the appetite in Congress for mandating standards had vanished when President Carter deregulated much of U.S. industry two decades earlier. Reversing this was not in the cards.

We recommended that HD products be launched on the back of fast-growing storage media like DVDs and computer hard drives. These would handle plenty of HD content and would eventually drive consumer demand for live HD signals that would be delivered over fiber or high-capacity wireless from the local telephone pole. Eventually.

Moreover, since the demand for storage was known and the rate of its capacity increases could be planned with reasonable accuracy, Matsushita could control market timing and packaging, and gain an edge for its own technologies across a broad front. We explained that the products Matsushita contemplated were *not* TVs; they were computer displays. Take the TV part out of your brain, we said, and the display-plus-computer horsepower market begins to make a lot of sense. And, because the market is unregulated and free of standards, you can launch now without waiting.

Our audience listened and then, as if we had been blowing smoke, asked again when over-the-air HD would be introduced. At that point, I gave up hope that Matsushita had any real future in the TV business.

By 2000, a lot had changed. Under Ohtsubo, Sakamoto, and Morita, the company's PDP grand strategy was based on several things:

- Specialize in PDPs, the high-quality end of the flat-panel display business.

- Outinvest everyone in a series of rapid capacity increases so the company could take 40 percent+ market worldwide share by 2006, unheard of in the CRT business.
- Build alliances that offloaded areas where the company is weak or where it will never add value.
- Drive the number of manufacturing steps down quickly to less than 50 percent of start-up.
- Drive PDP energy consumption and manufacturing energy consumption down quickly.
- Launch every new product PDP at once worldwide, something MEI had never done.

Morita told me that he "thought this was a high risk, and when we looked at it we could not make a return. But we had the support of the CEO, for two reasons. First, MEI was long in the consumer electronics business where TV is big. Second, the larger flat panels were going to attract consumers." In a significant break with past practices, "once we decided to enter, we had to prepare plants, technologies, and people, and fill in what we didn't have with joint ventures."

Morita himself is from the integrated-circuit business and he realized at once that "we had to bring in IC experts." This changed decision making. In legacy products, "we had to consult many people. But here I made all the decisions myself and reported to the boss." This was the benefit of using IC people who knew how to make decisions quickly, again short-circuiting the Japanese hierarchy, and on a very large scale. "We have to plan," Morita said, "to make twenty million units." Or ten times the company's 2005 output.

When Fumio Ohtsubo first took me on a tour of his pilot PDP plant in Ibaraki in early July 2002, the power of Matsushita's thrust into the treacherous PDP market was clear. Two years later, Ohtsubo took me through the expanded Ibaraki operation, and in late 2005 I saw the giant new PDP plant at Amagasaki.

Yield-Output Curve

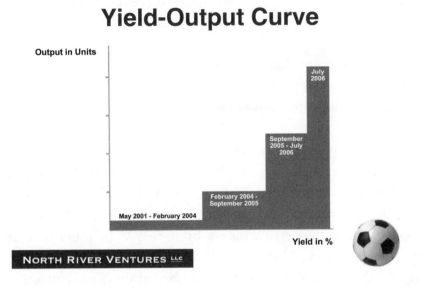

Output in Units

July 2006

September 2005 - July 2006

February 2004 - September 2005

May 2001 - February 2004

Yield in %

NORTH RIVER VENTURES LLC

The company put itself on a curve that was hard to beat: as the chart shows, it was pushing yield, volume, and market share way up and costs way down at the same time, accruing significant OFCF benefits at each step.

This may sound normal, and in traditional manufacturing it often is. But in the chip business, volume increases are often accompanied by a sharp drop in yield, with attendant customer service problems that take time to turn around. The reasons for this are complex and have a lot to do with the fragility of the chips and the disproportionate impact on quality of even small changes in production. Only the savviest chipmakers can double or triple output over and over again with minimal yield impact. The way they do this has much more to do with process management than with the specifics of manufacturing. Most companies stumble first on the making of the product and then fall hard on the management process. Picking themselves up is often publicly humiliating and leaves behind a lot of market share.

Morita told me that he felt MEI's success was based on three things:

- The ability to double capacity fast
- MEI's ever-higher yield rate
- The operation's profitability

Morita explained that the company has a proprietary method of continuous process simplification. As a result, he said, "Our yield went up even as our lead time went down."[136]

The contrast with ToughBook shows how much MEI learned about what is needed to take a high-risk V Product to market and make it stick. Matsushita today has a market share in PDP higher than it has ever had in any broad consumer electronics category. The company gets niche market shares and profits in a high-volume, big-ticket market. To do this, it had to go way beyond its manufacturing prowess, launching its PDPs simultaneously in all major world markets. This forced MEI not just to change how it made products, but to eliminate once and for all the deeply entrenched "parent alone" philosophy that had for decades encouraged the company to launch products in Japan first, iron out the kinks, secure volume advantages and control of manufacturing costs, and only then move into overseas markets. If you did this in a fast-moving digital market like PDP, you would be dead before you started. MEI had to launch everywhere at once, magnifying the risks of failure across the world stage, or not launch at all. It called this its vertical launch capability, about which I will write more later.

The PDP team was told bluntly to gain top market share within a month after release. The reason for this urgency was twofold. First, large parts of the company had to learn to compete in the world of rapidly deflating markets roiled by sharp shifts in price-performance and do it quickly or see the firm crushed. Second, to get to the company's 10 percent operating profit goal, it had to build up profitable growth businesses like PDPs faster than Matsushita's older businesses declined.

So the trick was, scale up a fast-deflating business profitably while managing down a business that wasn't just deflating. It was vanishing. Into the bargain, the whole thing had to work well enough to make up for the inevitable failures elsewhere in the V Product lineup. PDP itself was too big to fail.

Typically, Japanese companies are comfortable with a revenue bridge in nondeflating markets and focus more on market share than on earnings and shareholder value. Kirk, as we have seen, wanted to reverse this at MEI and PDP was to be his vehicle for doing so. If MEI could make it here, the rest of the company could as well. The message: get on the stick or get out.

First Matsushita had to develop a global platform for digital television in system LSI hardware and software. This black box, or proprietary core, is not as easy as it seems. Transmission standards differ around the world, and common modules had to serve them all. The platform uses the Linux operating system, which is robust and proven and, as open-source software, saves money.

Matsushita launched its PDP product in May 2001, pumping them out of its first Ibaraki plant at the rate of 30,000 a month. Seven months later the company opened its second Ibaraki factory and capacity climbed to 100,000 a month. Twenty months later, capacity jumped to 250,000 units a month with the opening of the Amagasaki plant. By the time this book is published, capacity will have reached 425,000 units a month with the opening of the second Amagasaki operation. Productivity has more than quadrupled during this ramp-up. In addition, the first Amagasaki factory was built in five months, three weeks ahead of schedule. It started production in just over nine months, two months ahead of plan. And it did so without a significant drop in yield, allowing Matsushita to drive step function increases in volume at high quality. Indeed, yield rates are now far above those achieved by the competition.

Where the initial plan called for a new factory every two years, Matsushita can get a 1.6 million-square-foot plant up and running in well under one.

But just before launch in Europe, the company discovered a glitch in panel circuitry, which is more complex than in most PCs, and had to fly 10,000 fixed units in four jumbo jets to make the launch date.

This quality problem brings up the main challenge facing Matsushita in improving yield. In this business, getting to 95 percent is only half the battle. It is usually twice as hard to get the next 3 percent and twice as hard again to get to 99 percent+. But once above this threshold, there are more opportunities for improving processes, which can eliminate whole steps in production, driving costs down further still. In addition, the PDP itself is only one-third the cost of the final display. The rest is in housing and electronics, offering lots of opportunities for major cost cutting.

The lesson here is that managing the capacity-yield curve well creates an operating free cash flow machine. Well positioned on this curve, Matsushita can pressure competitors as much, or as little, as it wants. For many, that is not a fun prospect. And coming from "Maneshita," it is unexpected.

Digital Still Cameras

The difference between digital still cameras and PDPs is that while Panasonic had a long history in the legacy TVs that PDPs replace, it never made film cameras and had only modest experience in DSCs. Matsushita Kotobuki and Kyushu Matsushita both commercialized products in 1997. But with the digital discontinuity, Kirk Nakamura and Kazuo Toda, his domestic marketing chief, both recognized an opportunity to launch a new DSC line and seize share quickly. If they could execute this move fast enough, Matsushita would have another high-selling, profitable V Product to reinforce its revenue bridge. DSC could be the first of MEI's "create" phase products, something entirely new, and if it succeeded, it would open a large new market for the company.

The risks were high: Matsushita would have to move quickly, something it was not used to doing, and into a market in which it had no experience. To make sure everyone was focused, Kirk ran the kickoff meeting personally.

The results of Matsushita's DSC efforts were astonishing. From a standing start in late 2001, by 2005 Panasonic was selling four million cameras worldwide, was number two in the Japanese market and closing fast on the market leader, Canon. Konica-Minolta left the camera market in January 2006,[137] the once mighty Olympus was at the exit door, and Sony was not far behind. Panasonic will soon have 10 percent of an eighty-million-unit global DSC market that is growing at 15 percent a year. In several Asian markets like Singapore, Hong Kong, and New Zealand, Panasonic's share is already 10 percent. Indeed, Panasonic's share in Asia, the world's fastest-growing and biggest DSC market, is its biggest share outside Japan.

But Mamoru Yoshida, who now runs the DSC business, reasoned that the risks were not so great. "We got into this business because we had all the basics already in house."[138] The company had decades of experience in video, optical zoom lenses, CCDs, and System LSIs that could be brought to bear at speed. It had a strong position in batteries since the days of its founder, and is known for battery management technology that gives its batteries a longer life than those of the competition, something camera users value highly. The company is part of the SD consortium and uses SD memory cards widely. But it had yet to leverage its SD investment into something big, and Kirk thought DSC was a killer app. Critically, Panasonic had brand recognition and large sales channels in every major market worldwide.

For the first time since Konosuke left the scene a generation earlier, an MEI CEO personally initiated a new product category and drove it through to completion. Like PDP, DSC was to be an example to all the other parts of the company of what Matsushita needed: innovation, speed, sales, and profit. Kirk kicked off DSC in October 2000, only a few months after becoming CEO. He pulled together all his top executives to manage the process—Toda, who was then running AVC, Koike from semiconductors, and Ohtsubo, who was the leader-in-waiting at AVC—and by November of the next year the first product was on the market. By taking a leading role, as he did in PDP, he made it clear to everyone that he was accountable: if he failed in DSC, he would go.

As elsewhere, Matsushita accelerated product introduction by making up for what it didn't have through joint ventures. Leica, for example, makes Panasonic's DSC lenses. West Electric makes the flash. LCDs come from Toshiba. This allows MEI to concentrate on CCD, System LSI, SD media, optics, and a part of the business that is almost as old as the company itself, batteries.

In 2002, Panasonic DSCs incorporated Matsushita's proprietary optical image stabilization technology, a critical feature given the susceptibility of point-and-shoot digital cameras to shutter shake and shutter delay. MEI also used its twenty years of video camera experience to put its aspherical lenses, of which it is the number one supplier to the global still and video camera industry, into its DSC to dramatically shorten focal lengths. To further ease the world of the point-and-shoot photographer, Panasonic launched its Venus line of image-processing LSI ICs designed to shorten shutter response and increase color saturation.

Yoshida told me that because the company had never been in film cameras and had done poorly in early DSCs, "Panasonic was not the first brand in cameras. We had to build a brand. We learned from our past failures that we had to create an entirely new image in cameras. We had to make it a full-scale commercial brand that could handle data and communications and be as useful for the professional as for the consumer."

Matsushita's goal in DSC is to create a new Panasonic photo culture that replaces the "Kodak Moment" of film days. Not only will those moments be delivered in a moment, something Kodak could not do using film, but they will be delivered directly through several media from storage, like SD and DVD, through wireline and wireless networks, to multiple Panasonic systems designed to manage these images simply and easily, especially its Viera line of plasma TVs.

On the user interface side, Panasonic pioneered the elimination of parallax lenses in point-and-shoot cameras, turning most of the entire back of the camera into a large, clear LCD, making composition much easier and allowing space for easy-to-read menus. I've long been a fan of Nikon film cameras and was surprised by the degree to which Panasonic point-and-shoot DSCs can be set manually for almost any condition. Ten years ago, when I first started advising Kirk, my son said to me with all the disgust that an eleven-year-old boy could muster, "You tell your friend Mr. Nakamura that kids today don't care about Panasonic. He has nothing for us." Needless to say, I didn't forward this abrasive message. But, a decade later, on July 4, 2006, acquaintances of ours put on an extravagant—$30,000 worth—fireworks display at a local lake. People came from all over to see this. Chris shot some video clips with an FX8 that he uploaded onto his Apple with its 21-inch display, running the sound through a stereo attached to the computer. The results were impressive. Shooting fireworks in film takes considerable skill. Chris just pointed the FX8 and took a set of 30-second clips. With sound. He sat back from the computer and said, "This camera is just amazing. The color saturation is incredible. It's the coolest thing I own." No small praise from a man who now makes his living as a theater lighting designer.

30-Degree Tilted-Drum Washer/Dryer

We don't see the Panasonic name on home appliances in North America, which is a shame. Some of them, like the tilted-drum integrated washer/dryer, are exceptional. Even without North America, however, Yoshitaka Hayashi, president of the Home Appliances Company, told me that his company is the most profitable in MEI and, with the merger with MEW, the largest and most profitable home appliances operation in the world.[139] This is due in large part to a curious result of the V Products system that I call the quantum effect.

In most of its computerized product line from DSCs to PDPs and ToughBooks, Matsushita behaves like a computer company; its new products hit the market in a rapid succession of blows hammering in ever greater price-performance along the Moore Curve. For most of the last half century, growing markets counteracted the deflationary impact of price-performance. Unit numbers always outpaced the drop in price. Even when demand for one generation of computers, like mainframes, slowed down, the demand for processing power kept growing quickly, shifting to newer markets like minicomputers, then PCs, and so on.

In white goods, Matsushita behaves unlike a computer company, selling either into mature, first-world markets with long replacement cycles or into fast-moving emerging economies like China. Either way, the white goods business is dominated by demographics, not processing power. You may be able to move a PC or digital camera owner rapidly through many generations of ever more powerful devices, or, like PDPs, you may be able to sell several to one home, but you cannot sell washers and dryers this way. You can sell only one washing machine to each home where it stays for years, while you can sell cameras and cell phones to individuals who may replace them in months. Either you ride a strong replacement cycle with a technological discontinuity, or you crack a new market, or both. Demographics determine the shape of the market.

Matsushita's V Product quantum effect comes from having a companywide system for driving digital and nondigital markets with sequential waves of infotech-like disruption. These waves allow the company to seek the value high ground in all its markets. This makes MEI like and unlike a computer company at the same time.

The result of this disarmingly simple stratagem—which would be impossible to do without a powerful digital product line to show the way—is a rapid series of product introductions that take shares of as much as 50 percent in the most profitable segments of the market. Doing this, Matsushita has effectively replaced its weak and broad-based product line with a much smaller one that is growing faster than the market and making a lot of money for the company.

The example here is the 30-degree tilted-drum washer/dryer. It is hard to think of anything special one can do with a washing machine and dryer. These products have long been commoditized, and suppliers forced into a decades-long struggle to make money as margins became razor thin and product development resources evaporated. The result of this downward cycle was a failure in demand creation. Customers have no reason to choose one product over another except for price, and perhaps reputation, neither of which offers the kind of differential advantage that creates enduring, profitable, long-term customer loyalty.

The big choice in washers and dryers is not so much function—they all work pretty much the same way—but whether they are top-loaded, as North Americans preferred until recently, or front-loaded, in the European tradition. They can, of course, be stacked to save space. And there is some variation in color, but not much. Creating new demand is not easy in this kind of market.

Into this unpromising market Kirk Nakamura insisted that Matsushita launch V Products with universal design characteristics simultaneously in multiple markets worldwide, and keep launching them. This meant rethinking the tried and true from scratch. The result was the 30-degree tilted-drum washer/dryer.

My first encounter with this washer/dryer came two years earlier, in late July 2004, when my wife Verna and I were visiting the Matsushita House of Technology in Osaka. Her father had just died and mine was to die shortly. We both had experience with the elderly and their problems doing simple things like washing clothes and dishes. Large products are often big, cumbersome, and hard to use. Increasing numbers of the elderly are moving into assisted-living facilities where space is at a premium and where ease of use is a blessing. Ease of use of major appliances can give distant relatives, even those close by, considerable comfort: Dad and Mom are not struggling to clean their clothes or wash their dishes.

At the House of Technology we saw all the things you would expect, like the latest plasma displays, cameras, and so on. But what really blew us away was the washer/dryer. First, the door opens on a single hinge at a 30-degree angle, making it easy for anyone to reach into. Even at six feet, I have trouble reaching into the bottom of my Maytags at home. With the 30-degree machine you can reach into the bottom from a wheelchair. There are no rough edges, and the door shuts with a light touch. Better still, you put in your clothes and the detergent, close the door, push a button, and do nothing until the clothes are completely dry. Not spun dry, but completely dry. And, our guide told us, the machine takes relatively little water, an increasingly scarce commodity in much of the world.

Verna took one look at this thing and said, "Every assisted-living facility on the planet." Then it hit me, a new category of washer/dryer sitting right in front of the greatest demographic event in market history: the tsunami of aging, rich consumers. Verna was so excited about this that when we stopped in Tokyo Station the next day for coffee with Harry Fujita, who managed our Japan trip and later arranged all the interviews and supporting data for this book, she was so forceful in her insistence on the market value of the product that we nearly missed our train to Narita and the flight back to New York.

When preparing *Panasonic*, I asked Matsushita to show me the product. In truth, I was presold. In March 2006, I went to the Laundry Systems Business Unit in Osaka to meet management and get some data on sales results.

At the Toyonaka City home of the Laundry Systems Business Unit, Kyosuke Kimura described the design and sales history of the product, known as the NAV series. The biggest challenge Matsushita had was to create a new washing culture in order to get out of the vicious cycle of commoditization and margin erosion. Previous products had been Japan-centric, solid products in a market of homogeneous competition that were built quickly and cheaply with existing technology. The new focus of the team was not on what to build but why. To do this the company looked at a range of factors:

- The environment
- The use of detergents
- Changing patterns in the lives of users
- Washing machine concepts
- Soiled clothes changing in type and use
- Housing patterns

The team also noticed that there are large secular shifts in washing machine styles every decade or so, and that the market was ready for a new cycle, but that no one had introduced information and knowledge technologies into the sector. Perhaps adding more design value to the product area could change the nature of clothes washing in its entirety, provoke a replacement cycle, and give Matsushita a powerful lead with a premium product where none had existed for generations. A break with the past had to be something for which there was no existing comparison table with other products, but which jumped out at buyers with its obvious usefulness and simplicity. Very un-Maneshita.

The company spent large amounts of time looking at how men, women, and children wash clothes, noting especially the angle of the body as it stoops and bends to load and unload washing and drying machines in a range of configurations and sizes. A tilted-drum made the most sense.

As in many other areas, like digital still cameras, Matsushita had spent some years before the V Products initiative experimenting with next-generation washers and dryers. The SK 60 front loader came out in 1997, and variations on a tilted-drum theme came out in 2001 and 2002. But the V Product discipline with its tight timeline for repeated waves of new products, and focus on value goods driving lifestyle changes, forced the team to think hard and come up with results quickly.

The idea of a tilted drum was not new, but there are several major problems with it. Tilted drums have inherent vibration problems that make them difficult to use reliably. Foam is "the archenemy of drum washing" Kimura said, but Japanese consumers prefer to see their clothes washed in foam because this convinces them that the job is being done. And the drying process had to be reconfigured to work properly.[140]

In addition to these problems, the Laundry Products Systems Group had to meet Kirk Nakamura's green strategy of products that take fewer resources to make and fewer to use than existing products. Kimura told me that the Japanese were used to top loaders that use a lot of water. Moreover, the Japanese believe that more water cleans better. Reduce water consumption and you risk convincing people that their clothes are not clean, scarcely a desirable result.

So the company not only had to change the culture of washing clothes, it also had to reeducate consumers about basic value perceptions. The two may look like the same thing, but anyone who has tried to compete with an iPod knows that just changing how consumers buy something does not mean automatic success in how they value it, and vice versa. Getting both right is tough. And Matsushita had to get it right in several countries at once, something that it really had never tried, in any product anywhere in the company.

When MEI's first tilted drum washer/dryer, the NA-V80, hit the Japanese market in late 2003, it took off like a rocket. The initial plan was to sell 80,000 units a year but Matsushita soon sold 250,000. Because of the volume of preorders, the NA-V80 entered the Japanese market in fourth place and four weeks later ranked first and did so at a ¥50,000 ($425) premium over washers and dryers sold as pairs. This premium was cut a bit by the cost of a stand to mount a washer and dryer one above the other in the same footprint as the NA-V80, but not by much. MEI had cracked an important piece of marketing code. You can take large shares of established, even stagnating, markets if you know how to manage technological discontinuities. And the way to do this is with the V Product quantum effect.

The NA-V80 uses 20 percent less water than a front loader and 40 percent less than a top loader. Exhaust air is condensed into water and expelled, eliminating costly ducting, filters, and the ever-present risk of lint buildup and fire in exhaust ducts that are overly long. During its first year, the NA-V80 won design awards in Japan, China, and even the United States, where it has not been introduced.

MEI only rarely attempted to create market discontinuities before the reform period. With the NA-V80, the company broke with this tradition, but did it in a business as far removed from information technology as possible, setting powerful new directions for the rest of the firm.

Matsushita had learned a vital lesson: study contemporary

clothes washing anthropology and you can sell fast-moving products at a premium. As Konosuke had drilled home half a century
earlier, add real value for people and you will make a lot of
money. And if you aren't making money, don't blame the competition; ask all over again what it is you need to do to add value.
Discounts are never the answer to the "how do we add value"
question.

Central to the V Products discipline, however, is the drive for
repeat hits within each category. So, having moved the NA-V80 to
the top of the market, it had to be replaced—the quantum effect—
with a new generation within three years. In December 2005, two
years after the introduction of the NA-V80, Matsushita launched
the VR1000. This product used a simple air-conditioning heat
pump—Matsushita is a major supplier of air conditioners—to get
the fastest drying speed in the industry and cut energy costs by 54
percent over the V80. To do this, Kimura showed me, Matsushita
fit the heat pump into dead space at the bottom of the tilted drum.
The team then introduced lower-temperature drying to minimize
damage to clothes, something that we in North America don't always think about because dryer damage is a way of life and new
clothes are relatively cheap. But in emerging economies like China
where disposable incomes are squeezed, this is no small advantage.
The VR1000 cut drying time by 46 percent into the bargain.

The VR1000 cut water consumption from 150 liters (40 gallons) to 69 (18 gallons), in part by introducing a warm-water jet
foam process. Water consumption is an increasingly big problem
in cities like New York, which looks like a water-soaked seaport,
but which is built on rock, retains little water, and suffers periodic
droughts. Even Japan cannot count on unlimited supplies of fresh
water, and large parts of the emerging world, especially China,
certainly cannot. With the tilted drum, MEI increased the rate of
information substitution for water and electricity, giving its customers significant control over their energy and water bills. MEI
has similar strategies elsewhere, like refrigeration. The Kusatsu

plant developed a new, easy-to-process insulating material for only $3,600 that is ten times more efficient than conventional material. It reduces energy consumption by 83 percent over the materials the company was using in its refrigerators in 1992. The new material is flexible and can be expanded to other commodities like cooking appliances, cars, PCs, and housing products.

MEI's newest tilted-drum washer/dryer entered the Japanese market ranked fifth, hit second place in a month, and quickly gained a 55 percent market share.

Matsushita did for clothes washing what Apple did for the iPod: create a new category (in Apple's case, managing entertainment), enter fast, dominate the category, and keep hitting the market with new products and new uses for those products that push the competition off a cliff. Rather than thinking of washers and dryers as products that can be tweaked a bit every year, but that otherwise sit in stores waiting for consumers to order replacements for worn-out parts, Matsushita decided to reinvent the concept of laundry from the ground up and then force the replacement cycle by coming up with a universal design–based product run through its V Products discipline and take the market by storm.

The tilted drum showed that the company could act like a computer company in two different, and far removed, spaces at the same time. Quantum weirdness as industrial strategy. For the competition, this is a threat. Most white goods specialists are just that, white goods specialists. MEI is an information specialist in the white goods business. It has a proprietary system for driving IT thinking into an otherwise bland market. This is seriously disruptive; it relieves Matsushita of the obligation to keep following up uncompetitive me-too products while increasing that obligation on its competitors. The quantum effect thus allows home appliances to inhale OFCF in a low-margined business, which is very hard to do. The lesson: Be an information specialist in *all* your markets.

Automotive Systems

The PDP story is about a hot new technology where Matsushita is doubling production every few months while maintaining high yield rates and crushing the competition with unremitting blows at their price-performance. Automotive systems are the polar opposite. This is a story of selling strong volumes into an established market—cars are consumer capital, the demand for which is reasonably well understood—where price-performance pressures are low, relatively, and where quality and logistics count for everything. What matters here are complex inventory and yield relationships that work the velocity of cash so critical to the Soccer Ball System.

This is also a story of a core MEI product in a troubled industry where the market shares of MEI's customers are shifting fast and their financial stability is questionable. Improving cash and capital environments in an industry like this is taxing. When Delphi entered Chapter 11, Panasonic Automotive Systems could have found itself on the hook for sizable sums. Only the deft moves of its managers avoided serious pain. Even Japan's much praised auto business is under assault. Mitsubishi has had years of troubles; Nissan went through painful restructuring and is trying to reconfigure itself in the North American market; Suzuki and Mazda may not make the next round. In North America, the entire industry is being roiled by market turbulence, and Europe, with one or two exceptions, is faring no better. MEI's mission is to sell into this mess and do it well and profitably.

At the same time, the car audio systems in which Matsushita specializes are becoming automotive information systems that keep drivers and passengers informed as much as entertained. Automotive navigation systems, already integrated with audio systems and a range of inputs and mass storage like CDs and SDs, are about to undergo even more changes as Toyota, for example, experiments with ultra-wideband wireless frequencies to exploit imaginative automotive information "environments."

Into this mix, automotive information systems are increasingly part of the branded in-car environment that automakers use to differentiate themselves. As BMW found with its iDrive system, this is easy to get wrong, and the branding risks are high. In such a scale-driven business, if a mistake in auto information systems cuts share even a small amount, the bottom line can be holed easily.

For this reason, car makers long relied on their suppliers to a degree only now being discovered by suppliers to retail powerhouses like Wal-Mart, and computer makers like Dell. Suppliers of automotive information systems have to deliver products that are easy to use, that don't fail, and that minimize inventories. This means a level of operational integration with customers that all businesses will have to imitate. The way PAS meets its operational challenges shows what everyone else will have to deal with sooner rather than later. Reflecting its leading edge position, PAS is Matsushita's only fully integrated domain with its own salesforce. Indeed, it is hard to imagine how anyone unfamiliar with the complexities of auto manufacturing could sell its systems.

In the worst of timing, just as Matsushita's reforms began and the tech crash threatened, PAS miscalculated Toyota's needs and wound up with a large inventory of products it could not sell. This forced the company to rethink how it operated. But when it tried to prevent a recurrence by cutting inventories, PAS found it had no way of doing this with its existing management and factory systems. PAS was forced to rethink its way of doing business. Yoshio Momose, assistant superintendent of the Matsumoto factory, told me, "We were appalled. We didn't know what to do. We had 560 employees and we were losing money. Unless we cut inventory we weren't going to make it. We had to understand reality and look at it square in the face."[141]

When it began, the changeover from conveyor lines to cell production and introduced the Toyota production system, Momose said, PAS quickly "realized that there were so many things that we didn't understand in detail." The biggest single problem, he explained, was that PAS worked on an inventory-heavy push system where production was calculated based on materials on hand. Toyota works the other way around, on a pull system, as Wal-Mart and Dell do, and sets demand backward from customer orders, using advanced communications to transmit purchase requirements into the supply chain in real time. Momose put this painfully: "We can understand this intellectually, of course, but the details of doing it are completely different from what we had ever done."

Meeting this challenge made Panasonic Automotive one of the first Matsushita operations to switch to cell manufacturing and slash inventories. Between 2001 and 2004, all eighteen production lines at the Matsumoto factory were switched to sixty-three cells and eight outsourced conveyor lines. The yield-inventory curve moved down. Productivity rose 150 percent, yields rose, and production more than tripled. While this made customers easier to serve, it made the yield questions multidimensional and that much harder to answer.

The company's yield rates are so high today that it frequently gets zero defects for *months* at a time. For those familiar with manufacturing, this is both a blessing and a curse. Defects have causes and these can be identified and fixed. Zero defects are the absence of something that can be identified. Which means that you get good results for reasons that you don't understand. But it is as important to know why something is perfect as to know why something else is imperfect. Zero defects, therefore, while the elusive gold standard of manufacturing, raise more questions than they answer. "Even now," Momose said, "some parts of the factory and some of the people understand this; others do not."

What Matsushita found, as most companies do in this position, is that testing products in stages is part of the problem. Hewlett-Packard learned years ago that as each test stage approaches six sigma quality (99.9999 percent yield), there is no

Yield-Inventory Curve

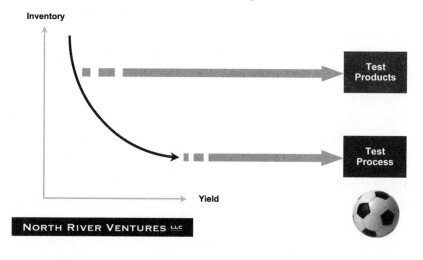

longer any point to testing the stage. Stage testing must be replaced by sophisticated systems for testing the entire process. Kouichi Hanada, manager of the plant management control team at Matsumoto, said this raised another challenge, that people are naturally reliant on inspection. But to analyze the process itself and to rely on it is much more complex.[142] In the past, for example, the factory ran routine overruns to make up for yield problems. Momose added, "We were relieved to have inventories. Now we have turned this thinking upside down."

PAS makes electronic toll collection systems, engine control units for managing engines, and smart entry systems, as well as DVD and CD decks, car navigation systems, and audio systems. Adding to its challenge in managing the yield-inventory curve is that it makes over 400 different models, some in very short runs—as little as one unit a day—that are scarcely economic but that must be made in order to keep the loyalty of major accounts. Moreover, the 400+ models can require as many as 1,200 line changes a month. This requires in-depth understanding of variable lot production.

Deliveries, too, are an issue. Most car factories run two shifts and each one takes four deliveries, meaning that PAS has to work its high-quality variable-lot system over eight deliveries a day. In addition, what the company learns has to be globalized, that is, it has to be translated from the Matsumoto mother plant to company factories in Thailand, China, Taiwan, the United States, Mexico, and the Czech Republic.

The company's challenge is to cut inventories and increase productivity and yields while doubling the number of deliveries it makes to customer production lines every day over a highly variable-lot production across a broad range of products.

The risk in the pull system is that while car makers still make forecasts that they use as indicators of future business, there is nothing firm about this and when the orders come in from customers there is always a discrepancy and the inventory risk gets pushed back on suppliers. Suppliers like PAS are car model–driven, not car maker–driven. That is, they are tied to certain models of Toyota, say, rather than to the company as a whole. When manufacturers plan a new model, they send auditors in to review all operations before they place an order, and often demand changes in the production system. Thus, the variable-lot system is also variable by car model and manufacturer so that inventory-yield issues are multidimensional. Nonetheless, Momose told me, "with our push system, we could not see the business. With pull we can actually see what is going on."[143]

The inventory-yield curve gives MEI two benefits. One, PAS gets improved tools for driving the velocity of cash. Two, PAS gets deeper levels of operational integration with customers so that it understands more about what drives their velocities of cash. Combined, these are core to major account management. What makes Panasonic tick in automotive is manufacturing DNA harnessed to what, in the Soccer Ball System, is the most critical thing of all: outbound logistics. No matter how well you make a product, if you can't deliver it effectively enough to impact directly your customers' working capital and your own, you can't compete.

Semiconductors

Like Kirk Nakamura himself, several of MEI's top executives experimented with reform long before the corporate-wide movement began in 2000. One of them, Susumu Koike, is chief technology officer and, when I met him, was president of the semiconductor company. Unlike the rest of MEI, which found change painful, radical change is part of the IC culture. "All the employees here have the background to understand the situation," Koike told me. "At least we have a culture that if the leadership asks for changes, we can, because we have always changed. It goes with the territory."[144] It is safe to say that no group in MEI understands management decisions in Moore Time better.

For MEI, this soft asset—the institutionalized understanding of the need for change and willingness to accept it—was rare when reforms started and this made Koike and his group central to their success. Elsewhere, MEI had strong and experienced individuals. Here it had an entire team.

Moreover, semiconductors have an outsized importance for MEI. When I interviewed Kirk in late 2005 for *Panasonic*, he pushed across the table a single 8″ × 6″ piece of paper that he had cut from a presentation. On it was an arrow showing the progressive consolidation of seventeen 250-nanometer DVR-R LSI chips in 2000, when he became CEO, to a single 65-nm System LSI in 2006, the year he planned to retire. The core of the company's rapid ascendance was on this curve. He was almost saying to me, "Chips and cash velocity, that's it."

By their nature, ICs are independent of the rest of the firm; there is a lot you can do to reform this part of the business without pushback from the other parts. The business also has to be out front to survive and investment commitments have risen sharply with each new IC generation. At the same time, however, while semiconductors have outgrown the electronics sector as a whole for the last decade, Japanese suppliers like MEI have lived through a major bust every four and one-quarter years.

So, you invest a fortune and get whacked before you can recover capital. This is a rough business. If you want to stay in it, you had better have a business model that can take a beating.

Koike's team faced two Moore Time cycles: their own in semiconductors; and the separate cycles of the products they support, like digital video recorders, where a generation might last three months and where price-performance drops are usually two or more times those in PCs, which are brutal enough as it is. In addition, the Big Bang chart (page 105) shows that the market is being turned upside down. What was a market decades ago for a few IC-based devices per business and soon became a market for IC devices per home, is now a market for multiple devices per person. The old TV market is about 150 million sets a year. Cell phones move in multiples of that. Future IC-driven devices will sell in the billions. And they will be cheap. To deal with this, Koike said, his team created a new business model based on three points:

- System LSI is like sushi—eat it quick—and must be a development-led rather than a capital-led business.
- Capital recovery, therefore, is the priority.
- Development efficiency, not manufacturing, is the source of competitive value-added.

Nothing is more contrary to MEI's manufacturing tradition. Koike's team, in effect, proposed reversing the way MEI thinks about its business. By getting an early start on this kind of thinking, the Semiconductor Company became core to MEI's new understanding of how the company should operate.

MEI's Semiconductor Company has a long history. Started as a joint venture with Philips in 1952, the Matsushita Electronics Corporation was folded into MEI in 1993 and became a domain company in April 2001. It is not a small operation, employing 16,000 people in seven countries, but neither is it anything like as large as Intel, which at $36 billion is half the size of MEI itself. Most of what Semiconductor makes is for consumer electronics and most of this is for the merchant market. So, while it has a strong captive business, it remains exposed to the vagaries of the global market where it ranks fourteenth in size by sales.

To survive in this market, the Semiconductor Company's strategy was to create the industry's first System LSI in sectors that are critical to the company's own V Products and to the merchant market:

- Optical disks
- Digital TVs
- Mobile communications
- Image sensors
- Automotive electronics

SC intends to create de facto standards by becoming the world's first mass producer of 65-nanometer system LSIs, and acquiring IPRs and technologies that allow a rapid recovery of investment. Central to Semiconductor's ability to gain share fast is its PDP-like ability to move to progressively smaller architectures while keeping yield high, slashing costs, and cutting the energy needed to both make and use its products.

Doing this will support MEI's V Products, like digital still cameras, on the one hand, and make it a leader in the merchant market on the other. Thus the Semiconductor Company would become a meaningful contributor to MEI's V-sales/profit bridge.

To Koike, "The key in digital consumer products is fast software development and knowing how to turn this software around fast. There is also the problem of obsolescence. We have to recover the costs of software development as soon as possible and sell the products as soon as possible."[145]

To make this work effectively, Semiconductor is consolidating hardware and software platforms in mobile phones, personal audiovisual (still and video cameras), automotive audiovisual, home audiovisual (PDPs, DVDs, networks), and home security into a single platform, UniPhier. This new CPU/media processor combined with a multimedia processing library should cut IC development costs, make software easier to develop and integrate, and increase cross-domain leverage, all things that were missing in the old business model. By cutting out specific platforms for individual products, the Semiconductor Company increased development efficiency two to three times and expects this to reach five times in the near future. Sharing digital TV software assets, for example, cut development man-hours 60 percent and a common DSP (digital signal processor) in the UniPhier core cut 30 percent.

Even this limited degree of vertical integration has its pitfalls, as all vertical systems do. When MEI's cell phone division, a pillar in the V Products sales bridge, ran into trouble, it caused the Semiconductor Company considerable pain by slowing sales of one of its core products. By taking the top off Semiconductor's growth potential, the mobile telephone group hit MEI with a double whammy.

Risks like these make operational controls vital. To keep yields high during product scale changes, the company created proprietary process acceptance criteria (PAC) for setting yield criteria in advance and working back from these into manufacturing and development. In the past, MEI had launched a product and then tried to ratchet up yields, always a tough, and often fruitless, process. Koike put it bluntly: "Improving yield incrementally is a mistake and bad practice."

PAC was Koike's own idea, and he told me, "There was a lot of resistance. Many people felt that they could come up with the same results without changing our methods. PAC cost ¥2 billion ($17 million) to do but the head of R&D said, 'Just give me the money and I'll give you the yield.' But now we have results, they are all converts." PAC is today standard operating procedure in many parts of the company, like PCC for example, where it is central to getting products to market quickly, reducing time for decision making, and getting to zero defects. The system is designed from one end to the other to drive OFCF in its own right and to create the discontinuities that drive OFCF for other domains by shifting the basis of competition away from price, allowing the new Matsushita to position itself in the value end of its Pragmatic Visionary BrandDriver.

Matsushita's Soccer Ball Operations

In a previous section, we saw how, with the prototypical V Product the ToughBook, it took Matsushita nearly a decade to generate growth and profitable domination of a fast-moving niche. Then we saw how, starting in 2000, the company compressed this cycle into months with the production of plasma TVs and digital still cameras. Following this, we looked at MEI's "quantum effect," its ability to act like a computer company and unlike a computer company at the same time by applying computer industry cycles to home appliances like the NA-V80 tilted-drum washer/dryer.

Here I will pull all these lessons together to show how MEI did this by translating my Soccer Ball Metrics into a set of operations that became a cross-company value engine. This section is the interface between my cash and capital velocity output based system—set your goals and work the decision tree back from those goals to determine your action plan—and the mechanics that MEI uses to make this work.

The application of these Soccer Ball Operations, as I call them, across so many parts of the company allowed the firm to take quick advantage of its reorganization, getting the most out of its domain companies and its newly acquired affiliates long before another company, faced with the same challenges, would have been able to. In addition, the system shifted the company from selling everything to everyone, regardless of margin, to a focused company that sells fast-growing, profitable products at a premium.

Such a reversal of direction looks to many, especially in Japan, like an elimination of the Konosuke Matsushita system. In fact it is not. It takes Konosuke's core strategy—put the company closer to its customers than the competition is—and applies it for the modern world where falling information costs drive disintermediation and flatten business organizations everywhere.

What you will see here is not the genius of Kirk Nakamura, who initiated the system, but a complex collective genius that extends far beyond his top team leaders, most of whom we have met in past sections, and deep into the factory floor and to marketing teams who have to devise these operations and make them work every day.

The more you understand about what MEI has done, the more it is apparent that the company established a powerful cross-sector system that will be difficult for competitors to displace.

MEI's biggest weakness in the late 1990s, as I described it in the introduction, was a Niagara Falls approach to products: pour as much product as possible across the broadest possible range in the most geographic markets with no coordinated brand, image, customer experience, or market impact. This diffusion of effort blunted any attempt by any group or executive, no matter how senior or influential, to make the firm enduringly profitable.

Moreover, this system had little proprietary advantage; MEI made mostly commodity products like TVs that had more in common with their competition than not. With this system, MEI had no choice but to compete on price, which meant putting its margins at risk with every sale.

In turn, salesmen around the world, who had the least impact on decisions, were made accountable for the success of the whole upstream operation. Naturally, so long as this dichotomy between accountability and authority continued to widen, effective decision making, or even knowing what to base decisions on, was elusive.

Also, as we saw in the section about *Panasonic Ideas For Life*, in 2000 MEI was not a single-company, multibrand entity like Procter and Gamble or Unilever with well-managed brands in each unit. Rather, it was a highly diffused multicompany, multibrand entity that was impossible to market effectively.

In order for a unified brand platform to have any effect, even after its reorganization into domains and absorption of its affiliates, MEI had to put in place a set of systems that would allow it to hit the market fast with profitable, proprietary products. The chart shows how MEI did this by tying together the management of several elements—inventories, yield, capacity, and time.

Starting in the upper-right-hand quadrant is the all-important inventory-yield curve that I discussed in detail in the section on

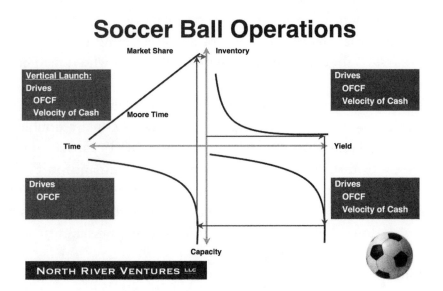

Soccer Ball Operations

Panasonic Automotive Systems. This curve has two powerful cash drivers:

- Lower inventory improves operating sources of free cash flow and increases the velocity of cash.
- Higher yield increases operating sources of free cash flow by cutting waste, improving customer service, and cutting returns.

Both of these cash drivers are vital to survival and growth. Companies weak in operating sources of cash and/or with a low velocity of cash have deep systemic problems. MEI's aggressive inventory-yield curve tackles this head-on.

MEI's ability to drive the inventory-yield curve down sharply—as the graph shows, it gets high yield even at relatively high levels of inventory—means that the company gets immediate benefit from even small decreases in inventory. Doing this requires managing a large number of upstream elements, both in-house and outsourced, as well as factory floor systems and outbound logistics. But once this knowledge is built into the system, its cash-generating flexibility is assured.

Management can turn its focus on inventory days in the sure knowledge that the system will not come back and bite it somewhere else. Subtle, but the number of companies who don't get it is legion.

As we saw in plasma TVs, MEI has accumulated experience in managing step function increases in capacity—usually doubling it—while increasing yield. We also saw how MEI's capacity-yield curve enabled the company to secure global dominance in PDPs quickly and to keep it product generation after product generation. As with the inventory-yield curve, MEI gets high yields at relatively low levels of capacity, allowing it to translate capacity increases into cash efficiently.

Once a company has the inventory-yield curve and the

capacity-yield curve in harness, it can sell aggressively with far less worry than the competition whose quality will fail once volume is cranked up—a sad story repeated almost daily in *The Wall Street Journal*.

When the two curves are combined, we have the core of a powerful manufacturing system, which MEI calls the super manufacturing model: a low-inventory, high-capacity, high-yield production system that extends from highly digitized products like digital still cameras to much less digitized ones like washing machines. The first two quadrants, therefore, lay the groundwork for a system that generates strong operating sources of cash and high velocities of cash, *regardless of sales volume*.

These quadrants also show a shift away from price competition based on product, to proprietary processes that run independently of the degree of vertical integration. Control of the first two quadrants lets a company mix and match outsourcing, insourcing, joint ventures, and black box technologies with relative ease so long as the curves are managed. This in turn allows it to surprise competitors almost at will.

In the third quadrant, I have added a fourth element, time. MEI's capacity-time curve, which I discussed in detail in the sections on digital still cameras and PDPs, shows the impact of being able to drive step function increases in capacity over ever-shorter periods of time. Again, a component of OFCF and cash velocity.

Taken together, we see the essentials of the new MEI business model: *generate profits by driving large increases in sales of unique products at higher yields and lower inventories, faster than the competition can.*

Soccer Ball Operations bring Wal-Mart efficiency to manufacturing. If we substitute companywide shelf space for capacity, and declining stockouts for yield, the Wal-Mart model jumps out: put more goods on the shelves with less inventory and fewer stockouts than the competition and the company scales quickly with maximum cash and capital efficiency.

You can also see another element of the Wal-Mart model: how to scale up profitably from unit one—a small store in Bentonville, Arkansas—to global superpower. It may make no sense to speak of a company the size of MEI in 2000—$72 billion in annual sales—as having to learn to scale up from unit one. But that is what it had to do. It had to "refound" itself, in Kirk's words, and to rediscover modern scale and scope economies from scratch.

Normally, scaling profitably and quickly is the province of newcomers, largely because newcomers have no baggage and have powerful founders to force the pace. But even that is not enough as DEC, Compaq, and Sun Microsystems discovered. To succeed, you have to understand, like Wal-Mart, how to manage cash and capital at super-efficient levels throughout your operation. Until Matsushita did it, IBM was the only established company ever to succeed at this. And Matsushita was significantly larger and more complex than IBM when it began the process. General Motors and Ford are now starting down this hard road.

The final quadrant brings together market share and Moore Time. For most of its history, as we saw, MEI and its affiliated companies took time out of the equation. They waited till markets reached a critical mass, then entered these markets with products that were made better and cheaper than competing products. Matsushita assumed this added the value the market was looking for and that this value would generate profitable sales. This strategy had the downside of forgoing proprietary technologies that locked up markets early and kept competitors out. So long as market share and time were not inversely related, MEI's strategy balanced the downside by reducing risk: others led the charge into markets and took all the casualties early. MEI could count on its manufacturing prowess and distribution to take a profitable piece once others had taken the hit.

Moore Time changed that. In 1996, when Sean White and I introduced the company to Moore Time in *The Digital Revolution*, Matsushita was not ready for decision making under the

Moore Curve and paid the price, not just in market leadership, but also in seeing whole markets foreclosed before it could move. Others were entering markets fast with proprietary, easy-to-use systems that prevented wannabes like MEI from ever getting off the ground. Moore Time rendered Matsushita's decades-long wait-and-see approach null. By the time MEI was ready to launch, the market was gone to someone else. Forever.

You can see what this looks like in the following chart, which I call Lead Ball Operations. In Moore Time, high inventories and low yields translate into small market shares that take a long time to build and that are inherently unprofitable and cash poor. Cash is taken out of the operation in all four quadrants.

You can also see how assuming, as Matsushita did, that Moore Time does not exist—the market share–time curve would have a slope of one—would turn your attention away from the other three quadrants: these quadrants wouldn't have the same impact on decision making. Or, at least, how responding to them would be a set of uncoordinated responses to unconnected inputs, and would not necessarily result in a coherent strategy. Or a quickly executed one.

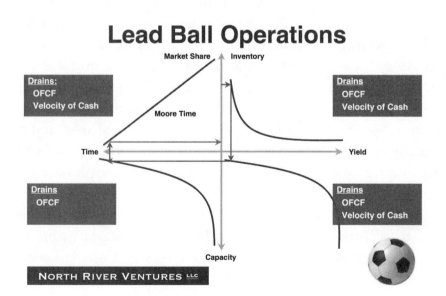

Lead Ball Operations

In the Soccer Ball System, responding to all four quadrants simultaneously is a function of the C-level drive for cash, which makes decisions and change happen fast. This, fundamentally, is what the MEI reforms of 2000 were about.

Soccer Ball Operations show how all the pieces of MEI's V Product strategy come together to give the firm a day-to-day management system that gets to markets fast and delivers fast. Rapid increases in market share over short time periods also drive customer information back into the system at accelerated speeds and, in doing so, quickly identify V Product improvements so that the cycle can repeat itself.

In feeding information back into the system quickly, the Moore Time curve, like the inventory-yield curve, has a direct effect on receivables, which like inventories are a key element in both operating sources of cash and the velocity of cash.

MEI's Soccer Ball Operations therefore drive the two most powerful elements of working capital at the same time.

Competitors trying to hit Matsushita with better products take the risk of being counterattacked by a superior cash engine, a risk that, as Michael Dell demonstrated for almost a decade, few companies ever think about when designing their market response.

It is not enough, either, to manage these curves in isolation. MEI's strength is in understanding that, at the operating level, an inventory-yield curve that inflects properly means nothing without a capacity-yield curve that also inflects properly. The same is true of the capacity-time curve. Indeed, managing these curves separately can easily decrease operating sources of cash and the velocity of cash, as more than one company has found out by trying to drive up capacity fast without adequate controls over yield and inventories.

To the extent that capacity is brought on stream without attention to the other two curves and hits the market early, product failures, returns, and customer service all suffer. Cash gets sucked out of the system rather than sucked into it. Companies with as much control of their operations as MEI has are, additionally, in a better position than others to sell interoperability to their customers. Instead of selling microwave ovens to Wal-Mart, for example, MEI is in a position to sell Wal-Mart superior inventories, the prime enabler of Wal-Mart's "Everyday Low Prices" brandline.

Without its market-leading cash velocity, Wal-Mart's business model would be too high-cost to offer low prices on a wide scale and Wal-Mart's brand promise would implode. MEI can sell to that concern directly. Selling cash flow this way enables a company to get much better terms from its customers than a competitor can get by selling products at a discount. Not only does this make major account management easier—rather than selling against your product weaknesses you are selling with your system. Selling cash flow also means lower receivables, which improves OFCF.

Finally, MEI's Soccer Ball Operations allow the company to raise the costs of switching suppliers to its customers, even though the company is selling premium-priced products.

All aspects of the model come down to doing more for less and improving cash flow in the process.

MEI's Soccer Ball Operations go a long way toward reestablishing what Konosuke always wanted: a system that is closer to customers than is anyone else's and that therefore adds more value for them than anyone else's. Moreover, as we saw earlier, Konosuke's major reorganizations, from his Division System to the Atami Conference, were all driven by crises in cash velocity. MEI's Soccer Ball Operations address these concerns directly by building cash sensitivity into the core of company operations. In effect, the new MEI model is more of what Konosuke had in mind, not less, the opinion of many in the Japanese press notwithstanding.

In most companies, sources of cash and cash velocity are the result of operations and are dealt with retrospectively. The MEI system does the reverse: it sets inventory days, then fixes yield, capacity, and time goals accordingly. This allows MEI to drive cash directly through operations to targeted results. Vital to MEI's thinking is that no number of V Products, no matter how ethnographically driven by the company's universal design strategy, and regardless of how much effort goes into *Panasonic Ideas For Life*, will succeed at any price unless the company's Soccer Ball Operations work.

MEI's Soccer Ball Operations, therefore, are essential to understanding the company's success. And they are also central to how the company will grow: the system provides feedback by design and can, therefore, be leveraged almost endlessly. Because the goal is operating sources of cash, there are, in MEI terms, "no taboos"; whatever has to be done to keep high levels of cash flow will be done.

Vertical Launch

Matsushita always had a timing problem with product launch. Divisions and affiliates launched products on their own timetables and in different geographies in different sequences and sometimes on different platforms. Certain of its markets, for example, TVs, had a range of incompatible systems and standards, exacerbating the situation. Commonly, a product was launched first in Japan. Once it moved in volume, it was sold overseas. Other products might be sold overseas and never in Japan. Marketing was diffused over products, countries, and time. In MEI's confusing structure it was in no one's interest to coordinate global marketing. The SG&A waste was phenomenal. Not to mention R&D and manufacturing inefficiencies. Eliminating the organizational clutter allowed management to address these problems and to coordinate product launches across the company to give Matsushita control of its brand.

All reform efforts from the domain restructuring to capital management, from universal design to V Products, and from super manufacturing to *Panasonic Ideas For Life* would bring few benefits if the resulting output of the firm didn't hit all markets all at once. Moore Time, too, would be a problem. Traditionally, products were dropped into markets slowly and only after they gained volume in their initial target countries, making them obsolete in Moore Time before they were universally available. This meant sacrificing R&D and SG&A for products that couldn't return their investment because of the way the system worked. The profitability of overseas markets like Europe and North America suffered because of this. MEI's best, most profitable products often didn't reach these markets until demand for them had gone to better products from someone else. Inventory piled up that had to be flamed off to make way for the next delayed product. The system designed profit out of the process.

Dick Kraft explained it this way: "Kirk and I used to say, 'MEI is not a global company. It is a Japanese company with global outlets for its excess production capacity.' "[146]

Because management was still thinking in the 1970s—the McLuhan Frontier again—it did not take Moore Time into account. Three decades ago, you could launch a new audio system in Japan, iron out the kinks, get good profits, then, after a couple of years, launch it in the United States and earn way more. This was a proven sales method, and no one thought to change it. Besides, the way the company was put together with so many piece parts, it was hard to think this problem through. Once computerization hit, computer-type product cycles hit sector after sector, eviscerating MEI's product launch methods. *That '70s Show* was over.

His decade in foreign markets made the challenge frighteningly obvious to Kirk. If MEI didn't market products everywhere at once, the entire Panasonic branding structure, weak though it was, would fail and with it the company's ability to generate cash predictably. Since cash is the priority of the Soccer Ball System, a coordinated global product launch capability was mandatory. In his big March 28, 2001, management conference where he introduced so many of the changes in *Panasonic*, he also initiated the idea of simultaneously launching new products around the world in a "worldwide explosion."[147] This became the company's vertical launch capability. Vertical launch was designed to overwhelm the competition with simultaneous, massive product launches worldwide. Kind of like VTOL aircraft, Kirk wanted product launches that had no ramp whatever; they appeared in force everywhere at once. It was the linchpin that held together his Braudel-like, everything-comes-together-at-once approach to reform. Without it, MEI would look like a flashy new car without wheels: looks great but it isn't going anywhere.

But getting to vertical launch in a company with no supply chain management system or global brand was a tall order, especially since, as he said in his March 28 address, so many MEI managers "had not even noticed" that the company's entire business model was obsolete. But, he pointed out, Matsushita had plenty of examples of products, like the tilted-drum washer/dryer, that were selling at a premium and beating up their markets. Properly done, he made clear, a vertical launch would have a salutary impact on profits.

Putting a vertical launch capability in place took some doing. For PDP, as we saw, it meant rethinking the planning process while going through generational reloads, expanding panel size, and regularly doubling production. For its V Products, the company had to replace its previous system of gates—get to the gate, then go through it, allowing almost anyone to slow down the process of getting to a gate for any reason—with a system of dates. In the new system, MEI sets D-day for a worldwide product explosion and works backward to define the gates through which it must pass and when. For a company used to launching new products in serial and which had never put everything into the line everywhere at once, this was stressful. It also forced managers to be infinitely more sensitive to global markets for their products, all the time. Knowing only what Japanese customers preferred moved from being at the center of decision making to being tangential. Even now the company has not made the full transition to the implications of vertical launch, and its global ethnographic capability lags its manufacturing capability.

There are additional stresses on management: to get to vertical launch everything that the company learned about sales and marketing from product conception and planning to manufacturing and delivery had to be replaced, just as it had in the shift from conventional TVs to plasma. Unlike plasma, which can be limited to a few factories, vertical launch affects every operation the company has in the world, from the smallest to the largest, regardless of function, and is still a work in progress.

In Japan, Steve Ushimaru synchs up vertical product launches by overnight construction of large, manned displays in hundreds of major retailers across the country that open the day the product is introduced. This is probably impossible to do in the United States.

Taken together with the mechanics of Matsushita's modern manufacturing, the company's ability to launch new products fast is forcing the less agile from its markets or reducing them to marginal players. It is also changing the OFCF generating capability of the company in ways that were impossible to think about before the reform began. The coordinated timing and frequency of a vertical launch can be sensibly planned for by the CFO. Problems can be identified, prioritized, and fixed. For the first time in its history, Matsushita can disrupt global markets and affect outcomes with fast-growing, profitable products. The days of Maneshita are over.

THE GREENING OF PANASONIC

Sean and I devoted the last chapter of *Beating Japan* to a new theory that as falling information costs drive ever-increased rates of information substitution for other inputs like land, labor, and capital, they will launch an era of green production. We called this the green wave. Several years later, we expanded this chapter into a full book, *The Total Quality Corporation* (Dutton 1995).

In *Total Quality*, we proposed that information substitution lets companies eliminate waste by dematerializing production, pushing costs down and quality up. Pollution signals management problems: waste indicates low quality and high cost. Our watchword became "Zero waste equals zero defects."[148] We gave examples of companies as diverse as Nissan and Lufthansa that were working toward our zero waste goals.

The environment was a big Konosuke concern and after he read *Total Quality*, Kirk told us that he was making the book the official policy of Panasonic North America. When he became CEO he embedded the concept in Matsushita worldwide: all MEI products must be a lot cheaper to make and cheaper to use than competing products; all must be information intense (the V Product system); and Matsushita must make green a proprietary edge in everything it does. He drove the point home hard, opening his December 2001 management conference with a blistering broadside saying that Japan's leading business paper, the *Nihon Keizai Shimbun*, ranked Matsushita only forty-fourth among Japanese manufacturers. "If this is true," he told his team, "we will have to stop advertising ourselves as an environmentally friendly corporation."[149]

Kirk returned to this theme constantly, and in March 2004 made a powerful statement of green production based on Toyota's "Seven Wastes" principle that a company must eliminate.[150]

- Waste from overproduction
- Waste from wait states

- Transportation waste
- Processing waste
- Inventory waste
- Waste of movement and motion
- Waste from defective products

He related low yield rates and, therefore, high levels of waste directly to poor customer service, telling his team, "Product quality mirrors corporate attitude to customers. In other words, without improving our quality, we can't evolve into a Customer Value Creation Company."[151]

MEI built these green goals into its cost-cutting program so that more green, as it were, and less cost would be seen as the same thing. Kirk intended this to be much more than a statement of intent or good public relations. What he wanted was a complete rethinking of how MEI products are made—cut energy and waste—and a rethinking of how products are used, again cutting energy and waste. Done right, he wanted to position MEI make products that pollute less and waste less by their nature. In this sense, he wanted to make the *Panasonic Ideas For Life* brand-line a complete corporate philosophy. Over the years as rates of information substitution rise, Matsushita will be seen, he hopes, as the indispensable agent of a cleaner environment.

In doing this, MEI is one of the few companies to recognize that phenomena like global warming are bad for business, not least because they shrink markets and contract economies. Large companies cannot prosper in a failing global economy. In an ironic rewrite of the old phrase "What's good for General Motors is good for America," Kirk was saying that what's good for the environment is good for Matsushita.

An example is the cut in water and energy consumption used in the tilted-drum washer/dryer. By 2002, Matsushita refrigerators used 17 percent of the energy they required in 1992. Black box technologies are often more energy efficient than the technologies they replace. In addition, MEI is big in air- and-water purification products. Its Aller Buster for allergies is used in ceramic fan heaters, air conditioners, nano water droplet air fresheners, and humidifiers.

The number of processes needed to make PDPs was reduced by 20 percent in recent years and process lead times cut by almost half. The Amagasaki PDP plant uses a photo catalytic coating on its 24,000 square meters of outer walls that reduces NOx gases by the equivalent of 1,800 poplar trees a day. Much of the plant's outside lighting is wind and sun generated and the plant uses its own rainwater for its grounds. The bulk of factory wastes from Styrofoam to glass panels and oil is recycled.

Within less than a generation, Matsushita may become the world's leading vendor of green products in its market segments. These will not be things that cost more for customers to buy and use, but less, making Matsushita's role ever more critical for its customers and shareholders.

The green concept is more obvious to consumers of Matsushita white goods where the need for less water, in a dishwasher, for example, or less electricity for a fridge, is well advertised. However, we see few of these products in the United States or Europe. But the countries where they now sell and have a large future, like Japan and China, are also countries with distinct limitations on their natural resources.

Digital cameras with no film mean no film processing, a really filthy—and unregulated—business. Battery management technology means longer times between recharges. Mass storage and communications mean fewer disks, and, in the case of CDs, all the packaging and even the retail sectors for distributing them.

Yield management is critical to a green operation. When chips can be mass-produced and sold for a few dollars each, low yield means one thing. But a plasma display, which is just one giant chip, costs thousands a pop and throwing these out means wasting real money. Yield management is essential to keeping wastage down.

Matsushita's biggest green move is the acquisition of control of MEW with its $13 billion in annual sales. As I wrote earlier in *Panasonic*, Matsushita Electric Works ran independently of MEI since MEW's founding in 1935 and its enforced estrangement by the postwar MacArthur regime. Today the company remains different enough that internal slides and charts show the company's 1935 founding as Showa 10, or the tenth year in the reign of the Showa emperor known in the West as Hirohito.

MEW suffered reversals in 2001–2002 but did not move into the red. Its operating profits were also stronger than MEI's had been for years. The company has six business lines:

- Lighting products
- Information equipment and wiring products
- Home appliances
- Building products
- Electronic and plastic materials
- Automation controls

What MEI picked up in MEW is, without a doubt, the deepest expertise in the world on the optimum management of space. MEW's products include complete kitchens, bathrooms, and other parts of homes designed to cut the cost of energy consumption and to make the use of space as efficient as possible. The company's mission, basically, is environmental efficiency in homes, businesses, and construction of all types. MEW has perfected just about everything a home needs, from lighting and security systems, and the materials to make them, to kitchen shelving units that drop down to the customer at the slightest touch. The concept is to surround the consumer with a complete *Panasonic Idea For Life* that the consumer lives in, rather than uses. MEW's modular bathrooms operate the same way, even to the extent of making bathroom cleaning simple, and automated, if need be.

MEW's office systems work the same way: simple and easy to use with the minimum energy consumption. To support these systems, the company makes energy-efficient materials. MEW CEO Koichi Hatanaka told me that MEW's main strategy is to "dig well and mine our best markets."[152] This company concentrates on fewer markets than MEI and has what it believes to be a "very powerful market share platform." MEW typically runs in the top four of its markets, making its operations more stable than those of its sister. The company was also quicker to cut losing divisions and direct resources elsewhere. This, Hatanaka says, forced a continued sense of crisis and a long-term effort to cut MEW's fixed costs. As a result, MEW did not share MEI's prolonged decline in profitability.

For MEW, the biggest benefit of its deal with MEI is that it is standing in front of the biggest demographic wave in history, a tsunami of wealthy, aging baby boomers. They will want simpler and cheaper space management. MEW doesn't have to do anything to capture this market; it is coming right at the company. With the miscellany in its portfolio moved off to MEI, MEW can exploit this green market with everything it has. There may be no other firm in the world positioned so well.

SOME THINGS DON'T WORK OUT: CELL PHONES

Everybody makes mistakes and MEI is no exception. Through its then majority-owned cellular affiliate, Matsushita Communications Industrial in Yokohama, Matsushita had the enviable position by the mid-1990s of being a leading supplier to Japan's homegrown and cutting-edge cellular carrier, NTT DoCoMo. Over the years DoCoMo, partly spun out from parent NTT, spent billions to buy roughly 15 percent of important carriers around the world, like AT&T Wireless, expecting that these companies would adopt DoCoMo's advanced services. As a preferred DoCoMo supplier,

Matsushita naturally expected to ride this wave to global market share. This seemingly insuperable advantage evaporated over the years as others like Nokia, Samsung, and Motorola came to dominate world markets. Matsushita faded into the "other" category, leaving a large hole in MEI's V Product sales bridge. How this happened and how Matsushita's expectations were scuttled is a story of major miscalculation and a salutary lesson for any company selling on a global stage.

The point of the V Product sales bridge was to get fast-growing, profitable, and highly differentiated V Products onto the bridge quickly enough to replace declining legacy products. In everyone's mind, the DoCoMo relationship made cellular a clear winner and a surefire V Product. Take cellular away and the bridge might collapse, or at the very least be much harder to build. One of Kirk Nakamura's priorities was to return MEI to 10 percent operating profit, and without cellular, the main support of corporate profit when he became CEO, 10 percent didn't look doable. In the event, it wasn't.

Putting a *Panasonic Idea For Life* into the hands, rather than the homes and offices, of everyone on the planet was vital to Panasonic's brand revival. Especially if MEI could drive a new range of DoCoMo-inspired services through generations of handheld Panasonic marvels. The major point that Sean and I made in *The Digital Revolution* and later in *FutureWealth* was that the time was coming when everything would be connected to the bitstream and that the more product-services that you could put on the bitstream, the more money you could make. Kirk made this the basis for his reform from the first day, saying that the networked society, rather than Konosuke's electric society, was to be the core of MEI's thinking. He even renamed the Audio Visual Computer Company (AVC) the AVC *Networks* Company.

Acquiring 100 percent of MCI was to be Matsushita's ticket to the networked universe, the link that tied its diverse consumer products into a coherent whole. Once the company was reorganized and the affiliates brought in, its financial polarity reversed, a new global brand platform in place, and its manufacturing restructured to generate cash flow, wireless would leverage its prodigious array of audiovisual and computing products, carrying the whole edifice on to a new phase of profitable growth and making the firm unbeatable on the global stage. Kirk shared my view that nothing the firm did would, or could, be excluded from this networked world. Sooner or later, even home appliances would be connected. If Matsushita alone had all the pieces, which it did, nothing could stand in its way. Moreover, with Toda's V Products operation aggressively filtering out products that couldn't bring top profits in the future, the internal mechanisms to ensure that the company approached the network future coherently were in place.

The risks in cellular seemed low in 2000 and much higher everywhere else, like in PDP. In his March 28, 2001, Value Creation 21 address to employees, Kirk said, "In the area of mobile phones, we plan to expand global business. In the area of GSM and IM2000, which will be launched in Japan this year, we will aim to become one of the world's top three companies, attaining a 10 percent share of the global market."[153] In early 2001, even though the tech crash had begun, starting with an implosion in telecommunications, this must have seemed achievable.

But the signs that it was not were clear for years. I don't think Kirk could accept these signs, however. He knew what MEI could do. Over the next few years he would be proven right everywhere else, so why not in wireless? In the end, the failure of Matsushita to beat out Nokia and Motorola on the global stage was probably inexplicable to him. It was his one major failure and left him with a bad taste in his mouth to the end of his presidency.

What made this bad taste extra hard to take was the certain knowledge that a wireless success would have pushed the company to its 10 percent operating profit goal, twice its level when Kirk retired. Had the company hit that number, its operating profits would have come achingly close to their peak of 1984 and restored Matsushita to a status in world business that would have been unimpeachable.

Another executive would have read the tea leaves and quickly exited the cellular business. Kirk couldn't let go. He kept coming back to cellular in his management conference addresses for years, alternatively promising great things, as he did in the VC 21 talk, and criticizing the cellular group for underperformance, as during the annus horribilis of 2001. But he never gave up. I am convinced that had he done so, MEI would have been on an even sounder footing than it was when he left it.

When the fall from grace in wireless came, it came fast. MCI's market share in Japan dropped from 34.5 percent in 1999 to just 15.2 percent in 2001.[154] In July 2001, at the depths of the dotcom collapse, a year after he had become CEO and just six months after his reforms had started to kick in, he gave a blunt assessment at his management conference. "During the past several years, the Matsushita Group has largely depended on mobile phone business for income. This disproportionate balance is primarily responsible for the present fragile business structure and slow growth. . . . The sudden decline in mobile phone demand has severely impacted our entire business performance."[155] Kirk went on to repeat to his senior managers that he expected the company to gain 10 percent of the world cell phone market. Without this, he said, "We will be unable to revive Matsushita." Instead, things got worse. In January 2002, Kirk told his managers that "another failure this year could witness the collapse of Matsushita Communications Industrial."[156]

From the vantage point of 2000, Kirk's plan for successful reorganization depended on cash from MCI. With that unit thriving, the company had the financial strength to launch all the other initiatives that would make the overhaul successful. But if that core unit began to fail, as it did, the underpinnings of Kirk's reforms would collapse, possibly quite quickly.

Kirk never got his 10 percent of the world market, or anything close. That he rebuilt Matsushita without this V Product pillar is impressive. But what MEI could have done with a big success in this sector would have been even more so. The failure of Matsushita to meet its goals in cellular is, without a doubt, the biggest disappointment of Kirk's career.

I've been in the telecom business all my working life. I know the business inside out. You will recall that Sean White and I built the largest telecommunications market research house in the world and sold it to McGraw-Hill in 1988. In my view two things wrecked MCI's ambitions.

One, common in the industry, was not understanding that telecommunications is driven by price-performance. Whoever offers more bandwidth for less wins. This is why the fiber business collapsed in 2001. Price-performance in what we call local access—the method used to connect you in your home, car, or office, to the network—was too poor to unleash demand from the hundreds of millions of powerful personal computers and game consoles that were waiting to be connected. As I explained to my clients all through the 1990s, you cannot give a man a new heart (long-haul fiber network) and expect it to work if he has no blood (local access) in his veins. Until price-performance reaches a point where it taps demand, nothing will happen—business models will stall, capital expenditures will fall, and most of the world's common carriers, and their suppliers, will suffer. In 2001, this is what happened.

Price-performance is a ratio. Fiber offers lots of performance but at a high price. Cellular offered neither price nor performance and would be eclipsed the same way mainframes were when the personal computer tapped a demand for computing power at a different point on the price-performance curve. If you understand price-performance you can get your customers ahead of the curve and keep them there profitably for both of you forever. Cellular's problem is that it is only a small part of the curve.

Once anything surpasses it, its day is over. Here MCI and most others made a subsidiary miscalculation. They pinned their hopes on a third-generation (3G) system that had too few price-performance benefits to be attractive. If MEI were to tie itself to cellular, rather than to wireless price-performance, it was increasing the risks to reform, not decreasing them.

The second thing that hurt MCI was the Japanese market. In this, MCI was not alone. No Japanese cell phone supplier ever broke out of the Japanese market. (Sony did, but in a joint venture with Ericsson of Sweden.) Japan's postwar industrial strategy was to close the IT gap with the United States in several sectors, one of which was telecommunications. As I mentioned at the opening of *Panasonic*, Japan's method of propelling itself forward was simple: direct the revenues of the government-owned telecom monopoly, Nippon Telephone and Telegraph, to buy advanced telecommunications technologies from a select group of Japanese companies: NEC, Fujitsu, Hitachi, and OKI. NTT would design a common product in its labs—say a telephone exchange—and each of the four suppliers would get an order for a certain amount, based on various criteria. Everyone else in the world did the same thing. In the United States, the Bell System had only one supplier for its territory, Western Electric. In the United Kingdom, the General Post Office, which doubled as the telephone company and had designed and built the world's first computer, had its stable of favored suppliers like GEC, Marconi, and Plessey. France did this with Alcatel, Germany with Siemens and ITT, and so on, country after country.

Every phone company had its own system architecture and none were compatible with the others. You couldn't ship an NEC-built telephone exchange designed for NTT to the United Kingdom or the States and expect it to work. Or vice versa.

Problems began to occur with the birth of the digital age about a quarter of a century ago. Development costs went through the roof and companies could not afford to sustain these without large markets. A simple solution for a Japanese telecommunications manufacturer would be to do what Japanese companies did with cars: sell in the big U.S. market. But in telecommunications doing this is not as simple as changing from left-hand drive to right-hand drive. Telecommunications standards and architectures were, and remain, wildly different the world over. Companies like MCI faced a dilemma: focus on Japan and watch margins shrink and market share go to others, or run the risk of doubling up on research and development costs to serve the Japanese market and a foreign one, like the United States. Either way, with this bifurcation of effort, the likelihood of gaining a dominant global position was slim. Moreover, NTT was a harsh taskmaster, demanding outsized support for its guaranteed orders. The result was that no matter how much a company wanted to develop products for overseas markets, its best engineers were always siphoned off to answer NTT's ever-pressing needs.

The simple solution, to have NTT adopt a more widely used architecture so that Japan's suppliers could gain economies of scale, was, for reasons that have never been clear, out of the question. Over the years, NTT was privatized and the Japanese market deregulated. Cellular came in and in 1991, NTT was split into two: the phone company in three parts and a wireless company, NTT DoCoMo, in which NTT owns the major share.

Old habits die hard. DoCoMo launched several wireless services unique to Japan. As always, in order to make products for foreign and Japanese markets, suppliers had to double up on their R&D. Not surprisingly, no Japanese or foreign company ever succeeded in bridging Japanese and overseas markets. DoCoMo insists that its brand, not that of Panasonic or anyone else, is on its cell phones. Today, the worldwide cell set business is dominated by non-Japanese companies: Motorola, Nokia, and Samsung. These firms market directly to their customers, selling branded features that are strong enough that customers will often switch carriers just to get their favorite cell phone. My daughter recently switched from a company that I know is better run and has higher levels of customer service to the worst performer in the United States because she wanted a Motorola RAZR, in hot pink. Panasonic, by contrast, gets no brand advantage from what it sells in Japan. To cellular consumers the world over, it doesn't exist.

When North America still had a single analog standard, it was at least possible for MCI to think of cracking the North American market by doubling up on development costs. MCI had an operation in Atlanta where it made analog cell phones. But when digital came in during the mid-nineties, the U.S. government refused to reenter the business of standards regulation that President Carter had exited two decades earlier. U.S. and Canadian carriers launched several networks based on a range of incompatible technologies.

In 1996, Matsushita Communications was aiming for the number four spot by 2000. But by the late 1990s, it found itself looking at three technologies in North America, another in the European Union, and still others in Japan. By 1996, therefore, it was clear that the company's efforts would have to be split across many fronts if it was to make its market share goal. Nokia, by contrast, had a large, homogeneous GSM base in the European Union from which to build solid cash flows. From this base, Nokia could attack everywhere and leave Japan aside with minimal impact.

While Matsushita was mulling over this problem, it was hit by two forces: one internal and one external. The internal force was the ever-present demand of DoCoMo, which sapped its attention. For quite a few years, this was not so bad: DoCoMo's volume demands were growing, Matsushita was a preferred supplier, and the business was extremely profitable. However, this only pulled engineering and marketing talent away from overseas efforts, effectively blinding the company to developments there. The external force was more subtle: as the Soccer Ball System shows, when information costs fall, human behavior changes, often in unpredictable ways. Wireless customers the world over rushed off in different directions, leaving suppliers like Matsushita facing customer needs that were nothing alike. A common platform was becoming more elusive, not less.

In Japan, the national infrastructure is so well managed that cell phone customers can walk up to a subway station, enter a few commands, and get directions, line changes and all, making a complex system easy to manage. In the West people love to yak aloud about their personal affairs on their cell phones. Who in America has not heard teenage girls bragging about their sexual conquests at the tops of their voices on trains, buses, even walking down the street, or investment bankers loudly proclaiming the art of their deal? In Japan, by contrast, people sit, or stand, on trains and quietly and politely text message each other so as to disturb no one. These differences go on and on.

For all this, MCI had superb opportunities to crack the North American market and did not take them.

In 1996, I got a call from Bob Ferchat, the head of Bell Mobility, Bell Canada's cellular arm in Toronto. Bob retired as Nortel Networks' CFO a year or so earlier and was hired out of retirement to run Mobility. Because I had advised every CEO at Nortel for the previous two decades, I knew him well. Bob had one relentless focus: customer churn. If he could keep this number down, his SG&A efficiency would be higher than his competitors' and he could outgrow them in revenue and profit at the same time. By 1996, he had reduced churn to 1 percent per month, a number still considered the industry gold standard and achieved by only one or two other companies in the world. He used to say that he would pay his competition to keep spending to increase their market shares. He would focus on levels of quality that keep customers so he didn't have to spend money to win new ones to replace them.

Bob knew of my relationship with Matsushita and asked if I could set up a meeting. He had been part of the team under visionary Nortel CEO Ed Fitzgerald that was the first non-Japa-

nese company to sell telecom gear to NTT and knew the people
there well. He had asked them to recommend a cell phone maker
that had the kind of differential advantages he was looking for to
keep his customers happy and his churn down. DoCoMo said that
the best supplier in Japan was Matsushita because its battery management circuitry gave phones more calling time between recharges. Japanese customers loved it. Bob wanted it.

I went in to see Kirk, who was blown away to have a customer
CEO call up and specify Matsushita. In the down and dirty business of price-driven commodity competition, this does not happen every day.

I explained to Kirk that we had an even bigger opportunity.
Bell Mobility had an operational agreement with Sprint PCS and
used the same technology. I knew the CEO of PCS and if we
could make something work in Canada, critically U.S.-like without being the United States itself, we could go to PCS with a
working business model with all the kinks ironed out. I added that
I also knew the folks at what is now Verizon. All three used the
same technology and with a bit of work, we had a shot at a clean
sweep of one of North America's main wireless technologies. He
agreed that this was an opportunity worth moving on (in Kirk
time, this means yesterday) and asked me to get into the loop
Steve Ushimaru, who then ran Panasonic Canada.

Steve, however, was not at all enthusiastic. He knew what Kirk
and I did not, that MCI was too DoCoMo-centric and was not
ready for this. He didn't want to risk a good relationship with Bell
Canada, where he sold Panasonic phones and answering machines
from Kyushu Matsushita. I did not fully grasp Steve's concerns
until later and naively pushed ahead. My results lived down to
Steve's expectations precisely. What I discovered was an operation
that had no major account capability, no understanding of customer needs, and no ability to gain this understanding. I wound
up dragging a reluctant Matsushita Communications executive to
Toronto who made no secret of his desire not to be there and who

did his level, and successful, best to ensure that no deal material-
ized. If Bell Canada wasn't going to do what DoCoMo was doing
in Japan, he wasn't interested. I was lucky to walk away with my
reputation with Bell and with Steve Ushimaru unscathed. The
whole thing was a fiasco. Matsushita never recovered its position on
the world stage.

But we weren't to know that then. Not long before he returned
to Japan in 1997, Kirk hired a sales executive from AT&T to sell
Panasonic wireless products to AT&T Wireless. She landed a $100
million order, only to have the thing bleed away in a series of Matsushita Communications blunders over the following months. She
left shortly thereafter, and Matsushita's attempts at selling in North
America were over for good.

In Japan, too, the warning signs were coming clearer by the day.
Between 1995 and 2001, DoCoMo grew at a 34 percent compounded annual rate and was inhaling cell phones from Matsushita.
But DoCoMo's average revenue per customer fell 53 percent over
the same period. Growth was about to hit a wall. In 2001, it did.
DoCoMo's market share peaked, and customer growth slowed.
Sales growth flattened and in 2005 actually declined. Matsushita
found itself locked into DoCoMo's cycle with no growth alternatives elsewhere. Once DoCoMo slowed, Matsushita slowed as well.

But when Kirk became CEO in 2000, a central part of his plan
was to bring MCI into the MEI tent. Atsushi Murayama told me
that the reforming team believed that because of the importance
of networking, without MCI restructuring the rest of the company would not make sense.[157] There was a problem, though it
was not insurmountable. As the 1990s wore on, MCI's sales to
DoCoMo grew and its stock rose to the point where it was not
economic to buy the company. Matsushita needed MCI for its
planned reintegration of brands and technologies, but could not
afford to buy it.

When MEI bought MCI, it did so against the combined backgrounds of the 2001 telecom collapse, which hit DoCoMo hard

and drove down the price of MCI's stock to the point where it was affordable, and the failure of a 3G cellular to take off elsewhere. The industry slid into a five-year stall. Panasonic Mobile Communications, as it is now called, then had to work its way out of a sales and profit decline with all the account management weaknesses that had been clear to me in 1996.

Some progress was made with Vodafone, and a factory was set up in the Czech Republic. But, in 2005, Vodafone suddenly dumped Panasonic—something a crack major account team would have seen coming and would have headed off at the pass—leaving MEI without any wireless presence outside Japan. The Czech operation was closed. Just before this happened, throughout 2004 and 2005, DoCoMo's revenues had started to fall, and the firm's operating free cash flow with them. Matsushita was squeezed on two sides.

Not only did one of the pillars in MEI's revenue bridge crumble, but a good piece of the company's semiconductor revenue that depended on its cell sets crumbled as well, threatening a domino effect in the heart of the company.

Yet this structural weakness was apparent in 1996, long before Kirk became CEO, and nearly a decade before the company was forced to retreat from foreign markets. As it is, by the time Matsushita musters the force to return to international cellular markets, consumer behaviors, already diverging away from simple phone calls in a big bang of new communications cultures, will have moved so far away from Matsushita that its position in traditional cellular will never recover. In retrospect, even buying MCI at a discount was not worth it. If anything, the operation has been a drain, a major drag on earnings, and a barrier to progress.

Nonetheless, Kirk is nothing if not stubborn. He told me before he retired that wireless is central to the Panasonic product range: modern consumer electronics won't work without it. One way or another, Matsushita must be in wireless. He was determined to make wireless work, no matter what it took.[158] So long, I must add, as it's not cellular.

Fortunately, there is an ever-widening range of wireless technologies with superior price-performance from WiMAX to IP wireless and ultra wideband that present large opportunities and minimal standards hurdles. Few companies—perhaps no other company in the world—have the range of semiconductor, imaging, camera, storage, and communications expertise to leverage these markets. Kirk told me emphatically that this leverage was so great it had to be used and that the whole structure of reform hung on networked technologies. Kazuyoshi Fujiyoshi sketched out how this would work. "Instead of separating into separate businesses like imaging, communications, and so on, we should have one focus, and to do this we need a corporate-wide matrix. There are opportunities in fixed/mobile convergence. This will merge Wi-Fi and mobile. We want to see how this will work, especially with WiMAX, but overall, this will create a new market for us."[159] Amen.

CHAPTER FOUR

A RENEWED JAPANESE POWERHOUSE

TODAY MATSUSHITA'S OPERATING EARNINGS ARE MOVING UP AND ITS cash velocity is also. The company is closing in on big earnings generators like Samsung and repositioning products to compete with Apple, Dell, and others. It has markedly outshone Sony and Philips in sectors like flat-panel TVs.

For all that, however, as the next chart shows, Matsushita is only now at the jumping-off point where Dell and Wal-Mart were a decade ago. The Nakamura period pulled together all the pieces, reformed all the firm's operations, and positioned the company for its future moves. Back when Sean White and I wrote *The Digital Revolution*, we divided MEI's challenge into two: its long internal lines of communication and long external lines to customers. The simplest way to look at where Matsushita is today is that the first of these has been addressed and the second only partly so.

The challenge for the next generation will be to push the limits of the envelope further and get the firm to scale profitably, as

Matsushita Restructures

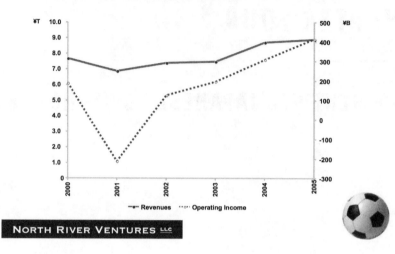

¥T 10.0 ... 500 ¥B

Revenues ···○··· Operating Income

NORTH RIVER VENTURES LLC

Wal-Mart and Dell did. This will require constant restructuring to make cash and capital velocities competitive. Moderate improvements will not be enough.

The market has rewarded MEI for its reforms to date. Unlike the Nikkei, Matsushita has more than recovered its December 1989 price, trading 62 percent higher than it did then.

Moreover, given its cash, leverage, and increasing stock price, MEI is in a position to acquire a company of at least $30 billion in sales and probably much more. Since there is nothing left in the Matsushita family to buy, this would be a "foreign" company in the sense that its DNA will be nothing like MEI's, even if it is Japanese. Possibly, it would be a non-Japanese company. To make a deal accretive, however, Matsushita will have to have the management controls of a high-velocity company. Personally, however, I think there are better uses for cash and pricey equity than a merger.

In his magisterial study of the development of capitalism worldwide, Fernand Braudel showed why some systems work and

Central Strategic Problem, 2006

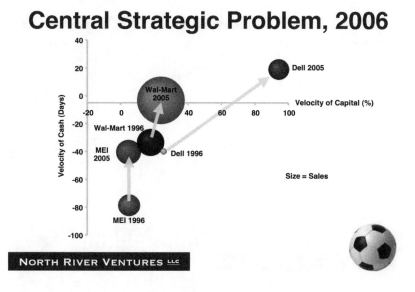

NORTH RIVER VENTURES LLC

others do not. At the University of Toronto, we studied Braudel closely. He was an inspiration and is central to my thinking about Matsushita. As I noted of him earlier, Braudel concluded that everything—political, economic, and social—has to pop at once for capitalism to emerge, and it has to keep popping at once for it to succeed.[1] I add to this the simple phrase "as the cost of information falls." But massive change in parallel is exceptionally difficult.

For CEOs the world over, there is a lesson here. Braudel said, in effect, that CEOs do not have to agree with Trotsky's unpleasant methods but they do have to accept his core principle that the revolution must be permanent to have any enduring impact. Kazuyoshi Fujiyoshi calls it "restructuring without interruption."[2]

Reorganizing a division or changing the product/service mix is a dead-end exercise. Everything must change at once, and keep changing, or the company will lose its place on the information cost curve. Fighting to get that place back is so hard that almost no one succeeds at it. That is what makes the Matsushita story so

Matsushita Share Performance

NIKKEI

NORTH RIVER VENTURES LLC

compelling. Matsushita fought back successfully on a scale that no one has ever seen before. In many ways, the MEI reforms are a Kitty Hawk event. Unless you see it for yourself—the Wrights were astute enough to take a camera—you have no logical reason to believe that it can be done.

MEI's restructuring has implications for Japan, of course, where few, even with all the publicity the company has received, understand what the company did, why it did it, and what the outcomes are likely to be. But to be sure, when a company of this size is on the move, more firms will be forced to change their ways and to rethink their own core principles, no matter how dearly held.

MEI's future challenge will be determined by its ability to do five things:

- Shift its corporate culture away from manufacturing into demand management.
- Directly manage customer experience of MEI products.

- Implement superior outbound logistics and inventory controls.
- Create deeper global account relationships.
- Globalize operations.

Looks simple, but this short list will be much harder to do than all the changes implemented so far. But without what has been done, this simple list would be unthinkable.

EXTERNAL RISKS

Matsushita faces several external risks that will try the company over the next few years. These are:

- the rate at which cyberspace is inflating
- deflation in digital markets
- the Internet black hole that is disintermediating markets everywhere

Cyberspace Inflation

Cyberspace is inflating rapidly. As price-performance drives down the cost of both computing and communications, the number of networkable devices increases at high rates, expanding cyberspace. The Big Bang chart at page 105 shows that soon every man, woman, and child in the middle-class world will have several devices in the tens of GHz. That means 1.5 billion people with, say, five 20 GHz products, or 7.5 billion devices, dwarfing all contemporary markets.

Matsushita's choices will have to be more focused than they are now and the company will have to choose markets more

Inflation in Cyberspace

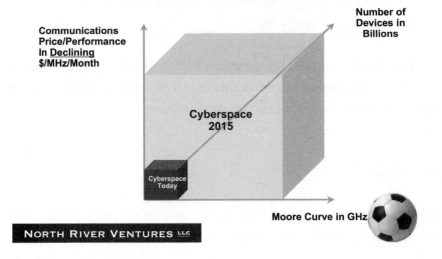

Communications Price/Performance In Declining $/MHz/Month

Number of Devices in Billions

Cyberspace 2015

Cyberspace Today

Moore Curve in GHz

NORTH RIVER VENTURES LLC

carefully. Inflated cyberspace will place a premium on using cyberspace itself to get close enough to customers to offer them profitable, proprietary services. Maintaining brand will be treacherous.

Inflated cyberspace will alter all MEI's markets, without exception.

There is no way to disguise how hard this will be for Matsushita, or any Japanese company. Three-dimensional product-service-content markets will be the prime pools of profit, and such offerings are not Japanese strengths. Matsushita will have to change this to exploit inflation successfully.

Market Deflation

There is another, equally powerful force: deflation. We saw this looking at MEI's sales bridge. Rapid downdrafts in price-performance mean you have to move ever-larger unit volumes just to keep sales even. Growing sales and profit in this environment is a killer. Deflation can be managed only by having good product-services that lock customers in to a product-service fabric with good cash flows. This is a Steve Jobs specialty. Few others have it, or understand it.

For instance, Kevin Maney suggested in his *USA Today* column that the Chinese market is the future for the recording industry.[3] If you can't charge for it, Kevin argues, figure out something else like treating CDs as free advertising for paid performances. Kevin raises a question for everybody in the information sector. What does a deflationary product-service-content business model look like?

For a company like Matsushita used to looking at its cost base for answers to deflation, Kevin is saying that it is nowhere near the right place to look. As I usually do, I agree with him.

Internet Black Hole

In August 1995, Sean White and I introduced the black hole in cyberspace, an Internet-driven point of price-performance powerful enough to swallow industries whole. Jim Crowe, CEO of Level 3, told *USA Today* that when he read this, he understood for the first time that the Internet was pure arithmetic—market physics, he called it—and that big money would be made by those companies who understood the physics of the black hole.[4] Crowe made a lot of it for himself.

The black hole is threatening everything in retail from computer sales to banking, is shaking up industries from music to television and all telecommunications, and its force is reshaping industries that are not being dragged over the event horizon. Matsushita will have to live with Internet black holes tearing at its structure. This will require constant reorganization over the coming decades if the Nakamura reforms are to keep bearing fruit.

The Future for Matsushita

Kirk Nakamura told his senior team in December 2003, "We cannot be perfectly confident that we can adapt to such changes. We should always be developing an agile management structure that can move lightly and responsively, like a soccer ball."[5] The job is not finished and probably never will be; change must be ongoing for the company to prosper. But the company now has a clear idea of *how* to change, something it lacked before. And it knows that it *can* change, and get good results for its efforts, both of which it had not experienced since the Atami Conference of 1964, over four decades ago.

To keep this process going the new CEO, Fumio Ohtsubo, set up task forces to cover key areas like the future organization of the company, what its most valuable technologies will be, and how customers should be best managed. Ohtsubo combines over five years working in Singapore with his time managing the AVC Company. Matsushita started a push into the Chinese TV market in 1994. By the late nineties the operation was going nowhere, and Ohtsubo went to China to find out why. Discovering that there was a mismatch between product and both Chinese household budgets and usage patterns, he developed a new product that made the operation one of the most profitable of MEI's overseas manufacturers. He was a big player on many of Kirk's task forces, oversaw a range of new AVC products like DSCs and PDPs, and put in place a new matrix management system to coordinate AVC operations.

No one understands better the challenges to the V-sales bridge and how carefully legacy products must be managed down and the V Product cycle kept tuned. DVD, which may seem new, is in its down phase already and must be replaced by new mass storage technologies. "We have to concentrate on growing categories and cut poor products quickly." His biggest issue, he says, is "how to manage these enormous changes on such a large scale and globally."[6]

Ohtsubo's single issue encapsulates the new Matsushita. Recall that in 1996 Sean White and I broke our recommendations into two parts:

- Shorten internal lines of communication, and
- Shorten external lines of communication.

When Kirk came in, I listed over thirty subsidiary elements to our first recommendation. The Value Creation 21 and Leap Ahead 21 plans addressed most of these. What remains is the second, which, for the most part, can be distilled to two words: demand management.

Demand management has its own subsidiary issues: global account management, outbound logistics, and globalized operations. But each of these is bigger than all the reforms that have gone before. Put another way, the Nakamura period put Matsushita in a position where it could *begin* its reforms. Fumio Ohtsubo will have to carry these out. "The next step," he told me, "is the most difficult. It will be how to implement the Soccer Ball."

In doing this, he thinks, like Kirk Nakamura, that the smoothest sales curve is the best. Kirk often led off Top Seminars with the injunction not to supercharge sales ahead of operations and he repeated this concern to me many times. Ohtsubo told me similarly that his priority in implementing the Soccer Ball System is "how we smoothly and quickly shift resources from one area to another to get to our 10 percent operating profit goal in a high velocity of cash and capital world."

Outbound logistics will be a priority—the external lines of *The Digital Revolution*—and, he says, "The problem we have is after shipping our products out. That is where we get hurt." He sees many opportunities to restructure SCM again to "minimize inventory." In other words, to extend the SCM system forward from factories into customers the way Panasonic Automotive works with its customers. Logistics reform has the potential to get Matsushita closer to negative working capital than it is, making profit targets easier to reach than they have been in the past.

Ohtsubo also realizes that this won't happen unless domain companies start working directly with their customers and this, I expect, will shake up operations worldwide.

He will also have to manage a renewed culture of growth, of which he says, ironically, "The most important part is figuring the timing to shut down products with weakening profits." In the past this was never done well, he says, and MEI has to learn to shut these operations down "as soon as possible." Indeed, knowing how and when to cut is what makes the V-sales bridge work.

Today, most of the operations Matsushita has reformed are in processes that get products to the end of production. Sales reform in Japan aside, Matsushita must learn that all profit today is made by those who manage the sales process. From this they derive the critical information that they use to further exploit profitable opportunities and add value to their products. Without first-class demand management, Matsushita could find itself once again struggling to cut costs in a commodity business.

The fundamental challenge in demand management is to understand where the highest-quality customer information comes from and then use this information to drive all operations. Companies that excel in outbound logistics—Wal-Mart, Apple, Dell, and Southwest Airlines—are no more than sophisticated logistical systems for delivering product-services to customers that backhaul large amounts of customer information. These companies use this information backhaul to add value to the fabric of their product-services and gain superior profits from hardware that may be no better, may even be worse, than Matsushita's. To get to its 10 percent operating profit goal, Matsushita must transform itself into an outbound logistics powerhouse capable of delivering product-services to its global customers and using information inflow to add ever-higher levels of value. That's demand management.

What links outbound logistics and demand management is information technology. IT is the dimension in which information comes together from all the cash touch points in the system, "informing" the system on what to do next to add value for customers and gain more profitable opportunities.

For Matsushita this will be yet another reversal of polarity. A company used to adding value through what it makes will have to learn how to add value through how it sells. This should not be so hard. If the firm applies the same vigor to demand management that it has applied to the 2000–2006 reform process, it will build handsome profits into its operations and will have little trouble staying ahead of low-cost manufacturers elsewhere in Asia. Indeed, the lesson of Steve Jobs and Michael Dell before him is that once you understand demand management and implement it in operational detail, you can hammer your competition with impunity for years.

And that will be the next chapter in this great story.

ACKNOWLEDGMENTS

A BOOK LIKE THIS CANNOT BE WRITTEN WITHOUT THE HELP OF A lot of people. I met hundreds of Matsushita employees in all ranks of the company over the years and had more access than any Japanese company may ever have granted an outsider. I cannot think of a single question that I asked in the last decade that was not answered openly and frankly with more data than I could imagine. This cannot be done by having one or two people answer a casual question or two. It takes a substantial and consistent commitment of resources over a long period of time. Many of those who helped out I never met and am unable to thank.

First and foremost I must thank David Chapin and Masa Kusumoto, who introduced Sean White and me to Kirk Nakamura in 1995, and Dick Kraft, who advised Kirk to go ahead with us. David worked with us during the critical year of 1996–97 when we supported Kirk directly and worked with his U.S. management team on a weekly basis. David's understanding of Japanese, and Kirk, made our work indescribably easier than it would have been.

I must also thank Shin Maegami, who, with David, escorted us to Japan in early 1997. Following David Chapin, I worked with Frank Yamanaka, Mike Miyata, Arthur Matsumoto (Arthur contributed much to this book and my thinking about MEI and Kirk Nakamura's U.S. period), John Burnham, Yasumoto Otsuka, Rudy Vidal, Hideo Nakano, and Hide Harada. Many of the ideas you see on these pages were worked out over the years in problem-solving sessions with them in Secaucus, New Jersey. At Panasonic North America I should also thank former CEO Don Iwatani and his successor, Yoshi Yamada. Also the head of PNA Public Relations, Jim Reilly, who in addition to his help over the years put me back in touch with retired executives who worked with Kirk in the States. There is one person who deserves more gratitude than I can ever measure, Rosemary Lopresto, who, I'm convinced, actually runs PNA. Only Rosemary knows the truth, and she's not talking.

In Japan, I have many to thank as well. Karl Takahashi and Osamu Takahashi (no relation) escorted me through Japanese operations for several years, smoothing the way through many meetings. In the late nineties, Karl did double duty as my translator. Nick Akamatsu, now personal secretary to CEO Fumio Ohtsubo, has been a big support for some time and became a vital player in the writing of *Panasonic*. Hank Ohsawa was Kirk's secretary while head of Panasonic North America, went with him to Japan when he took over AVC, and remained with him when he was CEO. He and I are the only two to have seen Kirk through the entire decade covered in *Panasonic* and this book would be nowhere without him.

I must also thank Makoto Nishikawa, Kirk Nakamura's translator during his time as CEO, who has translated many of my presentations at Matsushita over the years and who is an endless source of good advice on the nuances of speaking to a Japanese audience. As I mentioned in the text, Yoko Nakamizu of sports marketing restructured entirely my thinking about *Panasonic* and I owe her a great debt of gratitude.

Hisao Kato and Joe Ennokoshi gave me the Cook's tour of the Matsushita House of History in Kadoma, pointing out aspects of Konosuke's life and career that, for all my knowledge of the company, were new to me and very helpful to my understanding his thinking.

I have to thank Jun Ishii's entire team at corporate planning, especially Harry Fujita, Takayuki Uchida, Yuko Niwa, and Atsuko Shimizu. At corporate communications, I got great help from Tetsuo Egawa, Akira Kadota, and the redoubtable Megumi Kitagawa. Also at corporate planning, several people worked hard to translate *Panasonic* into Japanese: Eri Fukuda, Yuichi Takatoku, and Ryoko Ogawa.

How could I have done without Mami Katayama? One of MEI's top in-house translators, she took a great deal of her time from her family to travel with me to various parts of Japan, often simultaneously translating highly technical conversations both ways for hours, once to the point where she lost her voice. Also I must thank Sean Umezawa, who often translated with Makoto Nishikawa. At Intergroup, a fine translating firm—Etsuko Sasaki, Mutsumi Kawamura, Miyuki Komatsu, Yoshiko Myamoto, and Toyoko Ogino—assisted me for several years and through many, many meetings and presentations.

I must, of course, acknowledge my Japanese editor at Diamond, Hiromi Maesawa, and Mac Talley, my U.S. editor since 1992, first at Dutton and now at St. Martin's, and my longtime copyeditor, Sally Krefting. All have shown great patience with this complex project.

Absolutely nothing would have worked in the writing of a book as detailed as this one without a key person who pulls everything together. That person is Harry Fujita. Harry has worked with me since 2003 on various projects and for *Panasonic* managed all MEI's internal resources and arranged my many trips to Japan, eight in all. I must also thank his wife, Miyuki, for tolerating all the long absences this entailed.

I got a lot of help from senior executives and many are quoted in the text. But there are four who deserve special mention because they took much time during the last six years to give me their perspectives. Hiro Sakamoto ran corporate planning during the entire period of the reforms and spent many hours both asking and answering questions. Joe Shohtoku, who ran overseas sales, gave me valuable insights and made many useful suggestions. Atsushi Murayama's razor-sharp assessment of MEI's situation in the late 1990s, and progress since, was a constant guidepost for my thinking. Fumio Ohtsubo, the current CEO, kept me up to date on key operations like PDP over several years, giving me a clear sense of MEI's challenges.

This book would be nowhere without Sean White, my partner in many business ventures since 1976. Sean's incisive thinking and powerful intellect steered us both through business times good and bad for three decades, and his enormous contributions to understanding how companies scale—and therefore what would work for Matsushita—are too great to list. I hope the text gives some sense of this.

I must also thank Lisa Baisley, my executive assistant, for much of the period this book covers, who kept me traveling for as many as forty weeks in some years.

And I cannot fail to acknowledge Verna Mclean, my wife of over three decades, who advises me on every recommendation I make to all my clients worldwide.

Finally, of course, I have to thank Kirk Nakamura himself. This book reflects, I hope, the faith he put in Sean White and me to help him frame his approach to reform a decade ago and in allowing me to assess the company's performance on his retirement.

NOTES

INTRODUCTION

1. McInerney, Francis, and Sean White. *Beating Japan*. New York: Dutton, 1993, p. 102.
2. Matsushita Electric Annual Report, 2001, p. 3.
3. Nakamura, Kirk. "Embracing Reform." Management Conference speech, September 28, 2000.

1 THE CHALLENGE

1. Emmott, Bill. *The Sun Also Sets*. New York: Random House, 1989.
2. ———. "The Sun Also Rises, a Survey of Japan." *The Economist*, October 8, 2005.
3. "Japan's Chipmakers Search for a Strategy," *The New York Times*, January 3, 2006, p. B1.

4. Nakamura, Kirk. "Value Creation 21." Management Conference speech, November 30, 2000.

5. Kotter, John P. *Matsushita Leadership*. New York: The Free Press, 1997, p. 5.

6. Matsushita, Konosuke. *Quest for Prosperity: The Life of a Japanese Industrialist*. Tokyo: PHP Institute, 1988, p. 4.

7. Ibid., p. 8.

8. Ibid., p. 240.

9. Maney, Kevin. *The Maverick and His Machine: Thomas Watson Sr. and the Making of IBM*. New York: John Wiley and Sons, 2003, p. 324.

10. I am indebted to Tetsuya Kawakami, CFO, for this interesting observation about the pattern of Konosuke's mergers and acquisitions.

11. Interview by the Nomura School of Advanced Management, March 22, 2004.

12. Interview with the author, December 15, 2005.

13. Ibid.

14. Interview with the author, November 15, 2005.

15. Ibid.

16. Interview with the author, December 13, 2005.

17. Interview with the author, June 7, 2005.

18. Interview with the author, December 13, 2005.

19. Interview with the author, November 15, 2005.

20. Interview with the author, October 4, 2005.

21. Interview with the author, November 15, 2005.

22. McInerney and White. *Beating Japan*, p. 276.

23. Interview with Takao Tsumuji, February 15, 2005.

24. Nakamura, Kirk. "Transforming Matsushita into a Super Manufacturer." Management Conference speech, July 4, 2000.

25. Interview with the author, April 11, 2006.

26. Interview with the author, March 27, 2006.

27. Interview with the author, December 13, 2005.

28. Reihheld, Frederick. "Learning from Customer Defections." *The Harvard Business Review*, March–April 1996, p. 56.

29. Ibid., p. 59.

30. McInerney, Francis, and Sean White. *The Digital Revolution.* New York: North River Ventures, 1996, p. 28.

31. Silk, Joseph. *The Big Bang.* San Francisco: W. H. Freeman, 1980, p. 48.

32. Randall, Lisa. *Warped Passages: Unraveling the Mysteries of the Universe's Hidden Dimensions.* New York: HarperCollins, 2005.

33. McInerney and White. *The Digital Revolution*, p. 100.

34. Interview with the author, December 15, 2005.

2 THE SOCCER BALL COMPANY

1. McLuhan, Marshall. *The Gutenberg Galaxy.* Toronto: University of Toronto Press, 1962, p. 141.

2. *Financial Times.* Special Report, FT Global 500, May 21, 2004.

3. "PC Sales Accelerated During 4th Quarter." *The Wall Street Journal*, January 29, 1998, p. B2. During 1997, Dell sold 12,230 machines for each of 365 days. During 1998, it sold 20,167 machines a day, an increase of 65 percent. By the end of 1999, it sold 33,254 machines a day or 12,138,000 a year or 45 percent more than IBM by the same calculation.

4. "IBM, Georgia Tech Unveil 500-Gigahertz Chips." *The Wall Street Journal*, June 20, 2006, p. B3.

5. "Before Christmas, Wal-Mart Was Stirring." *The New York Times*, January 5, 2005.

6. I owe this observation to Stan Makita, executive officer in charge of Information Technology. Interview in New York on November 18, 2005.

7. Nakamura, Kirk. Management Conference speech, January 9, 2004.

8. "GM Aims to Become Build-to-Order Firm but Custom Online Sales Are Daunting Task." *The Wall Street Journal*, February 22, 2000, p. B23.

9. "Discounts. Cheap Gas. 0%." *The New York Times*, June 29, 2006, p. C1.

10. Braudel, Fernand. *Civilisation matérielle, économie et capitalisme*, Vol. 3. Paris: Le Livre de Poche, 1979, p. 48.
11. Maurois, André. *A History of France*. University Paperbacks, 1964, Paris, France, pp. 230–231.

3 BRINGING MATSUSHITA FORWARD

1. Nakamura, Kirk. "Overcoming Adversity." Management Conference speech, March 28, 2001.
2. ———. "Discovering Horizons for Future Growth." Management Conference speech, December 6, 2001.
3. ———. Management Conference speech, December 4, 2003.
4. Maney, Kevin. *The Maverick and His Machine: Thomas Watson Sr. and the Making of IBM*. New York: John Wiley & Sons, 2003, p. 445.
5. Gilmore, Dan. "One Heck of a Supply Chain Story." *Supply Chain Digest*, May 8, 2006, http://www.scdigest.com.
6. Nakamura. Management Conference speech, December 4, 2003.
7. ———. "Drastic Action Indispensable to Combat Declining Performance." Management Conference speech, July 5, 2001.
8. ———. "Creating a New Matsushita." Management Conference speech, January 2001.
9. Interview with the author, November 15, 2005.
10. Ibid.
11. Nakamura, Kirk. Management Conference speech, September 28, 2000.
12. In 2000, Matsushita had 455,336 finished products and 728,896 devices registered with the Global Code Management System. Over the next five years, these grew to 1,398,072 and 1,797,847 respectively. Presumably many of these are still registered even if no longer made, and many represent small variants in products and devices. Still, the total grew by over two million during the reform period.
13. Nakamura, Kirk. "Discovering New Horizons for Future Growth." Management Conference speech, December 6, 2001.

14. Interview with the author, December 12, 2005.
15. Interview with the author, November 15, 2005.
16. Ibid.
17. Ibid.
18. Ibid.
19. Interview with the author, December 15, 2005.
20. Interview by the Nomura School of Advanced Management, March 22, 2004.
21. Interview with the author, November 15, 2005.
22. Interview by the Nomura School of Advanced Management, March 22, 2004.
23. Interview with the author, December 15, 2005.
24. Nakamura, Kirk. Policy speech, March 28, 2003.
25. ———. "Challenges That We Face in FY '03." Management Conference speech, March 28, 2003.
26. ———. "Value Creation 21." Management Conference speech, November 30, 2000.
27. ———. Policy speech, January 14, 2002.
28. Ibid.
29. Nakamura, Kirk. Management Conference speech, December 5, 2001.
30. 2001 Global 500 at www.fortune.com.
31. Interview with the author, November 9, 2005.
32. Interview with the author, November 10, 2005.
33. Interview with the author, November 9, 2005.
34. Ibid.
35. Interview with the author, December 15, 2005.
36. Interview with the author, November 8, 2005.
37. Nakamura, Kirk. "Overcoming Adversity." Management Conference speech, March 28, 2001.
38. ———. "Drastic Action Indispensable to Combat Declining Performance." Management Conference speech, July 5, 2001.
39. ———. "Discovering New Horizons for Future Growth." Management Conference speech, December 6, 2001.
40. Interview with the author, November 11, 2005.
41. Ibid.

42. Ibid.
43. Nakamura, Kirk. Policy speech, January 14, 2002.
44. ———. Management Conference speech, July 5, 2001.
45. ———. "Exercise Leadership." Management Conference speech, March 28, 2002.
46. Interview with the author, December 15, 2005.
47. Nakamura, Kirk. "Overcoming Adversity." Management Conference speech, March 28, 2001. He returned to this theme in every one of his quarterly presentations over six years.
48. ———. Policy speech, January 14, 2002.
49. ———. Extraordinary Management Conference, February 7, 2002. He was still at this subject two and a half years later, criticizing managers in his July 1, 2004, Management Conference speech for second-quarter padding to avoid hard choices.
50. ———. "Exercise Leadership to Achieve V-Shaped Performance Recovery in 2002." Management Conference speech, March 28, 2002.
51. Interview with the author, December 15, 2005.
52. Ibid.
53. Interview with the author, November 11, 2005.
54. Interview with the author, November 15, 2005
55. Interview with the author, December 15, 2005.
56. Interview with the author, November 11, 2005.
57. Ibid.
58. Interview with the author, December 15, 2005.
59. Nakamura, Kirk. Policy speech, January 14, 2002.
60. ———. Management Conference speech, March 28, 2002.
61. ———. Management Conference speech, July 4, 2002.
62. "Top Volkswagen Executive Tries U.S.-Style Turnaround Tactics." *The Wall Street Journal*, July 18, 2006, p. A1.
63. Interview with the author, November 11, 2005.
64. Interview with the author, December 12, 2005.
65. Ibid.
66. Interview with the author, November 11, 2005.
67. Interview with the author, December 15, 2005.
68. Interview with the author, November 8, 2005.

69. Data from Tetsuya Kawakami in interview with the author, November 11, 2005.
70. "Case Study: Matsushita's Consumer Products Marketing Reforms," Matsushita internal document, June 20, 2004.
71. Interview with the author, October 25, 2005.
72. Interview with the author, November 15, 2005.
73. Interview with the author, December 12, 2005.
74. Interview with the author, October 4, 2005.
75. Gilmore, Dan. "One Heck of a Supply Chain Story." *Supply Chain Digest*, May 18, 2006.
76. Interview with the author, November 11, 2005.
77. Interview with the author, November 10, 2005.
78. Nakamura, Kirk. "Overcoming Adversity." Management Conference speech, March 28, 2001.
79. Ibid.
80. Ibid.
81. Interview with the author, November 9, 2005.
82. Interview with the author, December 15, 2005.
83. Nakamura, Kirk. "Issues and Actions for FY '03." Management Conference speech, December 5, 2002.
84. ———. "Discovering New Horizons for Future Growth." Management Conference speech, December 6, 2001.
85. ———. "Integrating Groupwide Efforts." Management Conference speech, September 26, 2002.
86. Interview with the author, November 11, 2005.
87. Interview with the author, December 15, 2005.
88. Interview with the author, November 10, 2005.
89. Nakamura, Kirk. "Overcoming Adversity." Management Conference speech, March 28, 2001.
90. For those of you of a certain age, like me, yes, Makita took his English name from the great Chicago Black Hawk and Hall of Fame legend, Stan Mikita—541 goals and 1,500 points.
91. Interview with the author, November 18, 2005.
92. Ibid.
93. Nakamura, Kirk. Management Conference speech, March 30, 2005.

94. Interview with the author, November 8, 2005.
95. Nakamura, Kirk. "Exercise Leadership." Management Conference speech, March 28, 2002.
96. Interview with the author, December 9, 2005.
97. Ibid.
98. Nakamura. "Value Creation 21."
99. ———. "New Management System and Structure in Full Operation." Management Conference speech, July 3, 2003.
100. Ibid.
101. Interview with the author, November 9, 2005.
102. Nakamura, Kirk. Management Conference speech, March 30, 2004.
103. McInerney, Francis, and Sean White. *The Digital Revolution.* New York: North River Ventures, 1996, p. 79.
104. Nakamura, Kirk. "Creating a New Matsushita." Management Conference speech, January 2001.
105. "Enter the House of Wal-Mart." *The New York Times*, September 10, 2006.
106. "Matsushita Plans to Take Control of Five Key Units." *The Wall Street Journal*, January 11, 2002.
107. Interview with the author, November 9, 2005.
108. Nakamura, Kirk. "Challenges That We Face in FY '03." Management Conference speech, March 28, 2003.
109. Interview with the author, December 15, 2005.
110. "Matsushita President Targets Change; Image Revamp, Mergers on To-Do List." *The Wall Street Journal*, July 24, 2000.
111. Interview with the author, December 13, 2005.
112. Interview with the author, April 13, 2006.
113. Interview with the author, March 29, 2006.
114. Interview with the author, April 13, 2006.
115. Interview with the author, November 9, 2005.
116. "Image 2000." MECA Internal Advertising Conference, October 31, 1995.
117. Interview with the author, December 12, 2005.
118. BAV is a global study by Young and Rubicam of 350,000 consumers in 44 countries that measures brand perceptions over a

brandscape of nearly 20,000 brands using 56 different brand metrics in ongoing quarterly tracking.

119. Nakamura, Kirk. Management Conference speech, September 26, 2003.
120. Interview with the author, April 10, 2006.
121. Ibid.
122. Interview with the author, February 1, 2006.
123. Interview with the author, November 15, 2005.
124. Nakamura, Kirk. "Surviving the 21st Century." Management Conference speech, October 30, 2001.
125. ———. "Extraordinary Management Conference." February 7, 2002, p. 7.
126. ———. "Integrating Groupwide Efforts." Management Conference speech, September 26, 2002.
127. Interview with the author, December 15, 2005.
128. Interview with the author, December 12, 2005.
129. Nakamura, Kirk. "Exercise Leadership." Management Conference speech, March 28, 2002.
130. Interview with the author, November 8, 2005.
131. Interview with the author, November 22, 2005.
132. *Consumer Reports*, March 2006, p. 18.
133. "U.S. TV Makers Win a Shelf at Best Buy." *The Wall Street Journal*, March 31, 2006, p. A11.
134. Interview with the author, November 8, 2005.
135. Ibid.
136. Ibid.
137. "Konica to Quit Cameras, Film." *The Wall Street Journal*, January 20, 2006, p. A11.
138. Interview with the author, November 7, 2005.
139. Interview with the author, November 16, 2005.
140. Interview with the author, March 29, 2006.
141. Interview with the author, November 14, 2005.
142. Ibid.
143. Ibid.
144. Interview with the author, December 8, 2005.
145. Ibid.

146. Email to the author, August 28, 2006.
147. Nakamura. "Overcoming Adversity."
148. McInerney, Francis, and Sean White. *The Total Quality Corporation*. New York: Dutton, 1995, p. 4.
149. Nakamura, Kirk. "Discovering New Horizons for Future Growth." Management Conference speech, December 6, 2001.
150. ———. Management Conference speech, March 30, 2004.
151. Ibid.
152. Interview with the author, November 11, 2005.
153. Nakamura, Kirk. Management Conference speech, March 28, 2001.
154. ———. Policy speech, January 14, 2002.
155. ———. Management Conference speech, July 5, 2001.
156. ———. Policy speech, January 14, 2002.
157. Interview with the author, December 15, 2005.
158. Interview with the author, December 13, 2005.
159. Interview with the author, December 12, 2005.

4 A RENEWED JAPANESE POWERHOUSE

1. Braudel, Fernand. *Civilisation matérielle, économie et capitalisme*, Vol. 3. Paris: Le Temps du monde, Armand Colin, 1979, p. 678.
2. Interview with the author, December 12, 2005.
3. Maney, Kevin. "No iTunes in China and the Future of Music." *USA Today*, May 4, 2005.
4 ———. "How Level 3 Worked Its Way to the Main Floor." *USA Today*, April 1, 1998, p. 1B.
5. Nakamura, Kirk. Management Conference speech, December 4, 2003.
6. Interview with the author, November 8, 2005.

INDEX

Aguilar, Mike, 207
Akamatsu, Nick, 86
Alcatel, 327
Alcatel-Lucent Technologies, 4,
    226
Aller Buster, 320
American Express, 189
Apple, *xiii*, 15, 36, 108, 122, 136,
    273, 344
  cash velocity, 119, 128–29
  IBM-compatibles and, 268
  iPod/iTunes/iLife, 7, 77, 92, 123,
    267, 268
  MEI and, 335
ARDIS (Advanced National Radio
    Data Service), 274
Asahi Shimbum, 66
AST, 273
AT&T, *xvii*, 273
  post-breakup, 4
AT&T Network Systems, 250
AT&T Wireless, 322, 332

Atami Conference (1964), 33, 45, 57,
    175, 313, 342
Audio Visual Computer Company
    (AVC), 323
Automotive Systems (MEI), 271,
    296–301
AVA Networks (Digital Networks)
    Area, 175–76
  automotive electronics, 176
  AVC, 176
  fixed line communications, 176
  mobile communications, 176
  systems solutions, 176
AVC Networks Company, 323

Beating Japan (McInerney/White),
    xii, xvi, xx, 1–2, 5, 8, 9, 28,
    64–66, 98, 101, 114, 135, 140,
    259, 318
  Iron Laws of Information/Impact
    on Markets, 65–67
Bank of England, 136